WOODEN OS: SHAKESPEARE'S THEATRES AND ENGLAND'S TREES

VIN NARDIZZI

Wooden Os: Shakespeare's Theatres and England's Trees

UNIVERSITY OF TORONTO PRESS
Toronto Buffalo London

© University of Toronto Press 2013
Toronto Buffalo London
www.utppublishing.com
Printed in Canada

ISBN 978-1-4426-4600-1

∞

Printed on acid-free, 100% post-consumer recycled paper with
vegetable-based inks.

Library and Archives Canada Cataloguing in Publication

Nardizzi, Vincent Joseph, 1978–
Wooden Os : Shakespeare's theatres and England's trees / Vin Nardizzi.

Includes bibliographical references and index.
ISBN 978-1-4426-4600-1

1. English drama – Early modern and Elizabethan, 1500–1600 – History and criticism.
2. Shakespeare, William, 1564–1616 – Criticism and interpretation.   3. Trees in
literature.   4. Forests in literature.   5. Deforestation – Environmental aspects – England
– History – 16th century.   6. Building, Wooden – Environmental aspects – England –
History – 16th century.   7. Theaters – England – History – 16th century.
I. Title.

PR658.E58N37 2013   822′.309364   C2012-908102-7

This book has been published with the help of a grant from the Canadian Federation
for the Humanities and Social Sciences, through the Aid to Scholarly Publications
Program, using funds provided by the Social Sciences and Humanities Research
Council of Canada.

University of Toronto Press acknowledges the financial assistance to its publishing
program of the Canada Council for the Arts and the Ontario
Arts Council.

ONTARIO ARTS COUNCIL
CONSEIL DES ARTS DE L'ONTARIO
50 YEARS OF ONTARIO GOVERNMENT SUPPORT OF THE ARTS
50 ANS DE SOUTIEN DU GOUVERNEMENT DE L'ONTARIO AUX ARTS

Canada Council   Conseil des Arts
for the Arts   du Canada

University of Toronto Press acknowledges the financial support of the Government of
Canada through the Canada Book Fund for its publishing activities.

for Carol Nardizzi
(1938–2010)

Contents

Illustrations

Acknowledgments

The final pleasure of writing this book is seeing all the trees – the colleagues, friends, family members, mentors, and students – growing in my forest.

At Duke University, where the pine tree abounds, I enjoyed the guidance and intellectual generosity of Laurie Shannon, Maureen Quilligan, Marc Schachter, Sarah Beckwith, Priscilla Wald, Tom Ferraro, Fiona Somerset, Sean Metzger, and Houston Baker. I also had the good fortune to traipse across the bosky terrain of graduate school with a host of inspiring fellow travellers: Monique Allewaert, Lara Bovilsky, Dan Breen, Max Brzezinski, Lauren Coats, Kate Crassons, Charles Del Dotto, Hillary Eklund, Alisha Gaines, Erin Gentry, Anne Gulick, Cara Hersh, Shannon Kelley, Nihad Farooq, Russ Leo, Kinohi Nishikawa, Eden Osucha, Jimmy Richardson, Britt Rusert, and Jini Watson. At the University of British Columbia, where the smell of cedar greets me on the way to my classrooms, I have had the immense pleasure of counting Dina al-Kassim, Patsy Badir, Mary Bryson, Miranda Burgess, Mary Chapman, Tony Dawson, Alex Dick, Bo Earle, Siân Echard, Stephen Guy-Bray, Liz Hodgson, Tom Kemple, Deanna Kreisel, Chris Lee, Tina Lupton, Scott MacKenzie, Laura Moss, Dory Nason, Alan Richardson, Robert Rouse, Judy Segal, Jeff Severs, Janice Stewart, and Sandy Tomc as colleagues and friends. SFU's Tiffany Werth and I arrived to Vancouver in 2006, and, as Tison Pugh predicted, we hit it off. I am grateful that she and Patsy commented on every word of this book. Not long after I started at UBC, I met Greg Mackie, the dearest Canadian I know. He responded to every possible incarnation of *Wooden Os* and made it smarter each time.

For their invitations to share my work at their universities and for their hospitality, I thank Cord Whitaker at the University of New Hampshire,

Joseph Campana at Rice University, and Jen Hill at the University of
Nevada, Reno. For their good company and support during the days of
writing and on the conference circuit, I thank Dan Brayton, Jim Bromley,
Lynne Bruckner, Joshua Calhoun, Jeffrey Cohen, Julie Crawford, Holly
Dugan, Simon Estok, Jennifer Feather, Jean Feerick, Will Fisher, Mary
Floyd-Wilson, Ed Geisweidt, Gil Harris, Jean Howard, Miriam Jacob-
son, Aaron Kunin, Rebecca Laroche, Scott Maisano, Gretchen Minton,
Jennifer Munroe, Madhavi Menon, Steve Mentz, Sharon O'Dair, David
Orvis, Alan Stewart, Will Stockton, Garrett Sullivan, Catherine Thomas,
Cliff Werier, Paul Yachnin, and Julian Yates. The image of the sawpit is for
Valerie Traub. Special thanks to Jeffrey Masten for the parachute.

I am lucky to count Suzanne Rancourt as my editor and Barb Porter
as my managing editor at UTP. The two anonymous readers for the press
both encouraged and productively challenged the book's contours; I am
grateful for their advice. Evan Choate did a marvellous job working as
my RA during the manuscript's final stages. Any mistakes that remain
are mine. A portion of the introduction first appeared as "Shakespeare's
Globe and England's Woods" in *Shakespeare Studies* 39 (2011): 54–63.
Sections of Chapter 2 are reprinted by permission of the publishers from
"Felling Falstaff in Windsor Park" in *Ecocritical Shakespeare*, ed. Lynne
Bruckner and Dan Brayton (Farnham: Ashgate, 2011), pp. 123–38. Sections of Chapter 3 are revised and reprinted by permission of the publishers from "'No Wood, No Kingdom': Planting Genealogy, Felling Trees,
and the Additions to *The Spanish Tragedy*" in *Modern Philology* 110.2
(2012): 202–25.

I dedicate this book to the memory of my mother, who died just as I was
starting to compose it. I like to think of it as a plant written in her honour.

WOODEN OS: SHAKESPEARE'S THEATRES AND ENGLAND'S TREES

Prologue: Evergreen Fantasies:
Utopia's Trees and Early Modern Theatre

In a passage that, according to a marginal gloss in the 1597 English edition of Thomas More's Latin text, records the "wealth and delcription [*sic*] of the Vtopians," the traveller Raphael explicates the island's program of woodland maintenance. He relates that Utopians "plucked up by the rootes" "a whole wood [*silvam*] by the handes" "in one place, & set [it] againe in an other place."[1] In his telling, this outlay of communal labour, which appears to our eyes as extravagant, proves altogether mundane. Raphael links it explicitly to "those things which husbandmen doo commonly in other countries, as by craft & cunning to remedy the barrennesse of the ground," among which practices he includes the "diligent trauaile" of agriculture and the careful tending of "cattle" (N3ᵛ). He here points towards an insight about woodlands that *Wooden Os* describes more abundantly in its introduction: trees were deemed as indispensable as grain, dairy products, and other consumable goods and resources that the land yielded to the livelihood of early modern English people. Indeed, as economic and environmental historians have christened it, early modernity was an "age of wood,"[2] and during this era the most vital measure of any polity's ecological "wealth" and welfare – from Utopia to England – was its available store of trees.[3]

In his narration, Raphael also enumerates the places where Utopians newly enrooted the island's "whole wood." Utopians, he reports, conveyed the trees "nigher to the sea, or the riuers, or the cities" (N3ᵛ). Such dispersal enacts a massive woodland clearance that recalls *Utopia*'s more famous depiction of England's enclosure crisis in Book I. But rather than circumscribing the use to which land can employed as an act of enclosure does, the reallocation of trees on the island affords Utopians more room for a range of unspecified purposes. And yet, Utopians do not immediately destroy the trees and produce lumber from them. Instead, the reconfiguration uproots and then replants still-living trees, effectively landscaping the natural world to the Utopians' liking and providing three kinds of location with a "standing reserve" of trees from which inhabitants could presumably extract "wood and timber" as required (N3ᵛ).[4] A precursor to the utilitarian regime of fiscal forestry, which simplifies a "habitat" into "the term 'natural resources'" (J. Scott 13), Utopian management is thus made possible by the island's plentitude and the collective pluck of its inhabitants. To readers of More's text in the late 1590s who were enduring what was then perceived as an unprecedented shortage of wood and timber, this "outlandish" instance of "Utopian husbandry" might have evoked that environmental crisis as well as the more fantastic solutions for its alleviation that were assayed and enacted in England during the reigns of Elizabeth I and James I.[5] This book aims, in part, to shed light on the environmental history of English woodlands and on the range of eco-fantasies – from colonial extraction to the reforestation of England – that this scarcity fuelled. Some remedies that early modern polemicists proposed to end or to mitigate the shortage could be as ingenious and as impossible to put into action as the program of woodland management conducted on Utopia.[6]

Wooden Os links the history of English woodlands glimpsed in More's *Utopia* to the advent of English "theatre," by which it intends the outdoor space where commercial drama was performed in London's suburbs. As the Prologue to *Henry V*, where the playhouse is called "this wooden O" (l. 13),[7] indicates, these venues were fashioned almost entirely from wood products. Less widely known to literary scholars, however, is the eco-material tie that connects early modern theatres and English woodlands. These venues were prefabricated, and the method by which they made their way to London's suburbs uncannily resembles the program of woodland clearance on Utopia: theatres were fashioned out of England's woods and then (surprisingly) framed there before they were disassembled and conveyed to the performance site, where they were erected again as they had previously stood in the woods.[8] London's theatres, where woodlands – forests, gardens, orchards, parks, and woods – were a favoured setting for plays, could thus display in performance "untimely" (to borrow Jonathan Gil Harris's term for signalling an object's polytemporality) traces of their placement as a theatrical frame in English woodlands and their former existence as living trees. These traces help to situate the study of the theatre's material fabric firmly within the ambit of early modern English environmental history.[9] Theatres required enormous outlays of a (seemingly) scarce resource and, as such, emerged at an opportunity cost. In an era of perceived and real shortage, theatres represent a massive investment in wood. Simon Schama might dub them sites of "cultural reafforestation," where the "literary and visual imagination" worked to "replant" diminished woodlands,[10] in part, by "transport[ing]" "the scene" (*Henry V*, Chorus 2, ll. 34–5) – as well as audience members sitting and standing inside the playhouse where that scene has been set – to the woods of ancient civilizations, of faraway lands, and of contemporary and historical England.[11] If the "price of art is the destruction of a living tree" (Bate 92), then early modern theatres could reimburse that outlay with evergreen fantasies.[12] Inside them, England's trees – replanted as the theatre – were virtually brought back to life whenever a character entered the woods. In the introduction, we'll wend our way towards these woods.

Introduction: Wood, Timber, and Theatre in Early Modern England

The Grain of Early Modern England

The late sixteenth-century English translation of More's *Utopia* provides no inventory of the explicit uses to which Utopians put the island's transplanted trees. We could follow Richard Halpern's lead and classify such woodland management as an example of the "blank absence of any motivation" on the island (156). We could also argue that since woodlands, like farms and fields, supplied many of the polity's most basic – and banal – wants,[1] to tell the story of what Utopians do with their trees after the Herculean feats of clearance and redistribution have occurred would make for dull conversation at the humanist table.[2] In 1597, More's English readers could nonetheless have made an educated guess about the benefits that rested on a plentiful and accessible store of "wood and timber" (*ligna*).[3] Perhaps they wished their island were as resource-rich as the Utopians'.

To our ears, the locution "wood and timber" in the translation of More's text sounds redundant. Both terms, after all, denote the product extracted from a tree. As Oliver Rackham, a preeminent historian of British woodlands, reminds us, though, the pairing "wood and timber" belongs to the idiom of woodmanship. Each half of the pair conveys a unique sense in this vocabulary of woodland economy. The salient distinction between them hinges on their utility. "*Timber* and *wood*," Rackham remarks, "traditionally mean different things." Timber includes "big stuff suitable for making planks, beams, and gate-posts," whereas wood encompasses "poles, brushwood, and similar smaller stuff suitable for light construction or for firewood" (23). The range of uses that Rackham taxonomizes highlights the plasticity of early modern wood and timber. Taken together, wood products were, as John F. Richards observes, the "all-purpose raw material in the early modern world" (240).

The pairing of "wood and timber" in More's *Utopia* thus functions as recognizable shorthand for these two categories of wood product. But the grammatical conjunction of "wood and timber" also suggests a similarity between these categories, and sometimes, as in the English translation of *Utopia* itself, one half of the pair encodes its counterpart. Raphael observes that the tract of woodland has been transplanted so "that wood and timber might be nigher to the sea, or the riuers, or the citties. For it is lesse labour and businesse to carrie grayne farre by land, then wood" (N3^v). The final "wood" (*ligna*) signals a definitional overlap, embracing the "wood and timber" (*ligna*) that precedes it,[4] as well as retrospectively comprehending the "whole wood" (*silvam*) that Utopians parcelled out. Although such knots of meaning, which confound a distinction between "nature" (living trees) and "culture" (lumbered wood), crop up regularly throughout these pages, I disentangle this Utopian knot below to illustrate more fully the ways that early modern England could not do without "wood," in its most capacious definitional scope, and the high stakes attendant upon maintaining an abundant stock of this resource during the period. Without "wood," some early modern witnesses, including the monarch, claimed there could be no England.

The inventory of items that Rackham classifies under the rubric "timber" – "planks, beams, and gate-posts" – suggests how these large pieces of wood worked literally to support England's people and to demarcate its land. Before the introduction of steel beams in construction and the widespread use of bricks, a topic to which we'll return in the context of theatre design, timber reinforced the infrastructure of an early modern England whose population was rapidly increasing and was putting an intense strain on existing institutions and resources. From wharves and bridges to warships, merchant vessels, and "stately Ship[s]" (Cavendish l. 77), to windmills and other machines employed in industry and agriculture, to "stately House[s]" outfitted with wood panelling (Cavendish ll. 104–13) and more modest cottages and farmhouses, to roofs of varying sumptuousness,[5] to fortifications for defence, and to resorts of public entertainment, the foremost of which in this study are London's commercial theatres, timber was early modern England's most ubiquitous building material. As William Harrison observed in 1577, it was the fabric of early modern English life: "The greatest parte of our buylding in the cities and good townes of Englande consisteth onely of timber" (84^v).

This elaboration of Rackham's list of things made with timber could be extended, but to continue it runs the risk of emphasizing breadth over depth. In other words, the expanded (and expandable) list is a mere sample of conspicuous uses for timber that proves all the more staggering when we factor in how much timber would have been required to construct any big-ticket item on it. The "typical" timber-framed farmhouse is one such item. Rackham reckons that "hundreds" of such farmhouses were erected in West Suffolk at the turn of the sixteenth century, and one of them, Grundle House, Stanton, "contains some 330 trees, a tenth of which are elm" (74–5). The seaworthy ship is another such item. According to environmental historian John F. Richards, the amount of timber harvested to manufacture one was "prodigious":

> The rule of thumb for warships was that each rated ton consumed about 1.5 to 2 "loads" (2.1 to 2.8 cubic meters) of timber. Each merchantman commonly used 1 load (1.4 cubic meters) per shipping ton. A great ship of the line [warship], averaging 2,000 tons capacity, swallowed 4,200 to 5,600 cubic meters of timber – the timber of several thousand mature trees. (224)

John Perlin, historian of the world's forests, simplifies and supplements these figures when he estimates that "a large warship took about 2,000 oaks, which had to be at least a century old (younger wood did not possess the necessary strength), thus stripping at least fifty acres of woods" (175–6).[6] Such outlays of oak for ship construction do not, however, comprise the total amount of timber felled for building a ship, for a seagoing vessel also required several masts, which were fashioned from conifers like pine, fir, and spruce.[7] According to J.R. McNeill, the amount of hard and softwood needed for launching a fleet of early modern ships as great as the Spanish Armada, a subject to which we'll return in the next chapter, was "6 million cubic meters of timber – oak and pine in equal portions" (398). When considered in the aggregate, then, the use of new timber in land and seagoing ventures would seem to defy full calculation. Moreover, this impossible sum does not take account of the timber that would have been essential to carry out the inevitable task of repairing ships, renovating and subdividing homes, and retrofitting places of worship in the wake of the Reformation.[8] Nor does it include estimates for building anew after fires, like the one London endured in 1666, which destroyed an urban core that an anonymous satire, commonly ascribed to John Evelyn, had described in 1659 as a "wooden City" whose "congestion" of "wooden" "Houses" constituted a perpetual hazard (10, 29).[9] In the wake of that fire, London is a timbered city no more.

Perhaps because timber supplied materials for the construction of a familiar and still desirable form of architecture (the half-timbered or "Tudor" house)[10] and for the build-up of a navy that would become, by the late seventeenth century, the most potent European commercial and imperial fleet, its importance in history obscures the more ephemeral and mundane, but equally manifold, applications of "wood" in early modern England. Carpenters and joiners crafted the everyday stuff of the household and workplace from this material.[11] From the joint-stool in the barroom of *Henry IV, Part One* to the banqueting table in *Macbeth*, to the bed in *Othello*, to the homely "dish of wood" conjured in *Richard II* (3.3.149) and other utensils that contemporaries called "treen,"[12] small, mid- and large-sized wooden objects furnished these domains. In addition, a range of items and goods not manufactured directly from wood, such as ale, glass, salt, and iron, could not have been made without it during the sixteenth century.[13] An iron griddle, for instance, would require firewood, purchased in bundles from urban vendors or plucked from nearby hedgerows, for preparing an evening meal. A smith whose forge was heated by charcoal, which is the product of an aged hardwood that has been evenly and slowly charred,[14] would have moulded such a pan. (Charcoal was also used in a range of other industries through the sixteenth century.)[15] The metal itself, which would have been extracted as ore from a mineral deposit, would have been smelted into pig iron in blast furnaces that were fuelled by charcoal until the second half of the eighteenth century, when coal became a viable source of energy in the industry.[16] In an era before the advent of railways and canals, all these wood products – charcoal, bundles of firewood culled from hedgerows and coppices as well as larger pieces of timber – were transported across England at varying distances on wooden carts, barges, and larger ships. As this imagined genealogy of an iron griddle intimates, there is no method for quantifying exactly how much wood, in sum, was used to heat early modern England and to provide inhabitants with many essential objects of everyday life.[17] It suffices to say that "wood" knew no social boundaries: every English person required it to sustain a minimal subsistence and maintain a modicum of shelter and warmth, especially during the winter months. Not all English people, of course, had equal or regular access to it.

As the chief support of infrastructure and the primary source of thermal energy, wood product was thus ubiquitous in early modern England: its countless applications in cities, in towns, and in the countryside must have been in plain view every day. But as Raphael's narration in *Utopia* indicates, such a material substrate barely breaks into discourse under ordinary circumstances. Then as now, the indispensability of a substrate like wood – or, for that matter, like petroleum and freshwater – is taken for granted, and its universal demand merits little attention in discourse until exorbitant prices and perceived shortages make it "urgently visible" (Fishman 24).[18] By the close of the sixteenth century, when the English translation of More's text was published in a third edition, conditions had altered drastically, so much so that the vignette about Utopia's woodlands would have taken on an unexpected cast. Late sixteenth-century England did not enjoy Utopia's woodland plentitude, and the sign of the "scarcitie" (90[v]) that William Harrison and other reporters observed was the rising cost of all wood products.[19] Price indices for the sixteenth and seventeenth centuries confirm that wood products were some of the most expensive items a consumer purchased. The index of timber prices more than tripled from 1501 to 1601, and, by 1649, the early sixteenth-century cost index had increased more than sixfold (Thirsk, *Agrarian* 846–50 ctd. in Richards 221); in the first half of the seventeenth century, timber's rate of increase nearly doubled that of agricultural goods (B. Thomas 127). Likewise, the cost of firewood began to outpace the general rise in prices for all goods in 1580s London, and between 1633 and 1642, its price was over two-and-a-half times higher than the cost of other products (M. Williams 170). Charcoal, too, became a more costly commodity for private and industrial consumption: its market value roughly tripled from 1590 to 1690 (B. Thomas 125). To turn-of-the-seventeenth-century readers, for whom such staple commodities were fast turning into luxuries, Utopia's limitless store of "wood and timber" could have been perceived as utopian indeed. They may well have worried, as Samuel Pepys would later do, "where materials" – in that word's fullest ligneous sense – "can be had" (qtd. in Albion ix).[20]

Such statistics about inflation helpfully frame a range of early modern texts that figure England, and especially London, in the grips of a severe shortage of wood and timber. In the logic of these texts, steep prices, compounded by an increase in demand, index a depleted supply of resources. In 1581, for instance, a law was enacted that "*touch[ed] iron-mills near unto the city of* London *and the river of* Thames" (23 Elizabeth c. 5). Among its stipulations, the law set a twenty-two mile boundary "about the city of *London* or the suburbs of the same" wherein woods could not be felled for making charcoal because "*the necessary provision of wood, as well timber fit for building and other uses, as also other sellable woods serving for fewel* [fuel], *doth daily decay and become scant, and will in time become much more scarce, by reason whereof the prices are grown to be very great and unreasonable, and in time to come will be much more, if some remedy be not provided*" [emphasis in original] (Pickering 341). Whereas Elizabethan statute law aimed to conserve precincts of wooded land from abuse by the iron industry and, in so doing, presumably lower and stabilize consumer prices, promotional literature for colonial expansion imagined the New World as both a quick fix to the present scarcity and a long-term solution to the resource crisis. To offset the "daily decay" codified in legal discourse, propagandists like Thomas Harriot hoped to augment homeland supply by exploiting the bounty of Virginia. According to his report, which was first published in 1588 and printed again in 1590, this territory contained an "infinite store" of coniferous trees whose instrumentalization would correct, in part, "the want of wood and deerenesse thereof in England" (B3^r).

In 1611 Arthur Standish recommended yet another strategy for alleviating the shortage: a full-scale program of planting trees in England. In *The Commons Complaint*, which he dedicated to James I, Standish delineates the potential fallout of an unremedied shortage of wood product. He does so in terms lifted directly from the monarch's "Princely speech to the Parliament" on the subject (A2^{r-v}).[21] For its bravura, the pamphlet's opening gambit, which concludes with a tag that compresses into the form of a motto a statement James addressed to Parliament ("The maintenance of woods is a thing so necessary for this Kingdome, as it cannot stand, nor be a Kingdome without it" [323]), warrants quotation at length:

Wee [the commons] doe in all humblenesse complaine vnto your Maiesty of the generall destruction and waste of wood made within this your Kingdome, more within twenty or thirty last yeares then in any hundred yeares before. Little respect is taken but by your Maiesty, for the posterity and prosperity of your Kingdom; too many destroyers, but few or none at al doth plant or preserue: by reason thereof there is not Timber left in this Kingdome at this instant onely to repaire the buildings thereof an other age, much lesse to build withall: whereby this greeuance doth daily increase. The reasons are many: first, the want of fire is expected, without the which mans life cannot be preserued: secondly, the want of Timber, Bricke, Tyle, Lime, Iron, Lead and Glasse for the building of habitations; Timber for the maintaining of husbandry, for nauigation, for vessels, for bruing [brewing] and the keeping of drinke, and all other necessaries for house-keeping: barke for the tanning of Leather, bridges for trauell, pales for Parkes, poles for Hoppes, and salt from the Wiches [salt-works]. The want of wood is, and will be a great decay to tillage, and cannot but bee the greatest cause of the dearth of corne, and hindreth greatly the yearly breeding of cattell, by reason that much straw is yearely burned, that to the breeding of cattell might be imployed: the want of wood in many places of this Kingdome constraineth the soyll [dung] of cattell to be burned, which should be imploied

to the strengthning of land, and so doth the want of hurdles for the folding
of sheepe, and the want of wood causeth too many great losses by fire, that
commeth by the burning of straw, and so it may be conceiued, no wood no
Kingdome. (1–2)

This jeremiad captures in the amplest terms possible the motivation behind the Utopian scheme of woodland management. There is no end to
the utility of trees, unless, of course, they prove finite and rapidly dimin-
ishing. With the mantra "want of wood," Standish's complaint describes
woodland impoverishment as an ecosystemic collapse: the cascade imperils traditions of agriculture, husbandry, industry, and polity. A lack of what
Standish calls "wood," by which he means woodland and wood product,
and the rise in cost that would surely attend upon uncurbed "destruction
and waste," put at risk the monarchy and the livelihoods of its subjects. By
this logic, the early modern English state rested on a precarious wooden
foundation.

Individual chapters on early modern English drama will take up in
greater detail the eco-solutions and fantasies – woodland conservation,
colonial exploitation, and systematic replanting – advocated in these three
examples for easing the resource crisis. Here we may highlight two general
points about these proposals. First, they correct the perception of early
modern English "policy" about deforestation as "laissez-faire" (Grove
56). Standish's program for intensive replanting may not have been implemented,[22] but it and the laws promulgated in Tudor and Stuart England
nonetheless indicate that the problems of woodland supply and energy
security persisted in public consciousness, so much so that regulatory solutions were sought. Second, these proposals challenge accounts by twen-
tieth- and twenty-first-century historians who have tended to regard the
crisis that this chorus of legal and extralegal voices articulates with a measure of incredulity. For the economic historian Michael Flinn, "contemporary pamphleteers," whom he does not identify, but which surely include
Standish, "are not perhaps the most reliable guides" for assessing the scope
of the scarcity (113).[23] Although Standish and figures like Harriot allude
to the impact of a lack of woods and wood product on England, their "occasional hysterical outbursts" in print are not, according to Flinn, descriptions of an actual "national" shortage; rather their writings manufacture
crisis.[24] He dismisses such panic as mere rhetoric and instead regards these
writers as the kin of present-day political lobbyists who "referred" "[a]t
best" "to local conditions" (113).[25] Keith Thomas has likewise sought to
temper the hyperbole of these early modern writers, maintaining that,

although deforestation was undoubtedly responsible for economic hard-
ship in early modern England, the "timber shortage was never more than
local" (193). And Michael Williams, from whose work *Wooden Os* draws
many of its statistics about price indices, also comprehends the scale of the
deficiency in a narrow way. "Generally speaking," he observes, "shortages
appeared in the economic core, first in England and the Netherlands during the later 1500s, but the scarcity was probably more local and limited
than widespread" (169).[26]

  In hindsight, it may well be that shortages were local, confined to urban centers and to those regions where the iron and shipbuilding industries depended on an abundant supply of wood and timber. Although the
total acreage of British woodland lost to the axe "cannot be quantified"
precisely, England's trees were not fully extirpated.[27] But correctives to
the narrative of scarcity that early modern pamphleteers told tend to pri-
oritize this ecofact above all other sources of evidence. Jeffrey S. Theis
has spotlighted the inadequacy of this stance in his recent study of early
modern English forests: "sometimes whether or not a people correctly
perceive their times is less important than what their perceptions, be
they empirically false or true, tell us about their era, for perceptions, not
empirical rationalism, typically govern human actions" (*Writing* 16–17).
Wooden Os subscribes to Theis's commonsensical approach to the debate and scrutinizes the logic by which local problems ballooned into a
national crisis in these pamphlets in order to explore perceptions of energy (in)security that have been too readily dismissed as exaggeration and
hysteria.

  The upgrade in scale from local to national in the early modern English
literature on resource scarcity stems, in part, from an individual writer's
insistence on his eyewitness account of woodland depletion across England. The decay and destruction of trees in multiple locales, in other words,
add up to the perception of a nationwide shortage. In an epistle to James
I in *The Commons Complaint*, for instance, Standish calls his treatise "the
fruits of my old age and trauell" (A2ʳ). His "best Schoolemaster" for the
task at hand has been "long experience": he "spent ... these foure last
yeares" since the anti-enclosure riots in the Midlands in 1607 "imployed"
in "study and trauel through some parts of most of the Countries [dis-
tricts] of this Kingdome." During this extended, albeit partial, expedition
through England, Standish observed wrecked woodlands and consulted
with "the best Commonwealths-men" about how to reverse the course
of destruction through a program of replanting (A2ᵛ). Like Standish, the
author of *An Olde Thrift Newly Revived* (1612), who is named "R.C." on

the title page,[28] bases his findings about the "lamentable scarcitie, and ex-
ceeding abuses" of English woodlands on first-hand experience (A3ʳ). But
unlike Standish, who figures himself as a garrulous, civic-minded peripa-
tetic, R.C. gathered his knowledge about woodland destruction while on
the royal payroll. His "employment [was] in the late Surueyes and Sales
of diuers his Maiesties Copies [coppices] and Woods." After this gesture
there follows a parenthetical statement suggesting that the Jacobean monarchy has been negligent in the care of its woodlands and complicit in the
liquidation of some of these assets for financial gain.[29] This supplemen-
tary comment casts doubt on R.C.'s further allegation about a widespread
shortage, however. It discloses a "feare" that abuse and scarcity exist
"vniuersally as wel ouer the Realme, as in the said particular places" (A3ʳ),
by which R.C. presumably means crown woodlands. Direct inspection of
"particular places" encourages an expert's surmise about dearth in other
places. If here, so the analogy ("as") goes, then so too must scarcity be
everywhere else, even if there is no ocular proof to support the charge. In
part, such anxious extrapolation about woodland supply in other locales
produces (then and now) the pervasive impression of national shortage.

   Although differently articulated in these pamphlets, the relations that
writers forged between and among locales across England on the basis
of personal observation are the rhetorical means by which a particular
shortage was magnified into a general scarcity. In early modern English
culture, transportation proves the material counterpart to such relation-
making, and its inadequacies at the local level contributed profoundly to
the perception of a national crisis.[30] Without the organization provided
by railways, canals, the postal and telegraph services, and an energy grid,
there was no reliable way for one community to correspond with another
about the need for more wood and timber, and there were few options
for conveying the requested supplies.[31] To complicate matters, a product
such as charcoal, which was an essential source of energy both in London
and in the countryside, could not be barged or carted at great distances; it
was too friable to make too a long journey (B. Thomas 139). When fresh
supplies of wood product arrived, they were often expensive, not necessarily because the woodlands at the point of origin were thinned. Instead,
merchants factored the costs of labour and transit as well as a profit margin into their prices (Hammersley, "Charcoal" 608; Rackham 90–1). In
regions that had an overabundance of woodland, according to economic
historian G. Hammersley, "wood was generally too expensive to be sold
readily at a distance but often too cheap for sale close at hand" ("Crown"
157). For communities crippled by a diminished stock of trees for wood

and timber, knowledge of plenty somewhere else in England must have been small consolation. Cheaper and more regular access to these resources would have been more desirable.

More's *Utopia* affords a fantastic literary solution – an evergreen fantasy – to precisely this sort of systemic predicament. According to Raphael, the transplantation of Utopian woodlands circumvents a persistent lack of "commodious carriage" by moving, in advance, parcels of trees to specific places – cities, for instance – where wood and timber would be consumed in a variety of ways (N3^v). Utopians also fix an inexhaustible store of woodland next to areas – rivers and seashores – where wood product could be both employed to build and repair other means of transport (bridges and seagoing vessels) and, if necessary, shipped to other locales at greater ease. More's text presciently recognizes a truth about transporting wood product: it is (and it would continue to be) an inconvenience.[32]

The Recycled Globe and Other Wooden Matters in the Architectural Archive

In the year following the publication of More's *Utopia* in its third English edition, London witnessed a series of events that, from our vantage, appears an uncanny instance of reality conforming to speculative fiction. Under the supervision of Richard Burbage, the son of a joiner, and Peter Street, a prominent London carpenter, a crew of workmen uprooted a "whole wood" in late December 1598. They dismantled the Theatre, a playhouse situated since 1576 in a "liberty," or precinct outside the jurisdiction of the City of London.[33] According to legal records, the crew "pull[ed] downe" "the woodde and tymber of the ... Playe house" (qtd. in Berry 5), and the disassembled Theatre was stored until more clement weather permitted its wood and timber to be barged down to a liberty on the south bank of the Thames, where the "whole wood" was replanted a short walk from the river's edge, not far from a rival playhouse, the Rose (Shapiro, *Year* 6–7). When the reconstructed Theatre launched its opening season in 1599, it did so under a new sign. Presenting the fare of its resident playwright, this transplanted venue, rechristened the Globe, welcomed its first customers.

As theatre historians have shown, a cluster of economic factors motivated the relocation. Andrew Gurr highlights the stress endured by Shakespeare's acting company at this time when he observes that, despite its present-day fame, the Globe was a last-ditch effort to find a permanent spot to play: "Constructed on a second-hand frame as a second-best option by the company which had hoped to use the Blackfriars hall instead, built for it three years before, the Globe's beginning was unpromising" (*Shakespearean* 142). The twenty-one year lease on the land where the Theatre's frame was situated had expired in 1597, and the landowner, Giles Allen, declined to renew it.[34] To make matters worse, citizens of London with a "NIMBY" sensibility thwarted the opening of Blackfriars, an indoor venue located inside the walls of the City that entrepreneur and joiner James Burbage (Richard's father) had purchased at the steep cost of £600 in 1596.[35] With both venues unavailable for performance after 1597, the company rented another theatre, the Curtain (Shapiro, *Year* 109). Such uncertain circumstances prompted six members of the Chamberlain's Men, including Shakespeare and Richard and Cuthbert Burbage, to embark on a bold economic venture: as "housekeepers" or shareholders, they rented a plot of land near the Rose and planned to build anew on it. But they did not contract Peter Street to furnish them with a new-fangled superstructure for the playhouse: the cost of fresh timber was too prohibitive, and they were likely looking to "economize" (Aaron 279). Instead, Richard and Cuthbert Burbage claimed possession of the property that the family owned – the old wood and timber of the Theatre – and carted it away in 1598; Allen responded by filing a suit for trespass.[36] As the decision to reuse the Theatre's frame suggests, the strained financial portfolio of the Chamberlain's Men shaped the Globe's architecture. Since this venture was spurred by scarcity and pragmatism, not Utopian abundance, we may say that the perceived and real shortage of timber also helped to shape the conditions under which the Globe was erected.

Although the Globe was unique among rival theatrical venues in that its frame consisted entirely of old timbers, the fabric of its superstructure was not unusual. Prior to the rebuilding of the Globe with substantial brickwork after a fire destroyed this "vertuous fabrique" in 1613,[37] all outdoor theatres, including the Theatre, were implicated materially in sixteenth- and seventeenth-century discourses about woodland scarcity. (Theatres and other edifices constructed in brick were also not unconnected to these discourses, since brick-making required a store of charcoal for fuelling kilns [Perlin 193].) Each "new" theatre, in other words, called for a vast stock of lumber to perfect a multistoried, polygonal frame[38] that, according to some estimates, accommodated as many as 3,000 patrons (Gurr, *Shakespearean* 116–17). For its sturdiness and its natural curvatures, which facilitated the construction of polygonal buildings, oak was the timber tree of choice for the theatrical superstructure. Archaeological research provides no clear sense of exactly how much timber was needed for assembling a theatre's frame, not only because these features were all demolished by the close of the seventeenth century, but also because extant contracts for early modern theatres include no precise details about the amount of timber required to build to the specifications they stipulate. Peter Street, for instance, agreed to model the dimensions of the Fortune theatre on the Globe, and the contractor for the Hope theatre used the "fforme, widenes, and height" of the Swan theatre as a pattern.[39] But neither contract itemizes the quantity of timber to be used in this "family tree" of venues.[40]

Notwithstanding such evidential gaps, a survey of custom-built outdoor amphitheatres erected in the sixteenth and early seventeenth centuries affords a sense of the financial extravagance and material outlay attendant upon the development of this entertainment industry in London's suburbs.[41] Traces of performance at permanent, outdoor venues erected prior to the opening of the Theatre are scant. A stage and a series of galleries set up without surrounding walls, the Red Lion was built to the east of London in 1567, and a playhouse at Newington Butts was raised to the south of the City around 1576; both had been dismantled by the end of the sixteenth century, although the playhouse at Newington outlasted the earlier venue.[42] The Curtain appeared in proximity to the Theatre on the northern suburban landscape in 1577.[43] When the Theatre was transformed into the Globe, this "house with the thatched roof"[44] nestled close to a new neighbour, the Rose, which sprung up in 1587 under the care of theatre impresario Philip Henslowe and remained in bloom until its plucking in 1606.[45] The south bank of the Thames was already crowded by 1599, for performances at Francis Langley's Swan had commenced there in 1595. The Dutch traveller Johannes de Witt visited the Swan in 1596 and described it in a letter as London's "largest" and "most magnificent" theatre; he was so impressed that he sketched its interior for his correspondent, and a duplicate of this sketch is the only contemporary drawing of an early modern theatre's interior that survives.[46] In the face of such competition and with the financial backing of his son-in-law, the famous tragedian Edward Alleyn, Henslowe took up residence to the north of the City in 1600, opening the Fortune playhouse.[47] The Red Bull, a former inn that seems to have been razed and custom-built again as a playhouse,[48] was also located to the north of the City's limits, and it welcomed customers within four years of the Fortune's début season. Ten years later, in 1614, Henslowe moved shop back across the Thames, where he raised the Hope, a venue that served a dual purpose. It was both a performance space and a bear-baiting arena; Ben Jonson's *Bartholomew Fair*, which features a vendor with a bear-like name (Ursula), had its first airing there.[49]

In all, then, nine new wooden theatres (excluding the recycled Globe) emerged as conspicuous fixtures in London's liberties from 1567 to 1614, and six of them remained visible throughout the early seventeenth century. William N. West observes that these "buildings," with their exposed timbers and plastered outer walls, "gave London a prospect unlike that of any other European city, distinctive enough in foreign travelers' eyes to characterize it" in their reports, diaries, and letters (43). The cost attached to this unique style of suburban architecture, if the fee for erecting one of these venues provides a reliable ballpark figure, was enormous. Peter Street, who supervised work at the site of the Globe, estimated that it would cost £440 for the building materials and for the labour necessary to erect the Fortune in 1600. Henslowe and Alleyn, in fact, paid him £520.[50] According to S.P. Cerasano, this figure balloons to £880 when the charges associated with "the development of the surrounding property in a preliminary fashion" are taken into account ("Fortune" 89). It is little wonder, then, that in 1598 the sharers of the Chamberlain's Men built their "new" theatre on the cheap.

As the legal documents surrounding the removal of the Theatre indicate, the frame was not the only conspicuous feature of an early modern theatre made from wood product. Once inside a theatre's timber walls, spectators would have encountered other major structural elements also fabricated from "woodde," such as the tiring house, where actors dressed for performance, and the stage. At the Fortune the stage was "to be bourded with good & sufficyent newe deale [fir or pine] bourdes of the whole thickness," and it was "to be paled in belowe with good, strong, and sufficyent newe oken bourdes" so that audience members could not see the actors' movements and preparations in the cellarage.[51] Above the stage was set "a shadowe or cover," which wooden posts that may have been painted likely supported;[52] Hamlet calls a similar piece of stage furniture at the Globe a "most majestical roof fretted with golden fire" (2.2.291–2), inspiring a widely used euphemism for this feature: the heavens. Indeed, the contract for the Hope names the stage canopy "the Heavens."[53] There were also, according to the Fortune's contract, wooden staircases that were to be "covered with Tyle" leading to upper galleries, where customers who paid more money upon entering watched the play while seated on wooden benches.

But a colossal, one-time investment for setting up a theatre hardly accounts for all the timber and wood that would have been required for the venue's upkeep. Evidence from the theatrical archive demonstrates that additional wood product was indeed employed for occasional renovation and general repair. The records of entrance receipts and expenditures that Henslowe kept for the Rose afford a glimpse of the expense of updating the theatre in 1592, just five years after its opening. According to these entries, which constitute part of a larger document that has come to be known as *Henslowe's Diary*, monies were paid out to labourers and suppliers during a hiatus from playing during Lent. The suppliers sold Henslowe "tymber," "dellberds" or deal boards, "a lode of quarters," which are a generic kind of wooden plank, among a variety of other building materials, while the labourers delivered timber by water, thatched a roof, and received wages (9–12).[54] Late twentieth-century excavations of the Rose's foundations reveal that Henslowe significantly altered the theatre's northern section in 1592 in an effort to augment seating capacity and to "enhance the attractions of the stage," likely by fitting it with a canopy (Bowsher and Miller 64).[55] Three years later Henslowe once again had carpenters and other craftsmen in his employ; this time, they worked with over 300 newly purchased "elmebordes" for undertaking unspecified "Repracyones," or repairs, to the theatre and perhaps for fashioning a "throne," which would have descended during performance in a fit of creaky spectacle from "the heauens" (6–7). Henslowe was perhaps sprucing up the Rose in advance of the Swan's opening. In *Pleasant Notes upon Don Quixot* (1654), Edmund Gayton recalls days at a "Play-house" that intimate another possible motive for renovations at a playhouse: raucous crowds. He vividly remembers how "the Benches, the tiles, the laths, the stones, Oranges, Apples, Nuts, flew about most liberally, and as there were Mechanicks of all professions, who fell every one to his owne trade, and dissolved a house in an instant, and made a ruine of a stately Fabrick" (271). Whatever the rationale, the price that Henslowe paid in 1595 for renovations to his "stately Fabrick" on the Bankside was over £115 (7), which turns out to be more than 20 per cent of his initial outlay for the Fortune.

The sheer amount of wood and timber necessary for building and maintaining a theatre suggests that the rapid development of this industry in the late sixteenth and early seventeenth centuries came at an opportunity cost. In an era of perceived and real scarcity, all that wood and timber could have been put to innumerable other uses, from commercial and residential construction in "wooden" London to the build-up of the English fleet. But it wasn't. So why were the many resistances to theatres in the period, which chapter 1 details, not enough to stop impresarios from buying and using massive amounts of the era's most precious material substrate? This question reconfigures the critical project of early modern studies since, at least, the advent of the new historicism. But no scholar, to my knowledge, has articulated the question in precisely these environmental terms. The theatre was indeed a site where early modern culture staged its ideological contradictions and struggles (J. Howard, *Stage*; Mullaney, *Place*), where forms of state power were put on display (Tennenhouse), arguably subverted (Dollimore), and then arguably re-contained (Greenblatt, *Shakespearean*),[56] where new social relations attendant upon an emergent market economy were modelled and solidified (Agnew; Bruster, *Drama*), where the identities of the City's new urban landmarks and precincts were shaped and consolidated (J. Howard, *Theater*), and where new modes of post-Reformation affect were explored (Mullaney, "Affective"). But none of this socio-economic and political work could have been accomplished without some measure of "wood," at the theatre and beyond its walls. Yet in this scholarship the fabric of theatrical structures tends to vanish: it does not contribute substantially to cultural change and self-reflection so much as serve as a disappearing "laboratory" where these assorted processes become manifest and can be observed.[57]

Wooden Os takes an altogether different approach to elaborating the role of theatre in early modern England. It details the theatre's constitutive woodenness in an age of this resource's perceived and real shortage in an effort to claim now that the gain derived from expending untold sums on wood and timber was, counter-intuitively, the erection and administration of "new woodlands" dotting the urban core. In London's theatres, consumers paid the price of admission to experience the pleasures and the frights of being inside virtual woods.[58]

Playing Inside Shakespeare's Woods

Early modern theatres invited spectators – many of whom would have encountered discourses of resource scarcity in print or in conversation and would surely have endured the pinch of rising prices – to behold a wood in the theatre.[59] Unlike other structures in "wooden" London, theatres called frequent (but not invariable) attention to themselves as woodlands in performance. As scholars of early modern drama well know, individual scenes and larger sections of plays take place in forests, woods, orchards, and parks.[60] A previous generation of scholars comprehended Shakespeare's woodlands as verbal constructs.[61] For instance, when *As You Like It*'s Rosalind exclaims, "Well, this is the forest of Ardenne" (2.4.11), she signals to audience members that, at her urging, they should see a forest mentally. Shakespeare's acting troupe could have supplemented such verbal prompting by employing tree stage props. These devices, which were likely wooden planks cut, redundantly, into the shapes of trees,[62] could have been trotted out for particular scenes or remained onstage as a backdrop for the duration of the performance.[63] But the inclusion of these objects in a late sixteenth-century inventory of stage props in *Henslowe's Diary* suggests that tree props worked to conjure a specific dramaturgical effect rather than create a general sense of "forest" or "woods": the Admiral's Men had on hand a "baye tree," a "tree of gowlden apelles," and a "Tantelouse tre" (319–21). More recently, Bruce R. Smith has illuminated the use of another theatrical accoutrement for vivifying settings like Arden. He focuses on the hangings (tapestries, arrases, traverses, and curtains) that prominently fronted the walls of tiring houses at outdoor venues and that were likely green in hue (*Key* 228). To this list of methods for inducing playgoers to believe that they were inside a virtual "green world" during performance,[64] I add the biggest and most solid theatrical instrument that an acting troupe had at its disposal: the playhouse itself.[65]

Shakespeare routinely conscripted the structural woodenness of the theatre to perform the role of tree, woods, forest, orchard, and park.[66] When a character invokes such a woodland setting verbally, his or her words indicate that the actor also physically motions towards some thing. This thing could be a tree stage prop, but it could just as easily have been one of the elongated, trunk-shaped posts of painted wood supporting the heavens. In *Antony and Cleopatra*, for instance, the play's eponymous Roman tells his friend that he will deliver news about the great sea battle to him where "yon pine does stand" (4.13.1). A "yon" is deictic: its meaning and referent depend upon its articulation in the present moment. Such a line also proves gestic: it functions like a pointing finger in the margin of a book, directing sight to that specific pine tree or stage post.[67] Other possible Shakespearean examples of post(s)-performing-tree(s) in this manner occur in *As You Like It* (2.5.26; 3.3.52), *King Lear* (5.2.1), *Richard II* (2.3.53; 3.4.26), *Romeo and Juliet* (2.1.30), *Timon of Athens* (4.3.223), and *Titus Andronicus* (2.3.277; 5.1.47). Sometimes actors drew other features of the theatre into the orbit of woodland settings. In the woods outside Athens, Peter Quince announces that "This green plot shall be our stage, this hawthorn brake our tiring-house" (3.1.3–4). More speculatively, in *Twelfth Night*, Maria may "plant" her partners in crime inside the room above the stage when she instructs them to hide inside "the box-tree" just before Malvolio discovers the forged letter that will be his undoing (2.3.153; 2.5.13).[68] Most grandly, the entire playhouse could also perform woodland. *As You Like It*'s Orlando's gesture to "the circle of this forest" encompasses all the Y-shaped arches and beams that support the theatrical superstructure and that form, overhead, a partial forest canopy (5.4.34). References to "this" "wood" in *Macbeth* (5.4.3) and *A Midsummer Night's Dream* (2.1.191–2; 2.1.223); "This shadowy desert, unfrequented woods" in *The Two Gentlemen of Verona* (5.4.2); "these woods" in *Timon of Athens* (4.3.208); and to "this forest" in *Henry IV, Part Two* (4.1.1) and *Titus Andronicus* (2.3.59) also encode comparable stage directions. Whatever differences there might be in the meaning assigned to these forests, woods, and trees – the woods outside Athens in *A Midsummer Night's Dream*, for example, do not reappear unaltered in *Timon of Athens* – it is the conscription of the theatrical superstructure into the role of forest, woods, and tree(s) that unites these richly disparate scenes and plays. In all cases, the actor signals to the audience to see one thing (a post) and another thing (a tree) simultaneously, as if the theatre were approximating the *trompe l'oeil* effect of anamorphic painting. He revivifies the wood of theatre, suggesting that in these moments there is no distinction between "nature" (living wood) and "culture" (lumbered wood).

Not intended to be comprehensive, this Shakespearean sampling does intimate that when the theatre and its features were scripted to perform the role of woodland, actors conjured this setting in a way that is qualitatively different from the ornamental backgrounds afforded by tree stage props and green curtains. We could describe such conjuration as ecomimesis, which, according to Timothy Morton, can exist in a "strong, magical form, a compelling illusion rather than a simple copy." In so doing, we pluck from an account of poetic ambience Morton's *very* "rough Greek translation for 'nature writing'" – indeed, it is a productive mistranslation for a phrase that could be rendered as "ecographesis" – and embed it into the realm of dramatic representation (54).[69] Such a move enables us to identify a curious eco-material effect of playing inside Shakespeare's woods. For when Quince nominates "this green plot" "our stage," he may pick up or kick around the green rushes covering the wooden floor (Gurr and Ichikawa 4); when he designates "this hawthorn brake" "our tiring house," he likely touches and points to the theatre's tiring house. In both instances, but more explicitly in the latter, Quince transforms the playhouse's structural features back into the vegetable matter that they were, or may have been. The joint force of such gesture and deictic language strips the interior of Shakespeare's wooden O of its cloth and paint and turns it into virtual woodland.[70] Michael D. Bristol's fine name for this force is "*fiat sylvius.*"[71] No doubt the success of such an imperative also rests on the audience's willingness to muster its "imaginary forces" (Prologue, *Henry V*, l. 18) and see trees in the wooden theatre.

Working on and in concert with the audience's "thoughts" (Prologue, *Henry V*, ll. 23, 28), Quince and his Shakespearean fellows thus revitalize woodlands during performance. But they do not do so by means of analogy and simile, the two rhetorical figures that scholars have recently employed to articulate the relation between early modern theatre and the natural world. Robert N. Watson, for example, wittily calls his landmark ecocritical discussion of Shakespeare's Arden "As You Liken It: Simile in the Forest" (77–107), and Jeffrey S. Theis christens the subtitle of his chapter on Shakespeare's bosky settings with a chiasmus, "The Stage as Forest and the Forest as Stage" (*Writing* 35–89). In Theis's reading, Shakespeare "blurs the distinction between sylvan and theatrical space and suggests that they are analogous realms": both are "sites of ambivalent contestation that can and do transform individuals as well as the nation itself" (*Writing* 35, 89).[72] Watson perhaps comes closer than does Theis to describing the operations of a *fiat sylvius* when he observes that *As You Like It* "insistently tests the membrane separating the biological world from human artifice and illusion"; in his analysis, Arden's "trees" are the preferred "test case" that Shakespeare uses to put pressure on this border (96, 97). But a *fiat sylvius* bursts through this "membrane" insofar as it proves a complex metaphor that reprises the eco-history of the theatre's fabric: Quince's "shall be" in the Athenian woods articulates an "is"; "this is the forest of Ardenne," Rosalind announces to her fellow travellers. In these utterances, the theatre is not simply similar or analogous to woodland. It *was* also once part of the woods, a forest, or tree, and now, in performance, its constitutive woodenness reverts to a former material condition. In Jonathan Gil Harris's terms, "the past" of the superstructure does not appear "as dead and buried, or even as a spectral visitor from beyond the grave, but as alive and active" (*Untimely* 31). In enchanting dead wood, actors can re-present, in an uncanny way, the woodland spot where trees were once lumbered to supply carpenters with the materials for erecting the theatre's frame.[73]

Like an escapist Hollywood film from the gritty 1930s that glamorizes sophistication and wealth, a play featuring an ecomimetic woodland proves an early modern English "ideological fantasy" that could afford audience members virtual compensation for the economic reality and the alleged environmental conditions outside the theatre's wooden walls (Morton 67). We might reason that a theatre transforms back into woodland for only the duration of the scenes requiring such settings. Yet the mobile nature of the repertory, in which some plays had long runs and many were revived and revised after their initial airings (as we shall observe about *The Spanish*

Tragedy) could have had an accretive effect that secured the material link between theatre and woodland. Multiple shows, adaptations, and revivals across the early modern period may have "typecast" the theatre in the role of woodland in the cultural imagination. An evergreen fantasy of the first order, such cultural reafforestation establishes a "woody theatre," which is Milton's verdant phrase for the space where the drama of Adam and Eve unfolds – Eden (Bk. IV, l. 141). Inside England's woody theatres, a rich array of eco-fantasies and nightmares about the shortage of wood and timber were staged.

Theatre *in* the Woods

Although there is no way to determine whether all early modern English playgoers comprehended the theatre in exactly this manner, two well-known examples from the theatrical archive further indicate the cultural pervasiveness of the material link between theatres and woodlands. Reminiscences logged in the diary of astrologer Simon Forman constitute the first example, and they suggest that at least one audience member may have beheld woods when he saw the theatre. After attending a performance of *Macbeth* in 1611, Forman noted in manuscript that "ther was to be observed, firste, howe Mackbeth and Bancko, 2 noble men of Scotland, Ridinge thorowe a wod, the[r] stode before them 3 women feiries or Nimphes."[74] Both Margreta de Grazia (55) and Stephen Orgel (32–5) have recently marshalled this entry to demonstrate how chronicle history conditioned Forman's reportage: there are no horses and no fairies (or nymphs) onstage in Shakespeare's play, but these figures do appear in an illustration that accompanies Holinshed's account of the story. Since there is also a lone tree in this woodcut, the allusion to "wod" or woods in this entry could be construed as another memory of reading chronicle history – Macbeth and Banquo "pass[] through the woodes and fieldes" in Holinshed (243ʳ) – rather than of seeing a play. But as we've already observed, later in Shakespeare's *Macbeth* there is a gestic reference to "this" "wood" (5.4.3), not to mention the march across the stage of Birnam Wood to Dunsinane, so it is possible that Forman's recollection has roots in an afternoon at the theatre. Two other pieces of evidence in Forman's diary lend support to the idea that he saw the "theatre" and remembered "woodland." He recollects watching the newborn Perdita "caried into Bohemia & ther laid in a forrest" and in another play the body of the presumed dead Fidele (Imogen) "laid … in the wodes." Yet neither *The Winter's Tale* nor *Cymbeline* refers to "forest," "woods," or "tree" in

Figure 0.1 Raphael Holinshed, *The First volume of the Chronicles of England, Scotlande, and Irelande* (London, 1577), detail. This item is reproduced by permission of The Huntington Library, San Marino, California.

the way that Forman would suggest that they do. Only *Cymbeline* comes close: one character refers to another as a "woodman" – that is, as a hunter (3.6.28) – and Fidele promises to strew the decapitated body (s)he thinks is Posthumous's with "wild wood-leaves and weeds" (4.2.392). In Forman's reconstruction of these scenes, the theatre is woodland even when a play does not call ostentatious attention to the theatre's woodenness. Indeed, it would seem that all that's needed to trigger the theatre-woodland connection for Forman is a play's gesture to the natural world: the Bohemian seacoast in *The Winter's Tale* and the Welsh mountains in *Cymbeline*.

Visual evidence from the period likewise intimates that outside performance, theatres and woodlands were regarded as kin. In John Norden's *Civitas Londini* (1600), a panorama of London, the trees on the Bankside are so dense that they make it difficult to spot the Globe. (The Rose is easier to discern because its walls are higher and its flag waves.) Such a profusion of foliage may not be simply artistic fancy. It may also tap into recent memory of the precinct's topography, which incurred some measure of alteration when the Globe, Rose, and Swan playhouses were erected. A report filed on 12 July 1578 by "Mr. Recorder Fletewoode" in-

Figure 0.2 John Norden, *Civitas Londini* (1600), detail. This image is reproduced
by kind permission of the National Library of Sweden.

dicates that the Bankside was densely wooded in the years before this trio
of theatres took root: Fleetwood observes that the "place" around Paris
Garden, an animal-baiting venue near the river, was "so dark with trees
that one man cannot see another, 'except they have the lynceos oculos or
els cattes eys'" (Lemon 595). One viewer of Norden's bosky cityscape
who might have benefited from the clarity of such feline vision was J.C.
Visscher, a Dutchman who modelled his panoramic vision of London on
Norden's example. In the estimation of theatre historian R.A. Foakes,
Visscher seems to have overlooked the Globe in his model: "It is very
possible," Foakes hypothesizes, that "Visscher elaborated here with an
artist's license what he found in the panorama of *Civitas Londini*; perhaps
not noticing the Globe in that, which is almost concealed by trees, he has
taken from it the Rose, Beargarden [an animal-baiting arena] and Swan,
and for pictorial effect has enlarged them, and located the Globe and the
Swan quite incorrectly and much too near the river" (18). Like its pre-

Figure 0.3 J.C. Visscher, *Londinum Florentiss[i]ma Britanniae Urbs* (1625), detail. This image is reproduced by permission of the Folger Shakespeare Library.

decessor, Visscher's panorama also clusters treetops around the "Globe" and the animal-baiting arena, in some cases obscuring architectural components near the base of the superstructure with foliage. In both images, then, representations of living trees overlay the playhouse's exterior timbers, reminding viewers that theatres were (made from) trees. In these images, the theatres disappear behind and into the woods.

One effect of visual superimposition in these panoramas is the radical compression of the distance between the theatre and the nearby lush grouping of trees. When forests, trees, and woods are revived in performance, matters of distance likewise manifest in complex ways. For this "new woodland" is, of course, far removed from its potentially multiple points of origin. By the emphatic force of metaphor, actors repeatedly transformed the theatre into the forest or a post into a tree, often at different venues across suburban London because the scripts of the repertory were mobile.[75] In uttering sylvan metaphors that self-consciously reprised the theatre's material past, actors transported – a term that was synonymous in the period with "metaphor" (Parker, *Literary* 93) and that names the figurative movement of playhouse and audience from one place to another in *Henry V* – the current location of performance (in)to the woods. In so doing, actors also reinvigorated the dead wood of the theatre's superstructure, undoing the actual labour required to build it. For the frame's oaken timbers were felled "somewhere out in the country,"[76] shaped into usable pieces, assembled through joining, marked sequentially in situ with Roman numerals,[77] taken apart there, and then conveyed to the location of the venue, where this "portable" (Hattaway 22) and prefabricated kit was easily reassembled on foundations, thanks to the numerical marks that indicated how the frame had fit together while it stood *in the woods*, likely very near the spot where its materials were formerly enrooted.[78] There were, then, theatres in the woods in sixteenth- and seventeenth-century England before labourers took them down and re-erected them around London.

When the Burbages and their company disassembled the "woodde and tymber" of the Theatre and shifted it to Bankside in 1598–9, their act of recycling put a penny-pinching twist on the "normal Elizabethan way" for constructing theatres (Orrell, "Theatres" 103).[79] As such, these efforts also serially repeated the building process initiated in the English woodlands in the mid-1570s that culminated in the erection of the Theatre. As the rich example of the Globe suggests, *Wooden Os* contributes to the burgeoning field of eco-historical study insofar as it discovers in early modern English culture and literature precursors to more modern environmentalist practices and habits of thought.[80] But it does not aim to celebrate them in unambiguous terms, as ecocritical scholars of early modern letters – and especially of the pastoral – have tended to do.[81] *Wooden Os* could not have been written without the pioneering eco-historical accounts of Todd A. Borlik, Gabriel Egan, Ken Hiltner, and Steve Mentz, among others, but it also aims to trouble the designation of Shakespeare, his fellow playwrights, and their art as "green," in the term's modern sense. This study presents a fuller picture of early modern woodland ecology and its stage representations by contemplating the darker shades of green in the contested, felled, fatal, logged, and razed trees of early modern drama.[82] It is as interested in telling the story of the recycled Globe as it is in describing the cancellation of the theatre industry's footprint on English woodlands made possible by cultural reafforestation.

Staging the Shortage of Wood in the Theatre

Since there is no method for accessing how audience members felt about the drama's complex spatial and temporal engagements with the ecological crisis while inside a wooden theatre or if they all felt the same way at the same time, *Wooden Os* teases out of the period's playtexts clues about how the scripts in performance could have shaped, intentionally or unwittingly, audience sentiment. In pursuit of the traces of such conditioning, this book turns to four plays that transformed the theatre back into a woodland – forests, gardens, parks, and woods – and then enacted (or proposed to enact) the felling of trees there. In so doing, *Wooden Os* takes as its primary object of study the individual "stage tree," in the form of a stage prop, a stage post, and, in a posthumanist twist, even the actor's body. It comprehends the "stage tree" as a synecdoche for the theatre and, as we have observed, as a metaphorical trace of the woodland from which that theatre had been fashioned. The stage tree is thus no backdrop to the play's main action. It instead proves an active and alive "star": collectively, these trees comprise the *dramatis arborae* of early modern commercial theatre. Because the stage tree is in danger of eradication – or has been lumbered into logs – in these plays and yet remains renewable because drama is an iterative art form, this stage object enables us to see how the drama scripted for outdoor venues participated in, amplified, and wished-away the discourses of resource shortage that this introduction has outlined. At the *topos* of a stage tree, matters pertaining to colonial extraction and the market in bulk goods (chapters 1 and 4), genealogical aspiration and conservation in England (chapters 2 and 3), and the stability of English governance at home and abroad (chapters 1 through 4) converge in complex ways. And since an individual tree (or log) is also a figure in miniature for the theatrical superstructure in which it is staged, such matters, which are designated "eco-political" in these pages, become imbricated with the history of English playhouses, from the erection of wooden Os around London to the persistent calls from antitheatrical writers who, as we shall see throughout these pages, wish to have the "crookéd figure[s]" of theatre plucked up, pulled down, and put to better use (Prologue, *Henry V*, l. 15).

The stage trees that *Wooden Os* explores are (admittedly) called upon to do much work, and the beginning of each chapter affords a thorough map through its argumentative thickets. Moreover, since this study elaborates the polyvalent meaning of the stage tree, it takes the palimpsest as its interpretive model. Jonathan Gil Harris regards this "material artifact[]," which layers and presents tissues of meaning in "obstinately antisequential" ways, as exemplifying untimely matter, the concept that has already enabled us to behold the trees in the theatre and the forest in the theatre's wooden fixtures and walls (*Untimely* 13, 16). Because a palimpsest superimposes but does not wipe out strata of significance, the structure of engagement with stage trees in *Wooden Os* is based on its principles. In

effect, *Wooden Os* has been composed as if it were a palimpsest: form attempts to approximate content, insofar as the many guises of England's
theatrical woodlands appear in the chapters that follow as layers of eco-
material context remembered and recalled from discussions in previous
chapters. Indeed, the argumentative point this book makes about English
woodlands is not teleological, in that it revels in a final moment of insight
or congratulation about the reversal of deforestation. Rather, *Wooden Os*
stresses and lays bare a logic that enables us to see the accretion of meaning
to the stage tree through time.

Four chapters about English woodlands range across theatres and
genres as they track the eco-material history of English theatre. They
travel from the Rose playhouse in the late 1580s (*Friar Bacon and Friar Bungay*) to the Globe theatre in the early 1610s (*The Tempest*). Stops
along the way include the Curtain (*The Merry Wives of Windsor*) and the
Fortune (a revised *Spanish Tragedy*). This eclectic selection of drama and
playhouses aims, in the first instance, to sample the rich fare of early modern theatrical experience: in Virginia Woolf's apt formulation, in *Wooden
Os* "we ramble through the jungle, forest, and wilderness of Elizabethan
[and early-Jacobean] drama" (56). The selection has the added advantage
of including some drama that did not premiere at the venue where we will
study its performance. Thomas Kyd's *Spanish Tragedy* was at least fifteen
years old when Henslowe had it retrofitted for revival at the Fortune in
1602, and Shakespeare's *Tempest* may have opened at court or at Blackfriars, the indoor theatre that finally became available to Shakespeare's
company (known then as the King's Men) in 1608, before it was probably
mounted at the Globe. Moreover, the drama on the playbill in *Wooden Os*
has proven difficult to date with certainty: excepting *The Tempest*, this
is a roster of plays whose composition and earliest performance history
are shrouded in some degree of mystery. In this respect, these plays seem
rooted in an impassable forest.

Yet there must be some sure way through this thicket of stage trees. And
so the story that *Wooden Os* narrates, in the second instance, correlates
roughly to the environmental history delineated in this introduction, from
the steady increase in prices of wood and timber that started in the 1580s
to the apocalyptic rhetoric propounded by Arthur Standish in the second
decade of the seventeenth century. Individual chapters do not pair drama
with a writer who reflects on environmental scarcity in order to demonstrate how the drama fully exemplifies and adheres to the writer's agenda.
Instead, they explore in the imperiled stage tree surprising points of
(dis)connection between the discourses of scarcity and the drama's depic-

tion of both the material theatre and English woodlands. At times, the drama actively participated in the fearmongering discourses of scarcity, while at other times it stridently resisted these darker-green scenarios, for to destroy a stage tree could be read as a prompt to eco-political disaster. And sometimes the drama invoked possibilities for resolving the scarcity that turned out to be dead ends – or, in hindsight, deferrals – such as the promise of resource abundance that was promoted in colonial literature on Virginia. This drama registers a range of potential responses to the shortage of wood and timber because, by the first decades of the seventeenth century, there was no end to it in sight. The perceived resource crisis had yet to be remedied at the close of Shakespeare's stage career, and England was still experimenting with and refining existing representational strategies for articulating, mitigating, and evading its ramifications.

1

"Vanish the tree": *Friar Bacon and Friar Bungay* at the Rose

Near the midway point of Robert Greene's *Friar Bacon and Friar Bungay*,[1] a tree prop takes centre stage for roughly eighty lines. "[L]eav'd with refined gold" (9.79), it may be the "tree of gowlden apelles" listed in the late sixteenth-century inventory of the Admiral's Men's stage props – or, at least, a forerunner of it. Thrust through the stage floor's trapdoor, the tree and the magicians interacting with it also "hold[] ... with a long suspense" (9.155) the attention of a double audience: the patrons who paid their coins for a performance of *Friar Bacon* at the Rose and the royal visitors who assemble in the play at thirteenth-century Oxford University to witness a scholarly dispute between rival magicians. Yet despite its prominence in *Friar Bacon*, descendants of the scholars who challenged one another in Oxford afford the tree prop only passing notice in their explorations of magic and dramaturgical innovation in the play.[2] In planting the tree at the heart of its analysis, this chapter crosshatches these scholarly interests with a third:[3] the link forged in the introduction between the (seeming) shortage of wood and timber in early modern England and the woodenness of the theatre. At the close of the disputation sequence, Bacon "Vanish[es] the tree" (9.161), a magic trick that opens a vista onto the play's engagement with these environmental and theatrical concerns.

Whether they are props conveyed onstage or one of the posts supporting the heavens, the "trees" of early modern drama, as the introduction outlined, have a material relation to the theatres in which the plays featuring them were performed. But in *Friar Bacon and Friar Bungay* such logic alone does not figure the golden tree as the Rose playhouse. The play associates tree prop and theatre not only by casting the scene of academic dispute as kin to drama, but also by employing a vocabulary of acting to name the exploits of the scholars who perform magic there. These exploits, however, work against expectation insofar as they are not steeped in the pastoral imagery that the play earlier invokes: the tree prop is not a backdrop for a Green(e)world of rustics and "bonny" milkmaids (1.16).[4] Instead, the renowned continental magician Vandermast supervises a spectacle of violence against the golden tree when he directs the "fiend appearing like great Hercules" that he summons to "tear the branches piecemeal from the root" (9.91, 99). *Friar Bacon's* treatment of the stage tree further elaborates its relation to material theatre by representing in this moment of violence the agenda of the early modern propaganda campaign against stage playing known as "antitheatricalism."[5] To its opponents, as Michael O'Connell observes, the "institution [of theatre] is corrupt at heart, and only a complete extirpation of all theaters and playing would satisfy them" (15).[6] O'Connell's word for the fate antitheatricalists wished against the theatre – "extirpation" – keys us into the botanical idiom for destruction that *Friar Bacon* shares with texts in this tradition; in 1633 William Prynne employs the exact term in his compendious tract *Histrio-Mastix* (6). In the pamphlets and treatises of Prynne's forebears, theatres were to be "plucked up," "razed," and "rooted out" as if they were trees – or perhaps a Rose. But by magically whisking the tree away, Bacon prevents the tree prop's utter obliteration. The art of vanishing thus preserves a figure for the theatre from an aggression that theatre's most vociferous detractors routinely expressed in the public arena of print and in civic correspondence posted between London's Lord Mayors and the Queen's Privy Council.

In this light, the sudden disappearance of the stage tree at the close of the dispute also proves an act of magical defence that has an affinity with the most ambitious experiment that Bacon conducts at "Brazen-nose" "college" in Oxford (2.166). With "the help of devils and ghastly fiends" (2.28), he plans to erect a brass wall that

> will strengthen England by my skill,
> That if ten Caesars liv'd and reign'd in Rome,
> With all the legions Europe doth contain,
> They should not touch a grass of English ground. (2.58–61)

In the late 1580s, when *Friar Bacon and Friar Bungay* debuted, Rome had yet again plotted to "touch" England. This time its agents manned the fleet of the Spanish Armada. There is, however, a noticeable drawback to enwalling England with a boundary that, in Bacon's estimation, would outstrip the historically feeble security afforded by "The work that Ninus rear'd at Babylon" and "The brazen walls fram'd by Semiramis"

(2.62–3). As Barbara Howard Traister observes, Bacon's design would sever "communication and interchange with other countries" (74).[7] These are not insignificant effects when we recall that essential goods that England required to deter a Spanish invasion in the late 1580s were obtained through overseas commerce. It imported iron, masts for ships, and naval stores, such as tar, pitch, and rope, all of which were products of forest economy, from a powerful alliance of northern European towns known as the Hanse. Interchange with this most favoured trading partner was strained during the period because the Hanse was also trafficking with the enemy. In the context of such tense trade dealings, Bacon's command that Vandermast and the tree be "Transport[ed] … unto Hapsburg straight" (9.158) gestures towards England's dependency on continental wood products whose security of supply was compromised in the late 1580s both by poor relations with German retailers and by competition over naval provisions with Spain. In Vandermast's violence, then, *Friar Bacon* imagines the unlikely marriage of English antitheatricalism and foreign invasion on English soil: both the assault on the tree prop and its vanishing constitute versions of an ecological disappearing act that could affect national security.

Friar Bacon and Friar Bungay's tree prop thus emerges as a rich stage icon rooted firmly in the economic, environmental, and religio-political controversies of sixteenth-century England. Not only does its presence onstage point towards the "trees" housed in the wooden walls of the Rose theatre that were unavailable for further use, but its disappearance also belongs to a discourse detailing a kingdom-wide need for wood product. The polyvalent meanings of the tree prop's exit, in other words, co-articulate a resource dilemma besetting England in the second half of the sixteenth century: uses of timber converge at the tree's trunk that, in their incompatibility, highlight the opportunity cost pegged to the expansion and maintenance of theatre.[8] Since *Friar Bacon* is dramatic fiction, it is little surprise that it delineates no direct resolution to the resource dilemma emblematized in its stage tree. But the play does obliquely allude to a project for relieving England's ecological needs that aimed to win government backing in the late 1580s: Thomas Harriot's promotion of Virginia as a paradise of woodlands as easily plucked as those in More's *Utopia*. Presided over by the name and the iconography of Queen Elizabeth, both Harriot's colonialist pamphlet and Bacon's final act of magic in the play – a prediction of the Tudor Queen's reign that the play's English king glosses as "Thus glories England over all the west" (16.76) – work to extend the trajectory of *translatio imperii*. The wide-ranging "all" of Bacon's prophecy "suggest[s] a deferral of closure, an evasion of narrow referents," whereas Harriot's contemporaneous pamphlet "points England to" an "imperial destin[y] yet to be pursued" (Feerick, *Strangers in Blood* 105):[9] Virginia is a land of "virgin" forests whose abundance could cure England of its dependence on continental sources of wood product. In so doing, Greene's westward-looking play at the Rose and Harriot's brochure jointly imagine an eco-fantasy of colonialism that promised to make the resource dilemma England was enduring, and to which the English theatre industry had contributed, vanish. This colonialist fantasy, however, failed to take root in the late 1580s.

The Magical Tree Prop

In elaborating the meanings of *Friar Bacon and Friar Bungay*'s stage tree, this chapter engages a scholarly conversation about the play's two other magical stage objects: Bacon's "glass prospective" (5.105) and his brazen head, which the 1630 edition of the play reproduces for the first time on its title page.[10] *Friar Bacon* associates scenes featuring these magical props with dramaturgical experiment and spectacular destruction. The glass prospective, for example, enables guests in Bacon's quarters at Oxford to witness events transpiring elsewhere as if they were watching a television on mute; Bacon tellingly dubs such sights "comedy" (6.48) and "tragedy" (13.36). The use of this magical object partitions the stage, but only audience members at the Rose could see and hear the double action unfolding; the characters huddled in Bacon's study observe dumb shows (Traister 82). After the magical glass shows and then prompts tragedy, strewing the stage with four corpses – two men "hard by Fressingfield" (13.62) who have duelled to the death over the milkmaid Margaret's love and their two sons who continued the mortal combat in Bacon's study after watching their fathers kill one another – Bacon decides to ruin the object. He does so in a way that amplifies the magical prop's capacity to split the stage: he smashes it to bits with a "poniard" (13.80). "So fade the glass," Bacon says, "and end with it the shows / That nigromancy did infuse the crystal with" (13.82–3). *Friar Bacon* had earlier accorded a similar fate to the brazen head, which, in addition to "ring[ing] the English strond" (2.65), promised to "unfold strange doubts and aphorisms / And read a lecture in philosophy" (2.26–7). After this automaton utters three gnomic phrases while Bacon (but not the audience) is out of earshot, "*lightning flasheth forth*," according to the stage direction, "*and a hand appears that breaketh down the* Head *with a hammer*." Kurt Tetzeli Von Rosador contends that

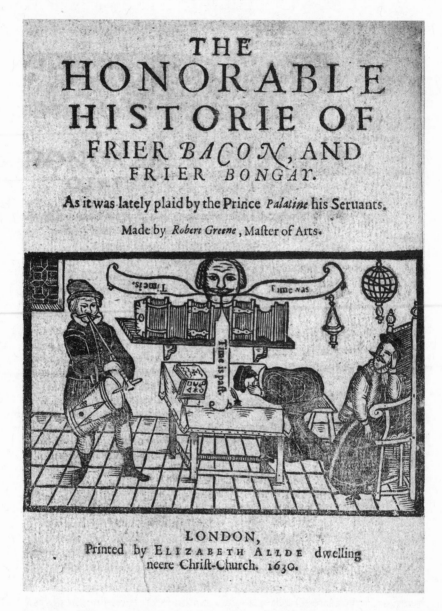

Figure 1.1 Title page to Robert Greene, *The Honorable Historie Of Frier Bacon, and Frier Bongay* (London, 1630). This item is reproduced by permission of The Huntington Library, San Marino, California.

at this moment the disembodied hand of God, a visual convention Greene likely lifted from emblem books, makes a smashing entrance in *Friar Bacon* (39).[11]

Such destructive stage business has led scholars to characterize *Friar Bacon and Friar Bungay* as an expression of its author's "endlessly vexed or divided relation" to antitheatricalism (Crewe 323).[12] For Todd Andrew Borlik, the brazen head is best understood "as a kind of humanist idol," and its (divine) destruction articulates the "genuine grievances" that Greene has "with the medium in which he works" ("'More than Art'" 131, 144). We could extend Borlik's comments to the shattered glass prospective, which Bacon aligned explicitly with forms of dramatic art – comedy, tragedy, and magical shows.[13] Yet the editors of a recent essay collection on Greene's writing challenge "the orthodox critical opinion that Greene consistently had an anti-theatrical bias." They adduce lines from a pamphlet called *Greene's Never Too Late* (1590) that heap praise on honest players to argue that the "passage points to a relationship with the theatre that is less adversarial than is often allowed to Greene" (Melnikoff and Gieskes, "Introduction" 8). In focusing on the magical tree prop, this chapter further readjusts the prevailing bias in Greene criticism by highlighting this play's multiple response to antitheatrical violence.[14] Neither Bacon nor a disembodied hand cut the tree down during the scene of magical disputation. Instead, the Oxford don protects it from the peril to which a foreign scholar has subjected it.

A recap of the scene starring the magical tree prop will help us better comprehend how *Friar Bacon and Friar Bungay* ultimately treats it in a way that is qualitatively different from its handling of the glass prospective and the brazen head. When the English monarch Henry III and the German Emperor Frederick II arrive in Oxford, Bungay and Vandermast engage in an esoteric debate about the relative merits of pyromancy and geomancy (9.26–72); for Bungay, the reward of victory is the glamour of being "use[d] ... as a royal king" (9.19). Once each disputant has argued his side, Vandermast challenges Bungay to "Prove" the "force" of geomancy (9.72, 74), which the English friar had advocated. In return, Bungay conjures a tree rooted in the ground and, according to Kent Cartwright, all but inaugurates a "theatrical commonplace" of Elizabethan drama: the appearance of a tree through the stage's trapdoor (226). More specifically, the tree Bungay conjures is the one "Whereon the fearful dragon held his seat, / That watch'd the garden call'd Hesperides" (9.80–1). Unfortunately for Bungay, however, this magical sally opens him up to a ready-made counterattack, for he has unwittingly recreated the eleventh labour of Hercu-

les. Vandermast summons a "fiend" in the guise of the mythological hero
(9.99), but the continental magician puts a twist on the story. His Hercules does not defeat the dragon Ladon in order to "win the golden fruit"
(9.96). Rather, Vandermast "raise[s]" (9.89) "Alcmena's bastard" – Hercules – who has formerly "raz'd this tree" (9.88) to do so all over again. The
pun that Vandermast indulges in here ("raz'd" and "raise") links violence
to magic and prepares the double audience for the assault against the tree
that Hercules will soon commence. Indeed, when Vandermast orders the
fiend to "tear the braches piecemeal from the root" (9.91) and to "Pull off
the sprigs from off the Hesperian tree" (9.95), Hercules simply responds,
"*Fiat*" (9.97). As Hercules supervises such botanical destruction, Vandermast addresses Bungay, goading his opponent to stop Hercules "From
pulling down the branches of the tree" (9.100). Bungay admits that he
"cannot" (9.102), and so he – and England – would seem to concede defeat in the magical disputation. Vandermast commands Hercules to desist
(9.103) and calls for a prize – a wreath of laurels (9.115). To borrow an apt
phrase from Marlowe's *Doctor Faustus*, Vandermast wishes to be crowned
"conjurer laureate" (scene 3, l. 33).

Enter Friar Bacon. With his arrival, the play sets up conditions for a
second round of magical contest, but Bacon declines twice in this scene
to debate Vandermast (9.129, 150). He instead dares his opponent to undo
his final act of magic by "Set[ting] Hercules to work" again and to "ruinate that tree" (9.131, 133). Vandermast fails to charm his fiend into motion
because, as Hercules discloses, the might of Bacon's "frown" "Binds me
from yielding unto Vandermast" (9.137, 143). The German Emperor realizes the geopolitical consequence of his champion's baffling so he prods
Bacon to "dispute with him and try his skill" (9.149), which request from
a superior in social rank Bacon rejects. Bacon then employs his preferred
method for dispatching enemies and irritants in this play: magical transportation (9.158; 12.129). He bids Hercules to take Vandermast to Hapsburg, where this "novice" magician can enrol in remedial studies (9.151),
and to "Vanish the tree" (9.161). The first labour Hercules performs for
Bacon underscores Vandermast's total humiliation, but the second task
suggests that in besting Vandermast for England's sake, Bacon also triumphs over Bungay. To secure victory Bacon defeats all competitors in
the scholarly competition, including a countryman with whom he keeps
close company, most ostentatiously in the play's title.[15] Bacon, in effect,
makes all traces of his predecessors' art vanish, likely back through the
trapdoor out of which the tree prop initially rose and perhaps under the

smoky cover of an exploding squib. In so doing he confirms his reputation as "England's only flower" (4.60).

In light of the spectacular violence directed against the glass prospective and the brazen head, the preservation of the magical tree prop from renewed assault in *Friar Bacon and Friar Bungay* proves anomalous.[16] The differential treatment of these props, however, does not stem from a fundamental distinction in kind. As the next section illustrates, *Friar Bacon* classes both the tree and the magical objects housed in Bacon's study as media of drama. The difference that does matter for us, that sets the tree prop apart from its kin and makes it worth safeguarding from obliteration, is its elemental woodenness. In Greene's play, the magical tree prop emerges as an emblematic figure for the theatre where actors mount *Friar Bacon and Friar Bungay*.

Magic Acts at the Rose

The appearance and disappearance of the magical tree prop is an exciting experiment in stage business. It is so in no small measure because audiences (playgoers and readers of the play alike) unfamiliar with *Friar Bacon and Friar Bungay*'s plot are not as prepared to witness its emergence at Oxford as they are to see the glass prospective and the brazen head. *Friar Bacon* alerts its audiences to these other objects before it stages them (2.25 and 5.105). The stage tree, then, is a genuine surprise in this play. It proves all the more unexpected because one of Oxford's scholars – a certain doctor Burden – had suggested that the university would ready a different form of entertainment "To welcome all western potentates" (7.12). "We must lay plots of stately tragedies," he says, "Strange comic shows, such as proud Roscius / Vaunted before the Roman emperors" (7.9–11). Burden eagerly describes here university drama, which would have been performed in Latin and, we can infer from its advocate's name, may well have been a taxing production to watch. Clement, a fellow of Burden's, adds further details about the royal visit that substantially alter the welcoming committee's plans: "But more, the king by letters hath foretold" that the German Emperor and his resident magician will be part of the noble train (7.13). The proposal to mount university drama gives way to a desire to see Bacon "Match and dispute with the learned Vandermast" (7.22). Anticipation for the scene of magical disputation thus overrides the opportunity to stage collegiate theatricals. Moreover, *Friar Bacon* both complicates and enriches the realization of this dispute: Bungay loses to Vandermast before

Bacon enters, and Bungay conjures the magical tree prop during the initial match. Such plot twists, the play intimates, are touches of the professional dramatist and not likely to have been the fruit of Burden's labour.

The logic of this conversation about planning is supercessional, and so the scene of magical disputation supplants, but does not eradicate, the performance of drama at Oxford. It is thus noteworthy that Burden's university drama ("stately tragedies" and "Strange comic shows") fuses the generic designations that Bacon uses to describe the effects produced by the two magical objects in his study – "comedy," "tragedy," and "shows." Burden connects the staging of drama more explicitly to Bacon's magic when, after Clement shares his news, he predicts England's victory: "Bacon, if he will hold the German play, / We'll teach him what an English friar can do" (7.23–4). The metaphor here ("hold ... play"), as one of *Friar Bacon and Friar Bungay*'s editors notes, stems from the discourse of "combat or dueling," and we can envision the scholars, *Harry Potter*-like, extending their wands in magical dispute.[17] By way of a pun, it also belongs to an idiom of performance, forecasting the use of terms that *Friar Bacon* associates with the art of playing in the sequence featuring the magical tree prop. With some haughtiness, Bacon there asks a crestfallen Bungay, "What, hath the German acted more than thou?" (9.119), and later in this scene Hercules informs Vandermast that Bacon's "frown doth act more than thy magic" (9.137). In both instances, to "act" names a struggle between opponents, and its subject in these passages is the victorious magician. Bacon, then, is the premier actor in the scene of disputation: his authority over Hercules and his facility at reversing Bungay's conjuration is unparalleled; later in the play, after the brazen head has been destroyed, Bungay remembers Bacon for having "act[ed] strange and uncouth miracles" (13.10). In the formulation of Bryan Reynolds and Henry S. Turner, "Bacon's power, in short, is nothing less than the power of Greene's theatre" ("From *Homo Academicus*" 92).[18]

Yet we need to follow *Friar Bacon and Friar Bungay*'s lead in construing "Greene's theatre" as a more specific location than do Reynolds and Turner. In the scene presaging the Oxford dispute, there are a number of hints suggesting that the theatre in question is the Rose. *Friar Bacon* affords one such clue after Oxford's scholars decide upon an entertainment and announce that they will "hie to Bacon straight / To see if he will take this task in hand" (7.30–1). They do not succeed in exiting because the arrival of a "hurly-burly" prevents them (7.33). The constable, Bacon's sizar Miles, and "a company of rufflers" (7.37), the members of which are English aristocrats accompanying the court fool (Rafe) disguised as the Prince of

Wales, comprise this comic version of the royal visit for which the scholars had just been making arrangements. The scholars rightly doubt the
fool Rafe's nobility, and so he takes it upon himself to prove his identity
by explicating the power that inheres in his royal office. The example he
hits upon casts the monarch's power as magical. "Doctors ... know that
I am Edward Plantagenet," he boasts, "whom if you displease, will make
a ship that shall hold all your colleges, and so carry away the Niniversity
with a fair wind to the Bankside in Southwark" (7.69–73). We'll return
to maritime matters in *Friar Bacon* later in this chapter. Here we should
observe how Rafe's sense of royal prerogative anticipates the conveyances
("carry away") that Bacon will supervise when he transports Vandermast
and vanishes the tree, and how the play associates Bacon's magic with the
entertainments on sale at the Bankside. Ermsby, a gentleman in the faux
monarch's retinue, elaborates Rafe's theme by threatening to have "pio-
neers ... undermine the town [of Oxford], that the very gardens and orchards be carried away" as well (7.79–80). Such green spaces may gesture
towards commercial venues with verdant names situated on the Thames in
Elizabethan England: the baiting arena known as Paris Garden and, most
provocatively in this context, the Rose.

The bragging of Rafe and his company reconfigures the spatial trajectory of Greene's dramaturgy, which in Robert W. Maslen's apt phrase
"unfolds within the purlieus of an English playhouse" (175). Rafe and
his betters assert that they can transport Oxford University's architectural and topographical features to London's purlieus, a legal term for a
precinct of land that was formerly designated royal forest,[19] but which
we can gloss in this context as a "liberty." The authority of Ben Jonson's
Bartholomew Fair (1614), where "purlieus" names the unsavoury suburban location of Smithfield Fair (4.4.199), permits us to do so. *Friar Bacon
and Friar Bungay*'s characters thus articulate, in reverse, the precise effect
that Greene accomplishes when the play's Oxford is virtually recreated
at the Rose. In laying bare a version of its own dramaturgical logic, *Friar
Bacon* arrogates to itself and displays in Bacon's magic the sovereignty
that the fool claims. Despite the parodic register of the hurly-burly scene,
the power of magic and the magic of theatre in *Friar Bacon* are princely
measures.

Greene's prince was, of course, Queen Elizabeth. As scholars routinely
note, *Friar Bacon and Friar Bungay* nods to her cosmic presence in its
closing moments, when Bacon performs a final act of magic inside "Windsor" Castle (14.68). He accompanies the royal pageant that celebrates the
play's double marriage – the happy nuptials of the real Prince of Wales

to the Princess of Castile and of Lacy, Earl of Lincoln, to the milkmaid
Margaret – with an imperial-themed prophecy:

> That here where Brute did build his Troynovant,
> From forth the royal garden of a king
> Shall flourish out so rich and fair a bud
> Whose brightness shall deface proud Phoebus' flower,
> And over-shadow Albion with her leaves.
> * * * * * * *
> And peace from heaven shall harbor in these leaves
> That gorgeous beautifies this matchless flower. (16.44–8, 55–6)

Although Bacon does not explicitly name the Tudor monarch in this
"mystical" oration (16.63), his last two words encode her identity: all other flowers in the garden, he forecasts, will "stoop and wonder at Diana's
rose" (16.62).[20] This image suggests that Greene tailored the auspicious
prediction to a botanical tradition for figuring both the Tudor monarchy
and its last queen.[21] To my knowledge, however, no scholar has excavated
the pun that the magic demonstrated by "England's only flower" in the
disputation scene and that Rafe's comic bluster about the prince's prerogative make available: that the prophecy's matchless flower is also the Rose
theatre, towering above – or so the play would like to imagine it doing –
all competitors. At play's end, then, Bacon rehearses and embroiders the
botanical imagery of the hurly-burly scene, which included the gardens
and orchards of Oxford conveyed, jokingly, to the Bankside, and gathers
that imagery under the "leaves" of the rose – the flower of Elizabethan
iconography that shares a name with Greene's playhouse.

Attacking the "Trees" of Theatre

In developing a connection between the contest among magicians at Oxford and the actions performed at the Rose playhouse, *Friar Bacon and
Friar Bungay* also links the tree at the centre of that contest to the timbered
space of the theatre in which Greene's play is being staged. That both objects, tree prop and theatre alike, were fashioned from wood is the basis
of this material relation. By the logic of synecdoche, we can comprehend
the tree prop's abuse in the scene as a microcosmic figure that realizes the
antitheatrical rhetoric that a diverse group of writers and public officials
had directed against London's theatres throughout the sixteenth and seventeenth centuries. Vandermast's magic thus comes into view as another

example of the play's iconoclastic impulses, but Greene does not necessarily endorse this instance of antitheatricality. For it is immediately undermined when Bacon wins victory over his German rival. The magician who will later forecast the reign of Elizabeth safeguards from a renewed attack the emblem for the theatre in which her liveried men – the troupe known as the Queen's Men – mount the play. Bacon's magic defends Diana's Rose from an English antitheatricalism that the play tellingly codes as a foreign incursion on English ground.[22]

In pamphlets and treatises labelled "antitheatrical" the material structure of the theatre makes brief but colourful appearances.[23] In *The Anatomie of Abuses* (1583; 1595), for instance, Philip Stubbes glosses two of the earliest permanent outdoor venues – the Theatre and the Curtain – as "Venus Pallaces." Later in the treatise, he places playhouses in apposition with "Schooles or Seminaries of pseudo-christianitie" (202, 204), a strategy that evokes the title of an antitheatrical antecedent, Stephen Gosson's *The S[c]hoole of Abuse* (1579). In *Playes Confuted in fiue Actions* (1582) Gosson later branded such false religion as devil worship, since Satan "erecteth Theatres to make vs fall backwarde and flie the fielde" (B6ᵛ). In *A Refvtation of the* Apology for Actors (1615), a certain J.G. continues the rhetorical recycling of his predecessors' metaphors when he dubs "Theaters" "*Venus Pallace* and *Sathans Synagogue*" (57). Taken together, these writers deploy arresting representations that imagine the theatre as (wooden) schoolhouses where students learned how to comport themselves outside the sumptuous playhouse in ways counter to orthodox Christianity.[24]

To this litany of common antitheatrical figures for vivifying the impropriety of theatres, I add an exceptional image drawn from the first antitheatrical salvo against the theatre to appear in print after the opening of the Theatre in 1576, John Northbooke's *Treatise wherein Dicing, Dauncing, Vaine playes, or Enterluds ... are reproued* (1577). Northbrooke's mouthpiece in this tract is a character called Age who names "such places and theaters" "vnfruitfull and barren trees" that he hopes "shall be cut downe" by the joint forces of God and London's civic authorities (103). Age's image has strong affinities with publications charting the incomplete status of English iconoclasm, such as Anthony Gilby's *Pleasavnt Dialogve, Betweene a Souldior of Barwicke, and an English Chaplaine* (1581), which advocates that "the great trees of popery" – presumably rood screens, statues, crucifixes, and other wooden objects of Catholic worship – be "hewed down" (qtd. in Aston 335). From our vantage, Age's imagery also accords with the eco-material relation between woods and playhouses that dramatists exploited when their characters prompt audiences to behold a woodland in the fixtures and walls of a theatre. But dramatists tended not to share Age's unflattering assessment of theatrical woodlands. Indeed, for many dramatists, the "trees" of theatre produced the opposite effect. Instead of betokening infertility and, if we push the un-Christian implication of Northbrooke's rhetoric, of establishing a bosky synagogue for superstitious worship, the "trees" of theatre generate "new woodlands" during an era of that resource's shortage.

Despite the uniqueness of Age's image, his words do share with other documents in the antitheatrical tradition a botanically inflected vocabulary for destroying the theatre. From Northbrooke's call for theatrical "trees" to "be cut downe" in a massive woodland clearance, we could sketch a line that connects the aggression of other antitheatrical writers to the violence endorsed by London's elected officials. In *A second and third blast of retrait from plaies and Theaters* (1580), the reformed playwright Anthony Munday claims to take up the quill so "that the intolerable exercise of plaies might be vtterlie put downe." He goes on to advise London's "Magistrate" to "pluck[] downe" "this schoole." At the close of this tract he admonishes city officials to "roote out the memorial of wickednes from the earth," by which he seems to intend both the art of playing and the space where playing occurred – the "Theaters" of his title (53, 102, 127).[25] Philip Stubbes likewise urges that "these places of abuse" be "pluck[ed] downe" (247). John Field twisted the report of an earthquake that toppled the scaffolding at Paris Garden on a Sunday in 1583 to forewarn of God's further retribution. A self-proclaimed "Minister of the word of God," Field disseminated within days of the disaster a tract that he dedicated to London's Lord Mayor, mainly because a number of those "iustly punished" for breaking the Sabbath on the Bankside "were of your citie." "For surely it is to be feared," he warned in his account, "besides the distruction of the bodye and soule, that many are brought vnto, by frequenting the *Theatre*, the *Curtin* and such like, that one day those places wyl likewise bee cast downe by God himselfe, and with them a huge heape of such contempners, and prophane persons vtterly killed and spoyled in their bodies" (front., 2, n.p.). It would be hard to distinguish the corpses from the ruined wooden walls of the baiting arena if this nightmarish vision of divine justice, which resembles the violence of the disembodied hand in *Friar Bacon and Friar Bungay*, were to come true. As Miles reports of the brazen head's crushing, so too might Field have said of the rubble at the playhouse: "The latter day is come" (11.79).

Such calls for the destruction of theatres were not restricted to the realm of print. They also echoed in chambers occupied by London's successive

Lord Mayors.[26] On 3 November 1594, for instance, Lord Mayor Sir John Spencer sent William Cecil, Lord Burghley, a petition asking him to halt plans to construct the Swan playhouse. He depicts theatres in terms similar to those employed in published antitheatrical materials to persuade Burghley to "bee a means for vs rather to suppresse all such places built for that kynd of exercise then to erect any more of the same sort" (qtd. in Rutter 86–7). There was a formula to such correspondence: Lord Mayors composed missives that rehearsed the same accusations against the theatre, which added up to a charge of fostering gross misconduct and disease, and the Privy Council routinely passed over the requests for tearing theatres down. But on 28 July 1597 the Privy Council responded to the City's petition with a surprising order. London's aldermen were to "send for the owners of the Curtayne, Theatre or anie other com*m*on playhouse, and Injoyne them by vertue hereof forthwi*th* to plucke downe quite the stages, Gallories and Roomes that are made for people to stand in, and so to deface the same as they *m*aie not be ymploied agayne to suche use" [emphasis in original] (qtd. in Rutter 117). This injunction, which, equally surprisingly, was never enforced, sponsors a demolition that afforded civic officials exactly what they had long desired and that, notwithstanding the huge heap of spoiled bodies, resembles the horrific vision of "bringing down the house" that Field imagined in 1583.

In this range of documents, then, there is evidence of an almost technical vocabulary for describing the destruction of theatres. We might go so far as to say that the flattening of wooden Os desired by civic officials and antitheatrical writers proves akin to the smashing of enormous wooden icons. For to "cast down," "cut down," "deface," "put down," "pluck down," "root out," and "suppress" all belong to an idiom of Reformation iconoclasm that Greene also employed in *The Spanish Masquerado* (1589), a post-Armada, anti-Spanish allegory whose publication is contemporaneous with *Friar Bacon and Friar Bungay*.[27] There, Greene describes Henry VIII as having "suppressed [Catholic] Abbeyes, pulled down their sumptuous buildings, & scarce left one stone vpon another"; Elizabeth continued her father's project when she "vtterly raced & abolished al [the Pope's] trash and traditions as absurdities & heresies, out of her Churches of England and Ireland" (B2ᵛ).[28] In light of this lexical overlap, we could regard the attendance at plays, from an antitheatrical perspective, as a form of depraved communal worship.[29] Indeed, antitheatrical documents like Prynne's *Histrio-Mastix* explicitly cast such improper devotion as idolatry,[30] and they may even punningly figure, as Anthony Munday's *A second and third blast* does, the theatres as colossal wooden idols when "those *idle* places" are derided for "empty[ing] the Lordes sanctuarie ... of his people" [emphasis added] (65). We could say, then, that figures for the playing space where such superstitious worship was presumably conducted encapsulates in antitheatrical polemics all the irregular transactions housed therein, and that such iconoclastic rhetoric had the effect of putting the "trees" of London's theatres against which Northbrooke had fulminated on the proverbial chopping block.

In staging Hercules's assault on the magical tree prop, it is as if *Friar Bacon and Friar Bungay* has so internalized antitheatrical sentiment that a word which, in other contexts, would signal the erection of a playhouse's wooden frame – "raise" – has been warped by an aggressive homonym into its opposite: "raze." As we observed, however, Bacon's presence is potent enough to put a stop to Hercules's second attack against the tree prop, a detail that suggests that the raised spirit had not, in the first instance, fully razed the tree. We could regard Hercules's ineffectiveness in completing his task as predictive of the fate of London's theatres. For despite all the bluster and vituperation of antitheatrical writers and city officials, the theatrical woodlands dotting the City's perimeter were not demolished at the command of Tudor and Stuart governments. Until the onset of political turbulence in the mid-seventeenth century, London's theatres received no physical harm from royal quarters. In the next chapter we'll explore the accidental fire that "razed" the Globe in 1613, which, according to Ben Jonson, proved the occasion for puritanical "brethren" to "noise[] it out for news" of divine intervention against these "idol[s] of the revels" ("Execration" ll. 136, 139, 155). But only theatre impresarios, it seems, pulled down playhouses intentionally in the sixty-odd years before the Civil Wars: the Burbages disarticulated the Theatre's frame in 1598, and Philip Henslowe plucked the Rose playhouse in 1606. Otherwise, London's "woody theatre[s]" remained green until the 1640s, when these venues were closed and lost to posterity.[31] In the context of *Friar Bacon*, we may regard them as charmed until then.

By linking the magical tree prop to commercial drama and by staging and then literally expelling a violence that enacts the rhetoric of English antitheatricalism against the prop, *Friar Bacon and Friar Bungay* presents the golden tree as a complex sign for the Rose playhouse. Bacon's magic defends the tree from further assault and would seem to put a conclusive end to the aggression (actual and rhetorical) by vanishing the tree and transporting away those who might persist in attacking it. Yet such emblematic weight is not the only burden that the play makes the tree prop bear. Like Bacon's glass, which literally divides the stage, the magical tree prop engenders multiple perspectives, and its onstage presence prompts us to hold them together and sift them out simultaneously.[32] In upcoming sections we'll explore how the golden tree encapsulates the ecological and the geopolitical conditions of a threatened England and its colonialist endeavours in the late 1580s.

The fact that *Friar Bacon and Friar Bungay* casts its agent of antitheatricalism as a foreigner will help prepare us to embark on a geopolitically more expansive set of contexts for comprehending the magical tree prop. By all accounts, Vandermast is German: not only does the Emperor inform the English monarch that his magician is "A German born" (4.48), but English characters also consistently refer to him as "German" (7.15, 23; 9.46). Yet as James Dow McCallum noted long ago, the magician's full "name," which is given as "Don Jacques Vandermast" in the play (7.16), "is a mixture of Spanish, French, and German (Dutch)" (213). Enshrined in the signifiers of his identity, such continental hybridity, which the play collates under the general rubric "Hapsburg," works to associate, as we shall see, the magician who claims victory on English soil with the threat posed to Elizabeth's realm by the Spanish Armada. Although *Friar Bacon* presents the thirteenth-century dynastic match between England and Spain in a sanguine key, it makes unlikely bedfellows of sixteenth-century English antitheatricalism and the risk of Spanish infiltration. Bacon's magic vanishes both threats – one Puritan and the other Catholic – when he ejects Vandermast from Oxford. A motto that Greene would later attach to his exposés of the criminal underworld – *Nascimur pro patria* ("Every man is not borne for himselfe, but for his country") – aptly captures the spirit of Bacon's preservation of the magical tree prop from the polyvalent assault of Don Jacques Vandermast (*Defence* A4[r]).

Vandermast and the Armada

After the wondrous defeat of the Armada in 1588, Bacon's foresight about the posture of subjection that Elizabeth's rose would enforce all other flowers to hold ("stoop and wonder") and Henry III's elaboration of this prediction ("Thus glories England over all the west") stroked England's feathers. Although Greene inherited Vandermast from his source text – a prose romance – he tailors Bacon's archenemy to fit the Armada context.[33] Associated with "Hapsburg," connected to the "Belgic schools" (9.17) and a host of continental universities, including Padua, "Sien, Florence, and Bologna" (9.110–11), where he "put down / The chiefest of them ['men of art'] in aphorisms, / In magic, and the mathematic rules" (4.51–3), decorated with a Spanish honorific ("Don"), and cast as a potent threat to the sovereignty of English letters,[34] Vandermast emerges in *Friar Bacon and Friar Bungay* as a dense figure for Spain's "navy invincible," which was supposed to have been supplemented by vessels from the Netherlands headed by the Duke of Parma (Meteren 313). Vandermast's surname records a coincidental link between the foreign magician and these seagoing vessels: it embeds the word "mast," and so he is "of the mast" or perhaps those woodlands where masts were extracted. In Thomas Nashe's remembrance, the Armada uncannily appeared "like a high wood" (C4[r]) that closed in on the island because, as chapter 3 will demonstrate, the image of a single tree has functioned since classical times as an emblem for both a convoy of ships and the forest out of which those ships were built.[35] Greene further exploits this wordplay and this iconographic tradition by planting onstage the tree featured in his (supposed) textual source and then positioning Vandermast next to it, as if to match a verbal pun with a visual one. Not unlike the Armada, the continental magician suffers an ignominious loss: he is, to borrow a phrase from Emanuel van Meteren's account of the defeat of "the magnificent, huge, and mighty fleet of the Spaniards," "vanished into smoke" (326). Such an exit constitutes a spectacular effect on the world's stage.

Vandermast's surprising transportation out of Oxford, which he likens to the force of a "wherlwind" in *John of Bordeaux, Or The Second Part of Friar Bacon* (1590–4),[36] dramaturgically repeats the dispersal of the Spanish fleet (l. 36). In so doing, the play aligns Bacon's magic with the tempest that was credited with the sea-rout, which an illustration from George Carleton's *A Thankfvll Remembrance of Gods Mercie* (1627) captures in the moment just before it has had a devastating impact on the blockade of ships. But unlike his historical antecedent, Vandermast touches English soil and briefly wreaks magical havoc at Oxford. Indeed, the assault against the tree that Vandermast supervises accords with depictions of what the Spanish would have done had their ships breached "the walls of Old Oceanus," the defenses in which *Friar Bacon*'s English monarch perhaps puts too much faith (4.2), and dropped anchor. No doubt in an effort to rouse public sentiment against the looming invasion, Thomas Deloney, for example, composed a ballad in 1588 about the torture devices conveyed inside the Spanish fleet. Before "torment[ing] most cruelly" English "bodies night and day" with an array of ghastly whips, "Our noble Queene and Countrie first, / they [the Spanish] did prepare to spoyle" and "To ruinate our liues and lands, / with trouble and turmoyle" (ll. 21–4, 27–8). Such

Figure 1.2 George Carleton, *A Thankfvll Remembrance of Gods Mercie* (London, 1627), detail. This item is reproduced by permission of The Huntington Library, San Marino, California.

imagery succeeds in ratcheting up the cruelty precisely because it trades on and unsettles pervasive Elizabethan iconography in which the Queen's impregnable body is coterminous with England itself.[37] The following year Greene would envision the designs that the Spanish had upon first disembarking in similar terms. In *The Spanish Masquerado*, which was issued twice in 1589, he casts Philip II's admirals as Caesars who, after exclaiming "*Veni, vidi, vici,*" intended to "deuid[e] our Land into portions" (D2^r, D3^v). Although sketchy in their details, the atrocities against English land and people that the Spanish were imagined as eager to perpetrate echo the way Hercules spoils the tree. He treats it, in effect, to a series of beatings that break off (some of) its branches and then scatter them across the stage floor.

The circulation of such texts in the late 1580s stressing the ruination of England by Spanish victors likely helped corroborate and fuel a rumour about a more specific plot that the Spanish had hatched for destroying England's woodlands. According to John Evelyn's *Sylva* (1664), the Spanish scheme was a backup plan that targeted the Forest of Dean,[38] a royal preserve in western England near the port of Gloucester:

> I have heard, that in the great Expedition of 88, it was expressly enjoyn'd the Spanish Commanders of that signal Armada; that if when landed they should not be able to subdue our Nation, and make good their Conquest; they should yet be sure not to leave a Tree standing in the Forest of Dean: It was like the Policy of the Philistines, when the poor Israelites went down to their Enemies Smiths to sharpen every man his Tools; for as they said, *lest the Hebrews make them Swords, or Spears*; so these, *lest the English build them Ships, and Men of War* ... [emphasis in original]

Evelyn admits that it is possible that the tale he has recounted and glossed with a biblical precedent (1 Samuel 13:19–23) might be hearsay ("Whether this were so, or not"), which is perhaps why he includes no precise sixteenth-century source for his information (318). Evelyn could have culled and then elaborated details from Thomas Fuller's *History Of the Worthies Of England* (1662), a mammoth historiography of renowned English persons and a county-by-county natural history of England. In Fuller's entry on Gloucestershire there appears this account of the Spanish stratagem, which is explicitly not remembered as Spain's backup plan:

> I have read that in the reign of Queen *Elizabeth*, the *Spaniard* sent an Embassador over purposely to get this *wood* destroyed (*by private practices* and

cunning contrivances) who had he effected his Embassie, deserved a good reward at his return. It is suspicious if not timely prevented, carelesness and waste will gratifie the *Spaniard*, with what then he could not accomplish. [emphasis in original] (349)

More confident than Evelyn in the report's reliability, Fuller includes a marginal notation that divulges Samuel Hartlib's *Legacy of Husbandry* (1655) as his guide in the matter. Yet in Hartlib there is a sense of uncertainty that is absent in Fuller's account, but which is present in Evelyn's: "the Common-people did use to say, that in Queen *Elizabeth's* dayes the Spaniard sent an *Ambassadour* purposely to get this *Wood* destroyed: how true this is I know not" [emphasis in original] (49). In this mid-seventeenth-century genealogy of printed texts, the rumour about Spain's nefarious aim to deface and make unusable the oaks of the Forest of Dean proves a stalk whose roots cannot be fully delved: they are as untraceable as the ephemeral communications of Elizabethan counter-intelligence.

Yet Robert Greenhalgh Albion, an aptly named twentieth-century chronicler of the British Navy, adds a fresh detail to the lineage of the rumour that, if true, could clarify the source from which the Elizabethan commoners invoked in Hartlib might have gained their knowledge. He records an anecdote in which the documents ordering woodland destruction in Dean were discovered inside the wreckage of an Armada ship that foundered on England's southern coast. In the vein of Evelyn's account, Albion explains why the woodlands of Gloucestershire might have been targeted. The devastation of oaks, he claims, would have dealt "a blow to England's sea power" insofar as this grain of wood was crucial for fashioning the hulls of the English fleet (108).[39] Without these trees, England, so this counter-factual version of naval history goes, would fail to have constructed "wooden walls" – an early modern expression for a barricade-like convoy of ships[40] – to match the strength of the Armada. The early modern rumour of woodland devastation thus expands upon the dread of landscape ruination that Deloney and Greene mongered in 1588–9, and adds a certain appeal to Bacon's plan to protect England with bronze walls in Greene's play.

Although Gloucestershire shares an eastern border with Oxfordshire on present-day county maps, *Friar Bacon and Friar Bungay*'s Oxford is not set in the Forest of Dean. But since Greene's *Spanish Masquerado* belongs to a tradition that has come to be known as "The Black Legend," which is the English propaganda campaign that aimed to tar Spain's reputation with accounts of its imperial atrocities, it is no coincidence that his play depicts Hercules attacking a tree on English land under Vandermast's guidance.[41] *Friar Bacon*'s assaulted tree is agitprop. It would be too bold to claim, however, that *Friar Bacon* inaugurates the tale about woodland devastation that began to spread, we could surmise, as early as 1588. Instead, my sense is that *Friar Bacon* innovatively contributes to the anxiety about the effects of invasion that *The Spanish Masquerado* had also retailed: it plucks the tree from a prose source and subjects it to an attack that would have had multiple geopolitical resonances. Yet the play's easy dismissal of Vandermast works to quell the fears associated with the attack. It is as if, within the wooden walls of Diana's Rose, *Friar Bacon* momentarily imagines in the scene of magical disputation the consequence of Spanish invasion. The sign of Vandermast's failure to complete the despoiling that the Spanish had planned is no different from the sign that encapsulates the failure of antitheatrical aggression: it is the talismanic magical tree prop, which is never fully eradicated.

A Baltic Vandermast

In spiriting Vandermast and the stage tree out of Oxford, *Friar Bacon and Friar Bungay* stages a triumphant re-defeat of the Spanish Armada. Bacon's magic has Hercules transport Vandermast – and presumably the tree along with him – to "his academy" in "Hapsburg" (9.156, 163). In the fool Rafe's terms, the English friar sends the baffled magician back to the Niniversity whence he came. But Vandermast has not been expelled to the territories of Hapsburg Spain, despite the play's witty figuration of him as an Armada-like threat. We get a better – but not a crystal-clear – idea of where Bacon sends magician and tree alike when we recall that he furnishes these coordinates in response to the German Emperor's solicitation: "there your highness at return / Shall find the German [Vandermast] in his study safe" (9.163–4). At the moment of magical dismissal, then, Vandermast's German identity reasserts itself in a way that links the Emperor and "Hapsburg," which, as the play's editor observes, refers to the dynastic house (24 n. 45). But the Armada context does not evaporate into thin air when Vandermast and the tree are transported to a German university town. Instead, such a detail works to deepen the play's engagement with international events leading up to and transpiring after the Armada's failure in 1588. For it hints at a tense, late sixteenth-century commercial matter that embroiled England, Spain, and the Baltic seaports of the German Hanse. At the centre of this triangulated relation were wartime provisions, among which was the very wood product embedded in the German magician's name: lumbered conifers needed for making the masts of seagoing vessels.

When the English scholars discuss the sort of entertainments that they could stage for the royal visit, they inventory the territories that might fall under the Emperor of Germany's rule and, in so doing, bring locales associated with the German Hanse into the play's geopolitical reach. Mason informs his fellow doctors that, in addition to the King of Castile, Henry III is

> troop'd with all the western kings
> That lie alongst the Dansig seas by east,
> North by the clime of frosty Germany,
> The Almain monarch, and the Saxon duke. (7.3–6)

The Duke of Saxony is a ghost character in *Friar Bacon and Friar Bungay*: although other characters mention him and editors interpolate his presence into stage directions, he never speaks. So too might be apparitional figures "all the western kings" from the "Dansig seas by east," a catchall phrase from the early modern period for "Eastland," or the Baltic region, that stretched from Germany to Poland and could even include Russia.[42] Both Saxony and the Baltic monarchs, then, are superfluous, perhaps unnecessary to the plot because another figure – "The Almain monarch" – functions as their surrogate. This king takes the stage as the Emperor of Germany (9.181), accruing to himself all the lands and power associated with the Saxon Duke and those monarchs geographically adjacent ("North by the clime of frosty Germany") to his domain. *Friar Bacon* concentrates all peoples and places roughly Germanic, including Vandermast, under the Emperor's aegis.

In light of such geopolitical cataloguing, we glimpse in Vandermast a double Hapsburg identity united by the "mast" of his surname. Whereas his Catholic connections cast him as a defeated Armada, his Germanic roots confer upon him a general Baltic character. This latter association is further relevant to the Armada context since traders from Baltic seaports straddled the confessional divide to supply the warring factions with an array of bulk goods without which a sustained sea battle and invasion would have been impossible. The Hanse's spiritual kin – the English – exported wool through the monopoly of the Eastland Company and, in return, imported from Baltic towns iron, flax, and hemp, out of which sailcloth and rope were fashioned, as well as tar, pitch, spars, and some masts.[43] (The final item on this list gives the lie to the love poetry of *Friar*

Bacon and Friar Bungay's Prince of Wales, who conjures an image of "frigates" "Topp'd with the lofty firs of Lebanon" in his wooing of Margaret [8.53–4].) According to a pamphlet "Prepared for the seruices for the King of *Spaine*" and published in England in 1589 by Christopher Barker, the Queen's printer, the Hanse exported to its spiritual enemy – the Spanish – grain and "prouisions of warre," which included "martiall furnitures," such as "cables, mastes, and like marchandise" (*A Declaration Of The Cavses* 2, 10, 15). This pamphlet marks a low point in diplomatic relations between the English and the Hanse: its inventory of items found inside Hanse vessels could be compiled because the English had hijacked Hanse ships in Lisbon in 1589. As early as 1585 England issued official warnings, like the one on the title page to this pamphlet, that it would "take and arrest" ships carrying so-called contraband goods conveyed from Baltic ports to Spain; it was also convinced that the Hanse traders were altering their routes by sailing around Scotland and Ireland in an effort to avoid detection. England's official policy of search and seizure lasted through the early 1590s, netting as many (or as few) as thirty-nine ships hailing from the East Seas.[44] Even after the Armada had been blown off its course, then, England wanted to ensure that no northern European wood product helped repair Spain's wooden walls. In the logic of the 1589 pamphlet, to persist in engaging in trade with a spiritual enemy equips a foe (Spain) that could also target its supplier (the Hanse); to permit such trade to continue unabated opens England's gates to the barbarians. The fear that this pamphlet articulates is the terrifying prospect of a convoy of Don Vandermasts that successfully and permanently invade England.

Coded as a foreign invader whose magic temporarily despoils a tree rooted in English ground and aligned broadly with the Germanic market in maritime provisions, Vandermast helps focus a complex set of ecological and economic conditions that obtained in England during the wartime years of the late 1580s. Despite being surrounded and, so the legend goes, outnumbered by Spanish galleons,[45] England wondrously – some might even say magically – overcame the Armada of 1588, only to continue worrying about the reprovisioning of the Spanish fleet. Such regrouping depended upon commerce with Baltic towns, which historical geographer Michael Williams has dubbed "Europe's 'internal America'" (197), and which were also furnishing England and Spain with comparable goods. With the long-standing trade for these staple maritime goods imperiled by a policy that, from the Hanse's perspective, must have appeared as nothing short of piracy, England had a pressing need in 1588–9 to locate more of the resources that it required to protect its shores. Confiscation is a short-term and unsustainable economic policy, and the broadly Germanic figure Vandermast cuts in *Friar Bacon and Friar Bungay* suggests a Baltic option that was becoming trickier to negotiate. Even Bacon's preservation of the emblematic tree highlights that homegrown trees were otherwise occupied. Early modern theatres could take on the role of woodland and, as we shall see, of well-fitted ships in performance, but they were not dismantled en masse to provision the wooden walls of England's naval defence.

Greene's Western Trees

With a vast store of native trees invested in its buildings, including the superstructures of London's theatres, and because of tense commercial relations with its Baltic trading partners, England was imagined in the late 1580s as poor in the very resources upon which national security depended. One solution to this dilemma, in the formulation of Thomas Harriot, was situated to England's far west in Virginia. With its advertisements for "Merchantable" "commodities," which could be extracted for use in the colony and at home, as well as its account of "the nature and maners of the people of the countrey" (B^r), Thomas Harriot's *briefe and true report of the new found land of Virginia* (1588) resembles modern-day "investment brochures" (Borlik, "Mute Timber?" 33) and "real estate promotion[s]" (Marx 38). David Quinn situates this development material squarely in the Armada context. He observes that Harriot printed his recollections of his Virginia experiences in February 1588 because the "war against Spain led [Sir Walter] Ralegh and [Sir Richard] Grenville to revive their plans for an American venture, this time a privateering base on Chesapeake Bay that would divert and weaken Spanish maritime power." Such a plan, as Quinn continues, failed to receive the government backing that its advocates sought because the mounting fear of invasion in the spring of 1588 necessitated that all English ships be stationed closer to home (22, 24). Yet the frame of Harriot's pamphlet also puts forward another remedy to the wartime dilemmas that the seizure of bulk goods from ships, whether the Hanse or the Spanish manned them, aimed to alleviate and surely helped to exacerbate. Harriot's proposal, in fact, would altogether do away with English dependency on the Hanse: for Virginia, Harriot contends, could provide great stores of the very staple items needed for battle with Spain without the complication of tense commercial relations. Colonial extraction in Virginia could supersede an established trade with Baltic seaports.

Harriot articulates his proposal to short circuit continental trade in his pamphlet's second prefatory document, a letter he addresses "To the

Aduenturers, Fauourers, *and Welwillers of the enterprise for the inhab-*
iting and planting in Virginia." Near the end of this prefatory letter, he
explicates the tripartite structure of the pamphlet. Here is his rationale for
the first section:

> In the first I will make declaration of such commodities there alreadie found
> or to be raised, which will not onely serue the ordinary turnes of you which
> are and shall bee the planters and inhabitants, but such an ouerplus suf-
> ficiently to bee yelded, or by men of skill to bee prouided, as by way of
> trafficke and exchaunge with our owne nation of England, will enrich your
> selues the prouiders; those that shal deal with you; the enterprisers in general;
> and greatly profit our owne countrey men, to supply them with most things
> which heretofore they haue been faine to prouide, either of strangers or of
> our enemies. [emphasis in original] (A4ᵛ–Bʳ)

Harriot here elaborates for possible investors a fantastic business model
that is a win-win-win situation for English colonists, for English middle-
men ("the enterprisers in general"), and for Englishmen and women who
purchase the "ouerplus" goods from Virginia. The scheme has the added
advantage of cutting out entirely contact with "strangers" and "enemies,"
categories that the either/or grammar of this complex sentence suggests
might be distinct groups. In early 1588, "enemies" undoubtedly refer to
Catholics, from Philip II's Spaniards to the Pope's followers across Europe. In the context of strained diplomacy surrounding the transport of
bulk goods from Baltic towns to Lisbon we can construe "strangers" as
Hanse traders who supervised commerce in London out of the Steelyard,
since "stranger" in early modern English discourses typically designated
foreign-born merchants who moved to the City to flee religious persecution on the continent.[46] Despite the separation of these categories in Harriot's account, wartime relations with the Hanse indicates how strangers
could transform into – and abet – enemies.

The inventory of merchantable commodities that Harriot groups together in the first part of the pamphlet further suggests "strangers" (if not
"enemies") as the towns of the German Hanse. Indeed, many of the bulk
commodities listed here are precisely those supplies that England and
Spain were importing from the Baltic region. According to Harriot, there
grows wildly in Virginia *"Flaxe and Hempe,"* which will prove a "benefite
… in cordage and linnens." "There are," he continues, also "those kindes
of trees which yeelde" *"Pitch, Tarre, Rozen* [resin], *and Turpentine"*
"abundantly and [in] great store." Since these goods are the liquid by-

products extracted from softwood trees like pines and firs, we could also add masts for ships to this list of goods. Trees make another appearance in Harriot's speculation that iron "maie bee allowed for a good marchantble commoditie, considering there the small charge for the labour and feeding of men: the infinite store of wood: the want of wood and deerenesse thereof in England: & the necessity of ballasting of shippes." Chapter 4 will return to the matter of labour in colonial Virginia. Here I want to stress the logic that implies a link between Harriot's imagined end run around continental trade for goods like iron and the consequence of a shortage of wood and timber in England. The colonial outpost, in other words, could solve two resource problems simultaneously besetting England, for not only did the expedition's mineral expert confirm the existence of iron ore in Virginia, but these deposits were discovered "neere the water side" and in proximity to all sorts of trees – to the ash, the bay, the beech, the cedar, possibly the cypress, the elm, the fir, the holly, the maple, the oak, the pine, the sassafras, the walnut, the willow, the witch-hazel, and "many other strange trees whose names," Harriot mysteriously says, "I knowe not but in the *Virginian* language" [emphasis in original] (B^v–$B2^r$, $B3^r$, $D4^v$). Spenserian in its variety, the catalogue of trees and tree products that *is* Virginia will ease "the want of wood and deerenesse thereof in England" and extract England from a delicate continental trade. In this fantasy of woodland instrumentalization, Virginia comes into view as an economic and ecological panacea. But it is a prospect that, as Quinn contends, disappears quickly because Harriot's sales pitch did not succeed in aiding Grenville and Ralegh to garner financial support in the Elizabethan court.

Although we seem to have drifted away from *Friar Bacon and Friar Bungay*'s Oxford and the Rose playhouse, we have actually been moving in the westerly direction from which Bungay calls the stage tree.[47] For he conjures the golden tree from "the garden call'd Hesperides" (9.81). In classical literature written in the Mediterranean basin, the Hesperides constituted the western-most horizon. Treasurer of the Virginia Company, George Sandys, for instance, places this "Hortyard" of horticultural wonder in his seventeenth-century translation of Ovid's *Metamorphoses* in the "westerne parts of *Africa*" [emphasis in original] (218). Intensified exploration during the sixteenth century had the effect of pushing the location of the Hesperides beyond the limit of Gibraltar into the archipelagos of the Atlantic. Fixing the coordinates of the Hesperides proved something of a *cause célèbre* in Spain: they were variously identified – or misidentified, depending on the writer – as the Azores, the Cape Verde Islands, "Española and Cuba," and, most broadly, as the "Indes."[48] Despite such contestation over their exact position, these floating islands trended to the west of continental Europe.[49] My sense is that the Hesperian tree that *Friar Bacon* conjures in the Rose carries with it such occidental and proto-colonial associations. The insistence on *translatio imperii* and Elizabethan supremacy at the close of a play whose final word is "west" perhaps links *Friar Bacon*'s Hesperian tree to places as far west as Harriot's Virginia: the play retrospectively casts the golden tree as a symbol for the tantalizing store of staples and luxuries, from wood byproduct to citrus fruit, that could be shipped back to England. Within a decade of Greene's play, the English printer and translator John Wolfe would cast the aim of England's overseas expansion as the securing of sources for "those *Necessities* where-of we stand in Neede: as *Hercules* did, when hee fetched away the *Golden Apples* out of the *Garden* of the *Hesperides*" [emphasis in original] (Lin-schoten A4[r]). East of the Hesperides, England could replenish itself with this land's supposed inexhaustible plenty and, in so doing, turn its back on the continent.

England was not, of course, a Hercules in the New World in 1588–9. The magical tree prop may suggest the desirability of Herculean colonial projects such as those promoted by Harriot, but *Friar Bacon and Friar Bungay* "vanishes" the option by transplanting the Hesperian tree to a German "Hapsburg," as if to reinforce the immediate foreclosure of such westward enterprises for supplying wartime provisions. By the sheer force of magic at the playhouse presided over by Diana's rose, Greene's play conjures an eco-fantasy of extractive colonialism. But this fantasy did not take root in the late 1580s.[50] English colonists were just as likely to clear cut Virginia's trees for their bulk goods during this period as antitheat-ricalists were to succeed in having the "trees" of London's theatres cut down. At the turn of the 1590s, neither woodland history could yet be said to be.

2
"Come, will this wood take fire?"
The Merry Wives of Windsor in Shakespeare's Theatres

At the close of *The Merry Wives of Windsor* there is a late-night invasion of Little Park,[1] a game preserve adjacent to Windsor Castle,[2] within the bounds of Windsor Forest, and thus the property of the English monarchy.[3] This trespass on crown land is not a terrifying literary realization of the woodland spoliation that the Spanish were alleged to have devised for Gloucestershire's woods in the late 1580s. Instead, in this first "nocturnal" park scene "in English drama" (Barton, *Essays* 353), the play's cast assembles to stage and watch amateur theatricals. Some of Windsor's children don fairy costumes to "publicly shame[]" Falstaff (4.2.192, 194), while a number of their elders duck "i'th' Castle ditch" (5.2.1) to revel in the pinches and burnings that "this greasy knight" endures (2.1.94). The ritualized humiliation of Falstaff not only satisfies a collective desire to chasten the sexual and pecuniary predations designed – but never fulfilled in the play – by this outsider.[4] Falstaff's comeuppance in the concluding moments of *Merry Wives* also enacts a socio-political feat, for it unifies, however temporarily, against the trouble-making knight a community heretofore fractured by asymmetries in social rank, competing jurisdictional allegiances, discordant gender and marital relations, and linguistic and national difference. By this logic, an unanticipated effect of Falstaff's abjection in the Park is the consolidation of an English middle class.[5] Since the otherwise uncooperative denizens of the town cohere precisely around Falstaff in the woods, an environmental discourse of forest management frames the emergence of this novel social paradigm. The keynote of this discourse in *Merry Wives* is a fiery question posed by the chief male fairy, "Come, will this wood take fire?" (5.5.85).

This "wood" does not, however, refer literally to the Park's trees. The fairy, for instance, does not touch flame to Herne's Oak, which the epon-

ymous wives designate as the rendezvous point for Falstaff (4.4.40) and
towards which they rush offstage in a later scene, shouting "To the Oak,
to the Oak!" (5.3.21). Rather, the "wood" subjected to fire is Falstaff's
body, fallen prostrate in fear as the faux supernatural creatures of the forest approach. More precisely, "wood" corresponds to Falstaff's "finger
end" (5.5.81), a detail that affords new purchase on the Ovidian logic that
governs the scene. Criticism on Falstaff's entrance into Little Park as a
"Windsor stag" (5.5.11) typically regards him as a mythical creature on the
basis of the "richly multivalent" headdress of horns that he wears (Kahn
147): he proves an amalgam of Herne the Hunter of Windsor lore, who has
"great ragg'd horns" protruding from his head (4.4.29), and of Actaeon,[6]
the hunter of deer (and other men's wives, in some glosses) who, after being metamorphosed into a stag by Diana, is devoured by his own hounds.[7]
During this incendiary moment, the antlered Falstaff undergoes a further
– and as yet unnoticed – transformation: he takes on the shape of a fallen
oak tree.[8] The fairy's taper wittily illuminates the "wood" embedded in
Fal*staff*'s name, and the male fairy's question intimates that the aggression
directed towards this debauched knight's wooden body substitutes for
an assault against the play's most conspicuous royal tree – Herne's Oak.
The encroachment upon land preserved for monarchical pleasure and the
scorching of aristocratic "wood" co-articulate an act of environmental
protest that gets displaced onto Falstaff: the play's younger generation,
supervised by Windsor's wives, figuratively assaults Windsor Forest by
literally besetting a "wooden" figure whose rank associates him, in broad
terms, with its park. In so doing, the play enacts in the idiom of social
unrest a version of the quasi-anthropological dictum that pits civilization
against forest.[9]

    In concentrating on the "trees" of Windsor's Little Park and bringing
into focus the ecological coordinates of community building in *The Merry
Wives of Windsor*, this chapter extends recent scholarship that regards the
scene of Falstaff's shaming as an iteration of the play's abiding interest in
the discourses of early modern household economy.[10] Natasha Korda observes how the merry wives, who deem themselves "ministers" of events
in Little Park (4.2.191), display there for a third time in the play their
"competence as disciplined, yet discreet, domestic supervisors" (*Shakespeare's* 83). Wendy Wall connects such household *oeconomia* specifically
to the English middle class. She contends that the "generative grammar" of
English "housewives and castigating fairies" animates a "female fantasy"
in which housewifery is "key to community formation" (114, 121). Both
Korda and Wall treat Shakespeare's Little Park as if it were the joint house-

hold of the merry wives, with all traces of its status as a royal game preserve subsumed under the rubric of female domestic management.[11] In doing so, these scholars repeat the strategy that the merry wives themselves implement, for their trespass "beyond the household" into Windsor Forest effectively converts Little Park into an at-least double household and all persons (excluding Falstaff) who gather there into the park's keepers (Wall 113). But Little Park is different from the household of the Fords, where the two previous humiliations of Falstaff transpired: it requires another sort of economy, a "forested practicality" (Zucker 9), that requires the use of a "saw-pit" (4.4.52) instead of a laundry basket, which features prominently in the former humiliations. Indeed, this object of forest economy in the Park – the sawpit – abets the usurpation of royal prerogative by the play's domestic supervisors. But its repurposing as the "green room," where pretend fairies await their cue to attack Falstaff, momentarily works against its customary use. Although the townspeople gather around and hurt Falstaff's wooden body, they do not employ the sawpit to cut down literal vegetation. Middle-class community stakes a strong claim on crown land and its forest economy, but not at the expense of its actual woods.

By the ecomimetic logic we explored in the introduction, matters pertaining to forest economy in *The Merry Wives of Windsor* are also matters pertaining to playhouse ecology. Herne's Oak, where the wives and Falstaff meet up in act five, was more likely "played" by one of the wooden posts holding up the stage canopy than by the sort of tree stage prop employed in Greene's *Friar Bacon and Friar Bungay*. The theatre's architecture represents an uncanny, albeit inexact, version of its past life as a tree in *Merry Wives*. On the basis of such representational logic, we can approach in an ecological key two matters that continue to vex scholars of the play: the date of composition for *Merry Wives*, and the location of its early staging. This chapter offers no new archival answers to such concerns and instead purposefully errs on the side of temporal flexibility by accepting a date for the Folio *Merry Wives* as early as 1597 and possibly as late as 1599.[12] It does so to establish a relation between the woods of Little Park and the woods of Shakespeare's playhouse and to shed light on the play's immersion in the complex microhistory of London's theatres and England's trees.[13] Salient moments in this sequence of events include the publication in 1598 of John Manwood's treatise on ways to correct the mismanagement of English forests; the issuance of an (unenforced) order to demolish all playhouses in 1597; and the legal dispute that led to the disarticulation of the Theatre's timbers in 1598 and their re-erection on the Bankside in the shape of the Globe playhouse in 1599. Insofar as the

transportation of this wood and timber is an act of "woodland" conservation whose proportions are Utopian, Shakespeare's Globe proves, from
our vantage, an eco-fantasy of recycling.

Manwood's Forest; or, What's Special about Vert

In *A Treatise And Discovrse Of the Lawes of the Forrest* (1598), John Manwood collated the history of the statutes regulating activity in England's
forests since, as he claims, their purported establishment during the reign
of "Canutus the Dane" in 1016 (15ᵛ).[14] In a preface dedicated to Lord
Charles Howard, whose titles, among others, are given in *A Treatise* as the
"Constable of the Castle and Forrest of Windsore" and "Lord high Admi-
rall of England, Ireland, and Wales," the aptly named judicial bureaucrat
of New Forest and gamekeeper at Waltham Forest – Manwood – observes
that, despite their ancientness, forest laws are "yet ... extant" in printed
form (*2ʳ).[15] Manwood would seem to misremember deliberately, since he
had published *A Brefe Collection of the Lawes of the Forest* six years earlier, while he was, according to the title page, a "Student in the Lawes of
this Realme." In contrast to this earlier publication, *A Treatise* is not substantially longer, but it is far better ordered. A border of printers' flowers,
for instance, beautifully hedges in the information on its title page (Fleming). After two prefatory letters, there follows a detailed table of chapters
and subheadings, which data return at the close of the book in altered form
as an index keyed to folio pages and section numbers. There is, then, an
organizational elegance to the 1598 publication, which no doubt makes it
easier for readers, not only law students but presumably also personages
like Howard who have a vested interest in the forest, to "*raunge in so large
a field*" [emphasis in original] (*3ʳ).

   This "*field*" refers, on the one hand, to the polyglot knowledge of forest
history that Manwood anthologizes. On the other, it names the book itself, which Manwood likens to "*a perfect survey of a Forrest*" [emphasis in
original] (*4ʳ). In Manwood's *Treatise* England's forests prove entities that
are complete and ideal because,[16] as we shall see, he imagines their counterparts in the natural world to be in a state of disrepair. It is as if the aim
of *A Treatise* is to rehearse in a methodical way the laws of the "*perfect*"
forest so that the administration of England's forests could be modelled
on it and thereby easily improved. However humbly he presents himself
in *A Treatise*'s prefatory documents, Manwood betrays an ambition that is
both civic minded and self-serving: he aims to take primary credit for the
renewal of a vital and ancient symbol of English monarchy.

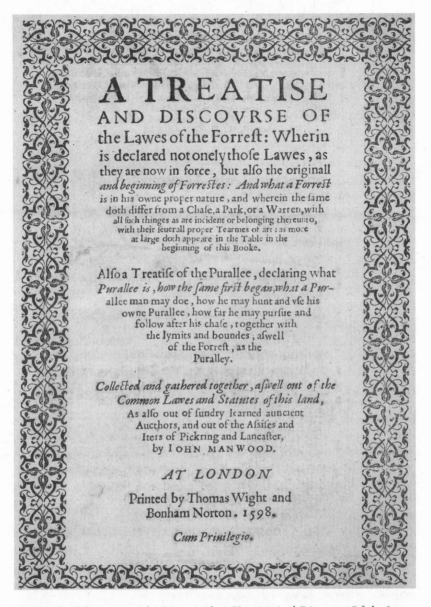

A TREATISE

AND DISCOVRSE OF
the Lawes of the Forreſt: Wherin
is declared not onely thoſe Lawes, as
they are now in force, but alſo the originall
and beginning of Forreſtes: And what a Forreſt
is in his owne proper nature, and wherein the ſame
doth differ from a Chaſe, a Park, or a Warren, with
all ſuch thinges as are incident or belonging thereunto,
with their ſeuerall proper Tearmes of art: as more
at large doth appeare in the Table in the
beginning of this Booke.

Alſo a Treatiſe of the Purallee, declaring what
Purallee is, how the ſame firſt began, what a Pur-
allee man may doe, how he may hunt and vſe his
owne Purallee, how far he may purſue and
follow after his chaſe, together with
the lymits and boundes, aſwell
of the Forreſt, as the
Puralley.

Collected and gathered together, aſwell out of the
Common Lawes and Statutes of this land,
As alſo out of ſundry learned aunciént
Aucthors, and out of the Aſſiſes and
Iters of Pickring and Lancaſter,
by IOHN MANWOOD.

AT LONDON

Printed by Thomas Wight and
Bonham Norton. 1598.

Cum Priuilegio.

Figure 2.1 Title page to John Manwood, *A Treatise And Discovrse Of the Lawes of the Forrest...* (London, 1598). This item is reproduced by permission of The Huntington Library, San Marino, California.

In Manwood's expert legal opinion, the forests of England are, in 1598, nowhere as faultless as they appear in his book. He explains to Howard that he has undertaken this project, in part, because "so many [English people] do daily so contemptuously commit such heynous spoiles and trespasses therein, that the greatest part of them [forests] are spoiled and decayed" (*2ʳ). The rhetoric Manwood invokes here is both plain and conventional. It echoes the language of statutes promulgated in the 1580s concerning the condition of England's woodlands. "*An act touching iron-mills near unto the city of* London *and the river of* Thames" (23 Elizabeth c. 5), which we looked at in the introduction, notes that the woods around London and in Sussex "*doth daily decay and become scant, and will in time to come become more scarce, by reason whereof the prices are grown to be very great and unreasonable*" [emphasis in original] (Pickering 341). Four years later, in 1585, another statute was ratified "*for the preservation of timber in the weilds of the counties of* Sussex, Surrey *and* Kent" (27 Elizabeth c. 19). It records that "*it is thought that the great plenty of tim-ber which hath grown in those parts hath been greatly decayed and spoiled, and will in short time be utterly consumed and wasted if some convenient remedy therein be not timely provided*" [emphasis in original] (Pickering 382). Yet although Manwood's text shares with these statutes a vocabulary for describing England's woodlands and a rhetoric of emergency, its intent is not to propose solutions for reducing prices for the English consumer or to recommend a wide-ranging program of replantation that would re-place those trees that have been heinously spoiled. In short, Manwood is no Arthur Standish: his sympathies are not with the men, women, and children living in – or off – English forests whose means of survival are the food and firewood that could be culled from the woodlands. Rather, his unabashed allegiance is to the crown, and his decision to reconceive and republish the treatise on forest law proves more invested in legislat-ing the misbehaviour of English subjects encroaching on royal property than in advocating, wholesale, for common rights in the forest.[17] Some scholars, such as Todd Andrew Borlik ("Mute Timber?" 40) and Jeffrey S. Theis (*Writing* 129), have observed that the policy Manwood advances in *A Treatise* figures him as a proto-environmentalist.[18] This may indeed be so, but the legal case Manwood makes for conservation in *A Treatise* is for the monarch's benefit.[19] As Simon Schama notes, in England "the greenwood generally votes conservative" (141).

Manwood thus hopes to put a stop to the pervasive misuse of crown land by reinvigorating the laws of the forest. His first step in resuscitat-ing these laws is to define the terrain they govern. For him a forest is a "certen Territorie of wooddy grounds & fruitfull pastures, priuiledged for wild beasts and foules ... to rest and abide in, in the safe protection of the King, for his princely delight and pleasure" (1ʳ). The limits of a forest can be ascertained by "unremoueable, markes, meeres, and boundaries, either knowen by matter of record, or els by prescription," and within its some-times visible – but always fixed – parameters there exist "certen particuler Lawes, Priuiledges and Officers, belonging to the same, meete for that purpose, that are onely proper vnto a Forrest, and not to any other place" (1ᵛ⁻ʳ). The legal borders of such royal precincts sometimes engulfed entire counties, such as Cornwall and Essex,[20] thus "pitt[ing] the people against the king, and by extension, against the forest" (Bowerbank 15).[21] A forest could also encompass or "comprehend" smaller units of woodland (7ʳ), each of which Manwood dubs a *"royall franchise of pleasure"* but none of which could be considered a forest in its own right [emphasis in original] (*3ᵛ). In order of relative "degree" to the forest, these franchises were the chase, the park, and finally the warren (7ʳ). Unlike its fellow forestial sub-divisions, a royal park, like Windsor's Little Park, was the only "inclosed" space within the larger comprehension (7ʳ). Usually a palisade of oaken stakes, which were sometimes aligned with a dense row of trees, delimited its boundary.[22] Nested within the "unremoueable ... boundaries" of a for-est, the park is a doubly safeguarded – and ordered – area. Its pale aimed to keep out forest trespassers as much as to hedge in its prized creatures.

As Manwood's emphasis on pleasure suggests, the purpose of a for-est, in its widest scope, is the enjoyment it provided the monarch and her noble guests during the hunt. For forests were established, according to Manwood's definition, as precincts "priuiledged for" the dwelling of "wild beasts and foules," all of which could then be pursued in "princely delight." Manwood later dubs such creatures "venison" (29ʳ), the most significant of which are the monarch's deer. We might say, then, that the store of healthy, available venison in a forest or in one of its franchises measures the potential use value – indeed the pleasure value – of that forest or franchise to the crown. But Manwood does not go so far as to reduce the forest to its animal life. There can be no pleasure of the royal hunt in any forest or franchise, Manwood insists, without the growth there of royal "plant[s]" that "beare greene leafe" such as "trees, woods, bushes" and "underwood" (33ᵛ). Like venison, plant life or "vert" is one of two "principall ornaments of a Forrest" (32ᵛ). Its presence enhances the de-light of the hunt because it offers "comlinesse and bewtie" to the "eye of a Prince" (33ᵛ). In forest law, however, the designation of "vert and Veni-son" as an essential decorative pair encodes an implicit hierarchy (1ᵛ), for

"Vert haue alwaies the first place, and is set before Venison, amongst the Canons of the Forrest Lawes" (28ᵛ–29ʳ). Manwood's initial definition of "forest" confirms this ordering. He accords "wooddy grounds & fruitfull pastures" (1ʳ) top billing in it because they constitute the "secret counselhouses" (33ʳ) *for* venison to *rest* in during daytime hours. (The pun is Manwood's: he contends that, in English, this term is "compounded of these two woords, For, and Rest," and then shows that the legal definition of "forest" "tak[es] his name of the nature of the place" [14ᵛ–15ʳ].) Vert also takes precedence in *A Treatise* because it serves as the key source of "continual feed" (2ʳ), especially during the winter months, without which the forest's herbivorous beasts could not survive. Lacking food supplies whose technical name is "mast," venison would be "exiled" from the forest (32ᵛ), compelled to "wander up and downe" like the human migrants that Manwood would keep out of the forest, searching for shelter and provisions outside the forest's bounds and, as a disastrous consequence, dashing through the sightline of poachers (2ʳ). Such wandering across borders by beasts and humans alike is precisely the sort of erratic movement that Manwood's highly ordered treatise is at pains to curb.

Since trees are instrumental to the survival of the monarch's deer in the forest and its franchises, forest laws "as greatly regard the preseruation of the vert of the Forrest, as they do the Venison" (32ᵛ). Indeed, the destruction of vert in a forest, and sometimes in those parcels of forestland which noblemen privately owned, was an actionable offence.[23] Burning ferns and heath, for instance, was punishable because both functioned as "couerts" for royal game (34ᵛ), although Manwood does not list here a penalty for this crime or elaborate the threat posed by forest fire. Especially protected by the statutes of forest law was the type of vegetation that Manwood dubs "Speciall vert" (35ʳ). This category encompasses all the plants growing within a monarch's "owne woods" as well as all those that produce fruit or nuts that venison find edible no matter where the plant grows in a forest, whether on a nobleman's land in that forest or in one of its franchises (35ʳ–37ᵛ). As an example of special vert, Manwood singles out the oak tree, which figures in literary texts from the period as royal: Spenser's *Faerie Queene* names it "sole king of forrests all" (Bk. I, Canto I, 8).[24] Because deer feed on acorns, the oak tree "shall not be cut downe," Manwood advises, even if it is rooted in "a mans owne freehold." Only under the supervision of royal officials known as foresters and as verderers could oaks and other kinds of special vert be felled. Depending on where the tree was felled, doing so without such permit could lead to a fine accompanied by the seizure of the logged wood as well as the confiscation of the cart and horse employed in hauling off the timbers (36ᵛ–37ᵛ).

Manwood's *Treatise*, which was republished in expanded form roughly contemporaneously with the composition and inaugural performance of *The Merry Wives of Windsor*, illuminates for eco-minded readers of the play the ideological and material indispensability of trees, and particularly of special vert, to the royal game park that Shakespeare selected for his *dénouement*. As we have observed, *Merry Wives* alludes to this crucial forest ornament by calling attention to the very special vert growing in Shakespeare's Little Park – Herne's Oak. But when an antlered Falstaff reaches this tree, shamelessly designating himself in mini-soliloquy as the "fattest," horniest deer "i'th' forest" (5.5.11) and the humiliation plot kicks into high gear, Little Park's special vert all but recedes into the playtext's background. In Elizabethan performance, however, the "woods" of Little Park would have persisted virtually in the fixtures and the walls of the outdoor theatre.

Indeed, the scene set in the park embeds a reference to the lumbering by which some species of vert were made into wooden products like the timbers and wooden planks used to build Shakespeare's playhouse. While describing details of the plan to discipline Falstaff, Mrs Ford explains that the town's children, disguised in fairy and elfish costumes, will "from forth a saw-pit rush at once" upon the unsuspecting horn wearer (4.4.52); in the next act they are crowded into a "pit" (5.4.2), which is likely the trapdoor in the stage's wooden floorboards.[25] The Windsor townspeople here avail themselves of an earthwork that was integral to early modern forest economy. As Oliver Rackham characterizes them, sawpits were temporary, usually rectangular excavations (118).[26] Like their more permanent technological cousins – sawmills – sawpits were employed to fashion tree trunks into smooth planks and boards, serviceable for building and construction.[27] In *Mechanick Exercises: Or, The Doctrine of Handy-Works*, a late seventeenth-century compendium on the arts of the smith, the joiner, and the carpenter, Joseph Moxon, better known for his description of the printing press, explains the labour of the sawyers who used this earthwork. The "*Pit-man*," according to Moxon, toiled from inside the ditch while his counterpart, the "*Top-man*," balanced himself on its rim, on a scaffold spanning the pit, or on the timber itself. These sawyers worked in unison to hew trunks perpendicularly with a long, double-framed implement called a "Sawyers Saw" or, appropriately enough, a "*Pit-Saw*" [emphasis in original] (96–8).[28] It was customary to refill these pits, presumably with earth, when there were no more trunks to be cut so that rainwater would not pool and stagnate in them (Rackham 118), a detail about early modern woodland management intimating that sawyers have not yet completed their toil in Shakespeare's Little Park. Some of the park's special vert, then,

Figure 2.2 "Engraving, woodcut or similar, of two men sawing a plank using a sawpit." This image is part of the Latrobe Photographic Collection, which contains an array of visual ephemera about the Latrobe area in Australia that dates from the nineteenth century and beyond. It is reproduced by kind permission of the National Trust of Australia (Tasmania) from its collection. Its provenance is unknown.

has recently been, or is soon to be, featured on the proverbial chopping block. Might Herne's Oak – or, in a metatheatrical nod, the "trees" of theatre – stand next in queue?[29]

We shall return to these questions in subsequent sections. Here we should note that *The Merry Wives of Windsor* affords no concrete information about the felling of any tree rooted in Little Park. We can infer that because the ditch has been excavated on monarchical property, this project would fall under the auspices of royal forest managers. But we cannot surmise the extent of felling in Little Park in the way that Gabriel Egan has done in his perceptive reading of large-scale deforestation in *The Tempest* (*Green* 155–7, 166). The provocative reference to the sawpit only points retrospectively to an anterior act of felling or proleptically to a future one. Since none of the park's actual special vert is cut down, sized, or lumbered in the play, we might be tempted to regard the sawpit in the park as an instance of Shakespearean local colour. But to do so risks overlooking how the scene of humiliation works by means of Ovidian logic to transform Falstaff simultaneously into special vert ("nature") and into a wood product ("culture"), and how it locates in Windsor's woods the process by which a new social configuration takes shape.

Burning "Woodman" Falstaff

Wearing a headdress of horns upon entering Little Park, Falstaff, we recall, deems himself a "Windsor stag." On the prowl for a quick buck in all senses of that phrase (1.3.60–2), this stud is eager for a "cool rut-time" with the merry wives (5.5.12). The rhetoric of Ovidian metamorphosis explicitly organizes his self-display in the park: he invokes the precedent of Jupiter's transformations into the "form" of a horned bull and into the "semblance" of a beaked swan to underwrite his own costuming as a spiky-headed "beast" (5.5.1–9). When the merry wives join him, they indulge his theriomorphic fantasy, responding to his hailing of them as his "doe" (5.5.13) by employing terms of punning endearment to name him – "deer" (5.5.14–15) and "sweetheart" (5.5.20). But as the merry wives had devised the plot against their aggressor, Falstaff was not meant to arrive in the park in the "shape" of a deer (4.4.43). Instead, he was to come "Disguised like Herne" the hunter, a figure of Windsor lore who is reported to wear "huge horns on his head," to "Walk round about an oak," and to "blast[] the trees" presumably with his chain, among other countryside menaces, at "still midnight" (4.4.28–30, 41).[30] According to Mrs Ford, some townspeople decline to "walk by this Herne's Oak" in the "deep of night" because they "fear" an encounter with this former "keeper ... in Windsor Forest" (4.4.27, 37–8); to borrow an apt phrase from *Friar Bacon and Friar Bungay*, some Windsor folk believe that "magic haunts the grounds" (9.46). Apparently, though, none of the participants in Falstaff's public shaming, including Falstaff himself, betrays anxiety about chancing upon this "spirit" (4.4.33). Indeed, once Falstaff and the wives assemble at the oak, he acknowledges the resemblance that they had intended all along: "Am I a woodman, ha? Speak I like Herne the hunter? ... As I am a true spirit, welcome!" (5.5.23–6).

   The scene's Ovidian logic can underwrite quick changes in subject position, and Falstaff's queries evidence the implicit dangers of such rapid switching. For in posing them, he transforms himself out of the stag into which he had self-metamorphosed and into the hunter-keeper or "woodman" whom he was supposed to resemble. Falstaff then rhetorically eviscerates his body. He treats it as if it were a carcass of venison: "Divide me like a bribed [stolen] buck, each a haunch," he directs the butcher-wives (5.5.21). But perhaps we might do better to regard Falstaff here as offering his flesh to dogs, for much scholarly criticism about his arrival in Little Park detects a debt to the figure of Actaeon. Metamorphosed into a stag by Diana for voyeurism and then devoured by his own hounds, the newly antlered Actaeon was customarily aligned with the cuckold, whose forehead sprouted horns as a result of his wife's infidelity. Through a logic of comic self-absorption, Falstaff wears the "horns" he would "bequeath" to the merry wives' "husbands" (5.5.23): he thinks, in other words, that he can both enjoy the wives' bodies sexually and take on the horns of "Actaeon" (2.1.105; 3.2.35–7). On the basis of this dynamic, scholars have aligned the elements comprising the shaming of an antlered Falstaff, which include, among other things, "rough music" and the handling of household implements in a communal procession, with the skimmington and the charivari, both of which were early modern rituals for publicly correcting households that suffered from sexual disorders like adultery.[31] Although the nexus of allusions to the communal management of household affairs certainly makes available this interpretation of Falstaff's treatment in the scene, a slightly different picture of the stakes of Falstaff's humiliation emerges when we shift our focus from the park's venison to its special vert.

As Manwood's *Treatise* demonstrates, without royal trees, there can be no royal hunt. Yet with the exception of Jeanne Addison Roberts, who observed some time ago a symbolic "connection" between Falstaff and Herne's Oak (*Shakespeare's* 113),[32] scholars invariably describe the animal that Falstaff becomes in Little Park and, in so doing, fail to see the forest for the trees. They pass over his metamorphosis into special vert. Such critical oversight might stem from the fact that Falstaff does not mark his tree-ness as he does his deer-ness, or that his transformation into Herne's Oak becomes most apparent in performance. For, despite affirming that they have designed to have Falstaff arrive in Little Park as Windsor's legendary hunter, the theatricals that the merry wives mount on crown land cast him in the role of "woodman" – that is, as a "man of wood." Even the horns Falstaff dons, which visibly align him with a Windsor stag and with the figure of Actaeon, could also index a bodily change into special vert during performance. Shakespeare elsewhere imagines "deer horns" worn on a hunter's head as "a branch" (*As You Like It*, 4.2.4–5), a tradition that extends as far back as Pliny's natural history, which consistently casts deer horns in arboreal terms – "braunches," "pollards," "tender stalkes," and "long knobs of the reed mace" (214). In this scene, then, a hardly upstanding member of the monarch's retinue who identifies with both the hunter and the hunted comes into view as a man metamorphosed into a tree of the monarch's forest.

The transformation of Falstaff into Herne's Oak works, in performance, by means of choreographed stage business. The fairies, we learn from the disguised Hugh Evans, keep a nightly habit: "But till 'tis one o'clock / Our dance of custom, round about the oak / Of Herne the hunter, let us not forget" (5.5.71–3). When Evans claims to "smell a man of middle earth," the fairies put off their usual "measure round about the tree" and instead are bid to go "About him" to "sing a scornful rhyme" and to "pinch him to [their] time" (5.5.76–7, 88–9). While chanting "some diffusèd song" that they have "practised well," the fairies "from forth a saw-pit rush" upon Falstaff (4.4.52–3, 64), so many tiny, shrill, otherworldly pitsaws swooping upon Falstaff, who *falls* to the ground in a recumbent posture when he first notices them (5.5.45). Accompanied by the infliction of violence, such circular movement around this "man" echoes the haunting course of action that Herne is said to pursue: "at still midnight" he "Walk[s] round about an oak" and "there … blasts the trees" (4.4.28–30). The "troop of fairies" encircle Falstaff as if they, collectively, were Herne the Hunter to his antlered oak tree (5.3.10). Courtesy of Falstaff, this landscape has been associated with the unpredictably translative and often punishing logic of Ovidianism, and here he bears the brunt of it.[33]

Mistress Quickly and Parson Evans reinforce the link between tree and Falstaff that this stage business conjures. In so doing, they also reconfigure the erotic coordinates of the midnight rendezvous in Little Park. Disguised as the Fairy Queen, Quickly commands her faux supernatural minions, all of whom balance "rounds of waxen tapers on their heads" (4.4.49), to administer a chastity test to Falstaff. "With trial-fire," she directs, "touch me his finger end": "If he be chaste, the flame will back descend, / And turn him to no pain; but if he start, / It is the flesh of a corrupted heart" (5.5.81–4). Wordplay on eroticized venison – heart / hart – transmogrifies here into wordplay on special vert – "heart" of oak, for instance. But whereas in an earlier scene to "put [a] finger in the fire" (1.4.75–6) proves a homey euphemism for wittingly endangering oneself, the wordplay engendered by this "trial-fire" imperils Falstaff because it subjects his body to a burning violence. For when the fairies are doing what they have been

ordered to do, Evans wonders, "Come, will this wood take fire?" (5.5.85).
It certainly can. If, as Peter Grav remarks, "the threat of Falstaff seems all
smoke with precious little fire" (219), then it is perhaps all the more ironi-
cal that little fire can cause Falstaff so much pain. Inside the wooden O,
he bursts into inarticulate pain, "O, O, O!" (5.5.86). The burning of fallen
"wood" may even figuratively endanger Falstaff's fal(se)-staff, especially
if we press, as so many scholars have done, the phallic pun that his name
encodes.[34]

The sexual torment Falstaff endures in the scene does not stop there; it's
only the singed (finger) tip of the iceberg. The fairies presumably recom-
mence their round after the fire has been touched to Falstaff's wooden
digit, and the theme of their song elaborates upon what the wives had earlier termed his "wicked fire of lust" (2.1.59).[35] While burning and pinching
him (5.5.98–9), they sing their "parts" (5.4.1):

> Lust is but a bloody fire,
> Kindled with unchaste desire,
> Fed in heart, whose flames aspire,
> As thoughts do blow them, higher and higher. (5.5.92–5)

The fallen counterpart to Herne's Oak is thus the target of a rhyming
punishment resembling a prescription for homeopathic "medicine"
(3.3.162). We may comprehend the fairy song as an attempt to rid Windsor of a social pathology, or a "dissolute disease" (3.3.161), that the wives
imagine Falstaff as having and embodying. As Jonathan Gil Harris has
demonstrated (Sick 29–51), the signs of syphilis in Elizabethan England
included economic acquisitiveness, sexual appetite, and burning, all of
which symptoms Falstaff abundantly presents throughout the play.[36] Pag-
ing Dr Caius, Windsor's resident physician, to procure relief would do
Falstaff no good, since he's already in disguised attendance during the theatricals.

Intentionally or not, then, the amateur theatricals of The Merry Wives
of Windsor cast Falstaff as a sexually dis-eased "man of wood." In Little
Park he turns into a human–tree hybrid whose body displays the lack
of distinction between tree and wood product that, in the introduction,
we observed to be in operation in the context of the playhouse's material fabric. Once the merry husbands step forward, the translative logic
of Ovidianism that Falstaff summoned upon entering Little Park spirals
uncontrollably, for, in David Landreth's apt formulation, "metamorphosis
initiates" in this play "endless possibilities ... which are not erotic but

punitive" (432). In quick succession, wooden Falstaff becomes, through name-calling, "Herne the hunter" (5.5.101), "Sir John" (5.5.103, 112), a "cuckold" by virtue of the horns (5.5.106), a "deer" (5.5.114), an "ass" (5.5.115), an "ox" (5.5.116), a "hodge-pudding, a bag of flax" (5.5.142), and a "puffed man" (5.5.143). Such mockery, some of which is self-directed, works to prolong the collective spirit of the community that has come to "watch[]" him (5.5.100) once Mrs Page has declared that "the jest" can go "no higher" (5.5.102).[37] Indeed, the verbal ribbing of Falstaff culminates pleasantly enough with an invitation for him to "eat a posset" of heated milk (5.5.158) at the Page household, which is the play's centre of local conviviality (1.1.162–4; 3.3.195–6).

This offer is standard evening fare in Windsor. Near the start of the play, Quickly assures her fellow servant, a young boy named John Rugby, that they will "have a posset … at night, in faith, at the latter end of a seacoal fire" (1.4.7–8). Unfortunately, Falstaff does not have an opportunity to accept – or reject – this conventional gesture of kindness among near-equals because the crisis of Anne Page's elopement interrupts him. When Mrs Page re-extends the invitation in the closing lines of the play, all the townspeople, and especially "Sir John," are bid to "laugh this sport o'er by a country fire" (5.5.219–20).[38] That Falstaff makes no reply to this warm invitation to a festive gathering around a bonfire that aims to secure "amitie amongest neighbours" is telling.[39] In a genial, yet authoritative, tone Mr Ford urges a noticeably silent Falstaff to join the party: "Let it be so, Sir John" (5.5.220). Already proven to be highly flammable, Falstaff, who has on several occasions expressed a personal anathema to excessive heat and to sweating (3.5.98–100; 4.5.79–81; 5.5.12, 31–3, 130–1), no doubt has serious qualms about being in such close proximity to fire once again. Unlike the seacoal fire around which Quickly and Rugby will keep themselves toasty, this bonfire would be fed by sticks, twigs, logs, and perhaps small staffs or staves of wood.

The Fall of Falstaff and the "English Middle Class"

The proposal to share a nightcap of posset at the end of *The Merry Wives of Windsor* seeks to guarantee the continuance of the social cohesion that the public shaming of Falstaff has produced. We glimpse the scope of the English community formed in Little Park by enumerating the roster of folk banded together against Falstaff. Often embroiled in neighbourly dispute and conjugal turmoil in earlier scenes, its members include the comically double-crossing servant Quickly; possibly Pistol, a "discarded" man

whom Falstaff has turned "out of service" for disobedience (2.1.154–5);
the state official Justice Shallow, who arrives in the play with a complaint
against Falstaff; the Frenchman Doctor Caius, who vies with the parson
in an erotic triangle and then joins forces with him against the Host of
the Garter Inn; Caius's rival and ally, Parson Evans, a Welshman who, in
disguise, speaks pitch-perfect English; several well-to-do townsmen and
women who are immersed in domestic squabbles throughout the play; and
Fenton, the impecunious aristocratic suitor of Anne Page, whose association with "the wild Prince [Hal] and Poins" indexes in her father's eyes
his unsuitability for Anne (3.2.61). United by a common action against
"woodman" Falstaff in Little Park, Windsor's "entire community," in
Wendy Wall's formulation, "busies itself with the work of producing the
spectacle of fairies" (123). Like Wall, Richard Helgerson comprehends this
community as an English middle class, but he astutely observes that it is
"generated ... more by narrative accident and theatrical opportunism than
by ideological design" (165).[40]

   We cannot, in other words, claim the emergence of the middle class as
the primary objective of Falstaff's humiliation. Rather, it is a surplus engendered by and through violence against Falstaff.[41] The unforeseen nature
of this social formation helps explain the tense inclusivity, the compulso-
ry quality, and the potential fragility of its survival. Not only is Falstaff
strongly urged to participate in an act of warm bonding, but also all members of the Page family employ the spectacle of his humiliation as a cover
for their various schemes to marry off Anne. If the Windsor middle class
shows signs of fracture before the play ends, then it does so because, as
Rosemary Kegl says, "Shakespeare's middle class" in Windsor "is a process
of constructing alliances among groups characterized by their simultane-
ous participation in very different structures of oppression and thus by
their multiple and often contradictory potential short- and long-term interests" (84). As Falstaff's disinclination to be merry and as the intrigue surrounding Anne's marriage at the close of The Merry Wives of Windsor both
indicate, sustaining this particular configuration of alliances and interests
outside the play's frame and within the domain of the Page household will
require a healthy supply of kindling to keep the communal fire vital.

   Hitherto unacknowledged in such criticism on the English middle
class in The Merry Wives of Windsor are the ecological coordinates of social consolidation. For the household "work," as Wendy Wall describes
it, required to shame Falstaff also has a complex impact on Little Park's
woodland ecology. This collective action against Falstaff encodes, but
only realizes by means of displacement, a belligerence against monarchi-

cal property. The social unit does not employ the sawpit, the work-a-day "green material" of communal effort,[42] to fashion saleable lumber from Herne's Oak or from any other of the park's royal trees. Its members burn tapers there, but not to set fire to actual ferns or heath. Actions that could have damaged Little Park's vert and could be construed as crimes against Windsor Forest as Manwood defines this precinct are instead perpetrated against Falstaff, the "man of wood" prostrated by fear. Were members of this merry cohort against Falstaff remanded to judicial administrators of forest law, not only would Fenton and Justice Shallow, who claims a relation to the crown by virtue of his bureaucratic position, be numbered among the offending parties, but the exact denomination of their crime, however convoluted in its elaboration, would amount, at most, to a finable trespass.[43] And that trespass is not reported in the world of the play, perhaps adding literary fuel to the idea, advanced by Manwood, that forest laws against trespassers and their accomplices were in need of reinvigoration in the Elizabethan era.[44]

In overstepping the legal bounds of the forest to harm Falstaff only, the Windsor townspeople also prove, paradoxically, to be guardians of Little Park's special vert. They do so because the actions that they "devise" (4.4.25) and "shape" (4.2.195) for the theatrical caper are of a piece with their duties as domestic managers. For Natasha Korda, the public shaming is "the culmination of [the wives'] diligent domestic supervision": they "protect the property and propriety of their households" in the royal forest as they do in their homes throughout the play. In this account, the "public arena" of Windsor's Little Park transforms (*Shakespeare's* 83, 95, 110), perhaps abetted by the Ovidian logic that Falstaff has injected into the scene, into "the home *per se*" (Wall 92). It may well be, though, that the Windsor townspeople *already* regard some part of Little Park as property that falls under their purview. In planning Falstaff's humiliation, the wives suggest how "an old tale" about the park's ghostly gamekeeper defines the community:[45] "You have heard of such a spirit, and well you know," Mrs Page tells her co-conspirators, "The superstitious idle-headed eld / Received, and did deliver to our age, / This tale of Herne the hunter for a truth" (4.4.33–6). In all senses of the term, Herne possesses the oak, and, because he was a royal agent, the monarchy retains ownership over the tree; but the spooky account of Herne's Oak belongs, according to Mrs Page, to the Windsor community. Indeed, by performing the broad contours of Herne's tale on royal ground, the merry cohort stakes a claim to posses it – the tale and, temporarily, the ground. But because the rules of household economy shade into the laws of forest ecology in the scene,[46] special vert in the park receives no damage. Instead, another figure associated with the crown – the interloping "woodman" Falstaff – shoulders the brunt of the townspeople's action inside the wives' "outdoor household."

And yet there is a hint that the extension of household ideology into forest ecology does not go uncontested by the crown in the play. Despite the wives' careful supervision of events in Little Park, all of its trees may not ultimately be protected by their homey appropriation of royal land. There is a small, but significant, detail in *The Merry Wives of Windsor* indicating that the felling of "wood" the merry wives oversee at night has a daytime counterpart. For the play hints that Little Park's special vert will soon fall to the ground (or may have already done so) and will not be able to pick itself up again as Falstaff does. (The fat knight has a knack for rising from a couchant position: in *Henry IV, Part One* he famously "counterfeit[s] dying" [5.4.115] on the battlefield and returns to an upright posture once the combatants have cleared the stage.) The unfilled sawpit is this clue, and it serves as a reminder that the monarchy could cut down Herne's Oak and all other special vert on its grounds because it deemed these forest ornaments royal property. The earthwork signals how the whim of royal prerogative can overrule the townspeople's communal memory and their customary use of the forest.

Windsor's Woods and Shakespeare's Theatres

The wives do not only convey into Little Park the ideology of household supervision. They also haul objects across its physical limits: stuff necessary for "a great scene" (4.6.17). Mr Ford says he will "buy them [the children] visors," and Mr Page volunteers to "buy" the "silk" for his daughter's costume (4.4.67, 70). Yet the wives know that much more than masks and expensive fabric will be required to put on a convincing show. Employing an idiom of professional theatre, Mrs Page instructs the two husbands and the Welsh Parson, "Go get us properties / And tricking for our fairies" (4.4.76–7). Some stage properties will be purchased, but others – perhaps the children's candles and "rattles" (4.4.50) – might come directly from the townspeople's homes. Sending Mr Ford on this mission, especially if he stops at his own household, is no bad idea, since, as Mrs Ford reported earlier in the play, her home contains "Neither press [cupboard], coffer, chest, trunk, well, vault, but he [Mr Ford] hath an abstract for the remembrance of such places, and goes to them by his note" (4.2.48–50). The likely circulation of objects from Windsor's households into Little Park proves a literary counterpart to the actual movement of goods, which sometimes were routed through a pawnshop,[47] from the early modern household to the theatre. As Natasha Korda observes, the household and the playhouse are best comprehended as "two material economies that together form a kind of Moebius strip, in which one side perpetually leads to the other" (*Shakespeare's* 207). *The Merry Wives of Windsor* confirms and complicates this thesis, for in its domestic spaces wives enter on "cue" (3.3.30), would-be adulterers speak "the prologue of [their] comedy" (3.5.66–67), and a jealous husband rehearses "old lines" (4.2.16), and in its theatrical space – the woods of Little Park – the merry wives oversee the application of household economy. Indeed, it is as if they discursively and materially treat the park as if it were a household *and* a playhouse, or a "playhousehold." We may say that the Moebius strip of the "playhousehold" that *Merry Wives* presents in its final act is fashioned, quite literally, from English wood.

In setting its amateur theatricals in this multivalent wooden space, *The Merry Wives of Windsor* unspools the material history of the theatre in which it is performed. The park setting not only casts the playhouse's superstructure in the role of Little Park's "trees," but it also resembles the sort of forested spot where the timbers and the planks of this superstructure were formerly enrooted as trees and where craftsmen erected these timbers into the rough shape of a theatre for the first time. From the sawpit in Little Park that the wives conscript for their scene springs this vision of the "playhousehold" in the woods, for it was an earthwork integral to the on-site preparation and construction of a theatre's superstructure. In a discussion of how master carpenter Peter Street undertook the building of the Fortune theatre in 1599–1600, John Orrell looks to the archives of the Royal Works to grasp "Something of the quality of [the] woodman's labor" that Street supervised. A meticulous account for the procurement of timber for the erection of the banqueting house at Whitehall in 1606 reveals that sawyers on the royal payroll earned 17 shillings and 2 pence for "makeinge" 68 "sawpitts and fillinge them upp againe" at 9 pence per "pitt," which tally added more than £3 to the total cost ("Building" 134). By rehearsing these figures, Orrell suggests that a similar operation, although perhaps not on so grand a scale, was necessary for the felling of trees for the Fortune playhouse; tellingly, S.P. Cerasano has surmised that the timber for the Fortune was extracted "probably from forests near Windsor" ("Fortune" 87). Although the specifics of the labour required for the frame of the Fortune remain conjectural, the broad details of its construction in the bush, which both Orrell and Cerasano provide, can be reasonably extended to imagine the landscape where timbers were felled and lumbered for the building of other early modern playhouses. In such a context, the sawpit in Little Park evokes a general sense of the material source of Shakespeare's theatre. By this complex logic, Herne's Oak, where the wives rendezvous with Falstaff, proves both the wooden post holding up the stage's canopy and a representation of the kind of tree out of which such a post would have been fashioned. The stage post performs here a ghostly version of its past status as living tree.

Such material contextualizing of the sawpit, however, affords no concrete information about why Shakespeare would include an allusion to it in this merry world of domestic farce. My conjecture is that the detail of the sawpit encodes in an environmental register the uncertain conditions of playing that Shakespeare's acting troupe endured during the late 1590s, as well as its endeavours to stabilize those conditions. As we did in chapter 1's discussion of *Friar Bacon and Friar Bungay*, we could regard the sawpit as a symbol that trades in antitheatrical tradition in a complex way. In this reading, it reworks a genealogy that can be traced back to John Northbrooke's 1577 call for the "trees" of theatre to "be cut downe" insofar as *The Merry Wives of Windsor* represents – but never employs – the means by which the larger timbers or "trees" of theatre could be felled. We would also do well to situate the sawpit in an antitheatrical context that updates Northbrooke's call for large-scale theatrical deforestation: the highly contested date of earliest performance for *Merry Wives* that scholars propose – 23 April 1597 – is roughly contemporaneous with a Privy Council order to destroy all theatres. Dated 28 July 1597, this unenforced directive, we recall from chapter 1, instructed London's aldermen to "send for the owners of the Curtayne, Theatre or anie other common playhouse, and Injoyne them by vertue hereof forthwith to plucke downe quite the stages, Gallories and Roomes that are made for people to stand in, and so to deface the same as they maie not be ymploied agayne to suche use" [emphasis in original] (qtd. in Rutter 117). In an effort "to deface" the playhouse's timbers so that "they maie not be ymploied agayne to suche use," an earthwork like a sawpit would have come in handy to redeem the investment in the playhouses' wood: it would help shape bulkier timbers into smaller logs serviceable for new building work and into scraps for firewood and small-scale repairs.

But *The Merry Wives of Windsor* cannot explicitly engage this 28 July directive in a cheeky manner *if* – and this is a big speculation – we take 23 April as the play's debut. We are on firmer ground, then, if we construe the sawpit as a wink-and-a-nod, a theatrical inside joke, to an even more immediate and personal matter that occupied Shakespeare's troupe around the time it first staged *Merry Wives*: the lack of a playhouse to call home. The company had been set up at the Theatre, for which James Burbage procured a twenty-one-year lease on 13 April 1576; this contract expired in April 1597.[48] It became clear that Giles Allen, the owner of the land on which the Theatre had been built, would not renew the lease, although it included a proviso that assigned ownership of the building erected on the land to Burbage. As early as 1596 Burbage decided not to stake a claim on this property and instead commenced efforts to purchase a new permanent location for playing indoors at the Blackfriars.[49] The opening of this venture was blocked and, when the lease agreement at the Theatre lapsed, Allen shut its doors to Shakespeare's company and, in the legal sense, *conveyed* to himself ownership of the theatrical super-structure.[50] In light of such tangled property relations, the most profound irony about *Merry Wives*, which is so obsessed with domesticity and well-executed household management, may well be that it was composed for and performed by a company of players that, for roughly two years in the late 1590s, had no permanent "playhousehold."[51] Like the dwellers that Manwood wants to turf out of the forest, the company migrated through London's theatrical woodlands, temporarily renting the Curtain and the Swan.[52] Meanwhile, the Theatre stood "vnfrequented," "in darke silence, and vast solitude."[53]

When framed by such uncertain conditions for playing, the allusion to the sawpit in *The Merry Wives of Windsor* works to signal "trees" that were out of the company's financial grasp, whether in the shape of the Theatre or in the form of lumber that could have been employed to set up a new venue. The company was, in effect, enduring a scarcity of timber of its own in the late 1590s because its wood and capital were tied up in other ventures and venues. "Trees" would have to be felled somewhere to provide the troupe with a fixed playing space, as they eventually were, in late 1598, at the site of the Theatre. By this logic, the recycling of the Theatre's frame for the Globe preserves theatrical woodlands in a way that resembles the conservationist use to which the merry wives put Little Park. For this project, carpenters excavated and employed no sawpit in the English countryside.

From Theatre to Globe

The Merry Wives of Windsor is keenly self-reflexive about the uncertain conditions of playing that its company faced in the late 1590s. Surprisingly, the play seems to process these conditions by translating them into the stuff of comedy. For instance, Mr Ford, who approaches Falstaff in disguise in an effort to persuade Falstaff to aid him in his pursuit of his own wife and, in so doing, prove Mrs Ford's unfaithfulness, describes the "quality" of his "love" to this would-be pander. It is, he says, "Like a fair house built on another man's ground, so that I have lost my edifice by mistaking the place where I erected it" (2.2.192–4). A variation of an early modern proverb ("Who builds on another man's ground loses both mortar and stones"), this one-liner, according to Andrew Gurr, allegorizes the legal situation surrounding the Theatre. It "reflect[s] Shakespeare's company's problem over the Theatre in the winter of 1596 with painful directness." Gurr further comprehends the disguised Ford's speech as "clinching" the case for the April 1597 dating of the play ("Intertextuality" 198). But the Theatre would surely have held a prominent place in the collective consciousness of Shakespeare's company through the winter of 1598, when the playhouse was disassembled and its constitutive timbers were transported off-site. The lines, then, indicate less the precise date of composition and first performance of *Merry Wives* than an approximation for when this comment would have retained strong topical purchase among the rank and file of the Chamberlain's Men.

More significant than its help in dating *The Merry Wives of Windsor* is the way that the comment made by an improbably disguised Ford couches the "problem" of the Theatre in the comic language of adultery. The desire for sexual consummation with a married woman proves, in this non-Ovidian formulation of adultery, akin to erecting (with all its punning implication) a house of "wood" on another man's plot of land. By this logic, adultery is a property relation that is transacted between men, one of whom is an unsuspecting party. Such attention to matters of rightful ownership and unlawful infringement accords with the play's general interest in the proprietary contest over forest utility, especially of Herne's Oak and its meanings. In the context of the legal history of the Theatre, it also recalls the wrangling that involved the Burbage family and Allen: the former owned the Theatre's "edifice" before the lease's expiration in 1597, but merely rented from the latter the "ground" on which it was "built." Tellingly, *Merry Wives* links adultery on two occasions to the sort of rental arrangement that obtained at the Theatre. It reprises this extramarital discourse when Falstaff converses with Quickly, a go-between who, in this capacity, proves his female counterpart.[54] She informs him that the servants who dumped him into the Thames as so much filthy linen "mistook their erection" – a malapropism for "directions" (3.5.34–5). In reply to this thoroughly misleading explanation of events, Falstaff says, "So did I mine, to build upon a foolish woman's promise" (3.5.36–7). If we accept a date for the play closer to 1599, then we could perhaps construe this revision of Ford's joke as a nod to the fact that the Chamberlain's Men had found itself in yet another potential legal knot, now on the other side of the Thames: its sharers or "housekeepers," including Shakespeare,[55] leased a plot of relatively undeveloped land to the south of Maiden Lane near the Rose on the Bankside on 21 February 1599 in an effort to settle the troupe once again into a permanent "playhousehold."[56] The solution that the company hit upon at least a year after it was barred from the Theatre – a thirty-one-year lease – transfers in a metaphoric sense the housing crisis that caused the problem in the first place from "another man's ground" to "foolish woman's" – a maid's – "promise."

A lease agreement, of course, was not the only household matter to follow the Chamberlain's Men across the Thames in the late 1590s. The Theatre's timbers were methodically "felled" under the cover of night and conveyed eventually, in 1599, to the site near Maiden Lane where the Globe was erected. No pitsaws were needed for this operation, for the labourers were not carrying out the 1597 orders of the Privy Council which directed that all playhouses be "deface[d]" so that "they maie not be ymploied agayne to suche use." Rather, the timbers of the Theatre were to be put to the very same use, although it would appear on the landscape under a new name. In performing this labour, the workers repeat a pattern: the site of the Theatre in 1598 stands in for the English woodlands lumbered for the erection of Burbage's first playhouse in the 1570s, and so the Theatre once again looks like the woods out of which it was first constructed, but this time outside the magic of performance. Under the cover of night, the workers also resemble the community gathered in Windsor Forest's Little Park that Mrs Ford and Mrs Page supervise as if they were forest keepers. For the workers preserve "trees" insofar as they recycle the Theatre's timbers for future reuse at the Globe. And yet, for Giles Allen, such antics in the winter of 1598 constituted fraudulence and theft – "steal" is a synonym for "convey" in *Merry Wives* (1.3.25) – not sound "playhousehold" management.[57] It would be hard to imagine this vexed landowner assenting to the idea that the most economical way for the Burbages to regain a "fair house" "lost" "on another man's ground" would be to play merry housewives and fell its "trees" to re-erect them, in a Utopian flourish, elsewhere. Indeed, Allen litigated such action as a trespass and valued the worth of *his* property stolen at £700. In the proceedings, he also claimed his plan was to disassemble this property to employ its materials "for a better purpose" (Gurr, "Money" 5, 8). One instance of repurposing wood and timber – the erection of the Globe – thus prevents another.

Playing with Fire at the Globe

Since pinpointing the date of composition and initial performance of *The Merry Wives of Windsor* with any certainty is a tricky enterprise, it is difficult to know if the story it tells about the business of playing in the late 1590s is an example of life imitating art, or of art designing a plan for life. Nevertheless, this coda ventures the untimely proposition that we comprehend the fallen and wooden body of Falstaff in Little Park as an emblem for Shakespeare's playhouse(s). This "globe of sinful continents" (*Henry IV, Part Two* 2.4.257) is, after all, a figure who is "conveyed out of [Ford's] house" in a laundry basket and then chucked into the Thames in *Merry Wives* (4.2.126–7).[58] Moreover, throughout his stage career, Falstaff consistently self-identifies as a rounded man, a "Plump Jack" who is "all the world" (*Henry IV, Part One* 2.5.438): in *Henry IV, Part One* he says that he used to be "an eagle's talon in the waist" (2.5.303); in *Henry IV, Part Two* he wishes that his "means were greater and [his] waist slenderer" (1.2.130–1); and in *Merry Wives*, he admits that he is "in the waist two yards about" (1.3.35–6). Two of these three examples, however, would seem to militate against such a reading if we accept the proposition of *Merry Wives* that thrift and economy define "playhousehold" management: "waist" in these passages slides easily into "waste" or domestic improvidence. Although the recycling of the Theatre's timbers for use in the construction of the Globe could earn this institution a place in the halls of environmentalism, we should recall that the initial erection of the Theatre would have left a large imprint on English woodlands in just those years that prices for timber and wood product began to rise rapidly in London. We could speculate that, for some Londoners, the building of the Theatre was nothing short of a waste of good wood and sturdy timber. The building of the Globe, according to Giles Allen, was indeed so.

By imagining Falstaff's wooden body in Little Park as a figure for the Globe, we can return briefly to the moment of his burning. For his body is wood that does take fire. At the close of *The Merry Wives of Windsor* the detail of a controlled fire reappears, we recall, in altered form as the roaring bonfire that the Pages will build offstage, outside the frame of the play. It perhaps returns in this way for safety reasons: since the onstage use of "dramatic pyrotechnics," as Ellen Mackay observers, "necessarily quotes the theater's susceptibility to burning" (166, 168), it is dicey business to employ a candle, torch, or squib inside the playhouse. By this citational logic, the singing of a wooden Falstaff toys with setting a fire that could engulf the entire theatre and add fuel to the righteous flames of antitheatrical polemicists. One such conflagration consumed the Globe in 1613 when, during a performance of Shakespeare's *All is True (Henry VIII)*, a small shot of artillery "did light on the thatch" roof of the Globe and "kindleth inwardly, and ran round like a train, consuming within less then an hour the whole house to the very grounds." This famous fire demarcated, in Sir Henry Wotton's remembrance, "the fatal period of that vertuous fabrique."[59] In a sporting – and yet potentially hazardous – key, Falstaff's burning in Windsor as a wooden O flirts with staging a version of a similar catastrophe.

And like Falstaff in Little Park, and like the disassembled timbers of the Theatre in 1598, the "glory of the Bank," which is Ben Jonson's moniker for the Globe, would rise again. In Jonson's poem, which, as we observed in chapter 1, records traces of antitheatrical self-satisfaction about the Globe's burning, Shakespeare's rival playwright and fellow actor says that the playhouse was "burnt ... to be better built" ("Execration" ll. 132, 166). The second Globe's construction, in 1613, would also take vast sums of wood, possibly some brickwork,[60] and capital – to the tune of £1,400, according to Andrew Gurr ("Money" 10) – to regain its pre-eminence in the suburban cityscape. We could speculate that, for some Londoners, this project was an extravagance; theatre historians seem to think it was so for Shakespeare, since he showed little interest in financing Globe 2.0.[61] But as Jonson's poem also suggests, the erection of a theatre on the Bankside, this time with an unchanged name, was a welcome homecoming.

3

"Down with these branches and these loathsome boughs / Of this unfortunate and fatal pine": The Composite *Spanish Tragedy* at the Fortune

In 1601, theatre impresario Philip Henslowe recorded an order for additional scenes to be used in a revival of Thomas Kyd's revenge drama *The Spanish Tragedy* at the new Fortune playhouse. He furnished Ben Jonson a handsome sum for "writtinge of his adicians in geronymo," a reference to the father Hieronimo whose son is murdered on a "fatal" tree in Kyd's play (4.2.7).[1] A year later Henslowe logged another disbursement to Jonson, a portion of which he earmarked specifically for "new adicyons for Jeronymo" (182, 203). Despite such evidence from *Henslowe's Diary* pointing to Jonson, there is no scholarly consensus about his hand in these five scenes, and the tantalizing mystery of the Additions' author – Jonson, Shakespeare, Thomas Dekker, John Webster, or even Kyd himself – accounts for a good deal of the criticism that this extended version of the play has received.[2] Moreover, it is not evident that the five scenes interpolated into the edition of the play printed in 1602 were composed in the early seventeenth century. Roslyn L. Knutson contends that the early seventeenth-century edition "most probably represents" the playtext as it was revived in 1597, and so "Jonson's" additions have been lost to the dustbin of print history.[3] The focus on such compositional matters has absorbed scholars to the extent that very little has been written about the content of the Additions, or their relation to Kyd's play.[4]

It is time to give the Additions their due. In so doing, this chapter remains productively flexible about the dating of these five scenes and brackets the question of authorship, while retaining the metaphors of amendment and writing over to explore how the seventeenth-century play engages one of this book's central themes: the relation between woodland ecology and English polity. Such matters circle around the iconic star of the composite *Spanish Tragedy*, a trellis-like stage prop. Kin of the magical tree that makes a cameo appearance in Greene's *Friar Bacon and Friar Bungay*, the composite *Spanish Tragedy*'s tree is a centre around which "actors" perform "in th' accursed tragedy" (3.7.41), the death of Horatio. But it proves a richer vehicle of meaning than Greene's tree because in this play it has an extended stage presence: characters treat the tree in a variety of ways, memorializing and representing it idolatrously, casting it in terms of social aspiration and epic genealogy, and, most spectacularly, destroying its "branches and … loathsome boughs" (4.2.6). In elaborating such engagements with the tree prop, which correspond roughly to the structure of this chapter's interpretive assays, the composite play affords us a glimpse of how it participates in wider early modern discourses on arboriculture and deforestation, and their role in defining England's governmental stability. In the obliterated tree, we see an image of England whose nationalistic fervour and triumphalism appear less firmly rooted than they did in the late 1580s when Kyd's *Spanish Tragedy* was first performed.[5]

In pursuit of the composite *Spanish Tragedy*'s eco-political currency, we can adapt a question that Zachary Lesser has asked about a play's first printing to consider the new context framing revision: why were these particular Additions written by some author(s) on Henslowe's orders (4)? In posing this question, we elaborate Charles K. Cannon's useful observation that the Additions "enrich[]," "develop[]," "heighten," and "illumine" the themes of the "old parts" (231, 234, 235, 236).[6] We may regard these heavily marketed scenes as textual prostheses: they supplement *The Spanish Tragedy* insofar as they introduce, in Leah S. Marcus's terms, "a new set of structural elements that create new possibilities for signification and cause those elements remaining from the old to take on different nuances of meaning" (*Unediting* 55).[7] By such commercial and textual logic, the Additions were probably as much a box-office draw to seventeenth-century audiences as was the sixteenth-century play that inspired them and which they partially replaced.[8]

In answering a version of Lesser's question for the 1602 *Spanish Tragedy*, we can speculate about the composite play's eco-currency, especially its relation to late-Elizabethan and Jacobean discourses about an uncurbed felling of trees whose ramifications, we observed in the introduction, were cast in explicitly political terms. The same year that the updated play was published for a third time, for instance, Arthur Standish prognosticated about the severity of the resource crisis in *The Commons Complaint* (1611), when he cautioned, "it may be conceiued, no wood no Kingdome" (2). The composite *Spanish Tragedy* taps into the mix of vulnerable ecology and polity that Standish articulated because it avails itself of – and crosshatches – the genealogical meanings for "tree." In early modern letters, a tree could embody a family's heritage, its "family tree," as well as a government's durability and perpetuity;[9] the pervasive figure of the monarchical tree, such as an oak in Windsor Forest, exemplifies the latter kind of emblem. Such iconographic uses perhaps derive from the capacity of some trees – oaks and pines, for example – to outlast several human generations if they are not felled or harmed by storm or disease. John Donne underscores the tree's maturity in relation to mankind's shorter lifespan when he dubs "the ... tree" "long-liv'd" in "The First Anniversary" (l. 115). Then as now, woodland health is one measure – an enormous yardstick – of a polity's genealogical futurity (Diamond).

The eco-political currency of the composite *Spanish Tragedy* comes into sharpest focus when we realize that the tree planted to enroot a family's genealogy does not extend beyond the first generation. In the Fourth Addition or the "Painters part," Hieronimo, a civil servant whose acclaim in judicial matters has earned him a favoured place at the Spanish court, contemplates a lethal trauma to the family tree he planted.[10] This grieving father of "unremarkable lineage" (Maus 57)[11] returns in this interpolated scene to the tree upon which his son Horatio was murdered in an earlier act and discloses that he nursed it from the moment he placed its seed in the soil. As the Fourth Addition revisits it, Horatio's death proves a harsh rebuke for his family's social pretension, a "green desire" (Bushnell, *Green* 14–15) that is embodied in a household whose architectures, according to Hieronimo, have their source in Vergilian epic. Such emphasis on the genealogical and social coordinates of Hieronimo's tree planting and its implications for political and social instability, in turn, invests with new meaning act four, scene two, a holdover from the 1580s play in which Hieronimo's wife Isabella hacks down the tree. In her act of destruction, which is quickly succeeded by a suicidal attack on the maternal breast, Isabella displaces vengeance onto the garden's fertility and then onto her body. In the revised play, her violence lays exorbitant waste to the family tree.

The woody refuse of such spectacular stage action signals how the composite *Spanish Tragedy* reflects and perhaps intensifies anxiety about the grim eco-political consequences of a shortage of timber and wood in England at the turn of the seventeenth century. In assaulting the stage prop, Isabella designates it a pine tree and, in so doing, introduces into the play an allusion to the denuded pine forests in Ovid's retelling of the Golden Age's fall. In the ruination of the pine tree, a complex emblem for the lamented and possibly dire fate of England's woodlands crystalizes. Unlike the fantasies of colonial extraction and recycling that we have explored in previous chapters, this play stages in this moment a never-green nightmare about English woodlands.

Tellingly, Isabella calls the pine tree she destroys "unfortunate" (4.2.7). This designation reinforces the fact that the tree has brought only ill luck to her family: Hieronimo, for instance, applies the term in this inauspicious sense to himself (3.2.63). Yet when the spruced-up *Spanish Tragedy* was revived at the turn of the century, its site of performance – the newly built Fortune theatre, where the renowned tragedian Edward Alleyn also launched a comeback[12] – adds fresh resonance to the more than twenty variant uses of "fortune" in the sixteenth-century play (1.1.7, 39–40; 1.2.3, 6, 103, 139; 1.3.10, 16, 18–19, 23, 54; 2.4.16; 3.1.1, 9; 3.2.63; 3.3.2; 3.4.78; 4.2.7; 4.4.148). All those "fortunes" reverberate against the playhouse's wooden walls, connecting the updated *Spanish Tragedy* to other plays in the repertory of the Admiral's Men that were retrofitted – *Old Fortunatus* (c. late 1599) and *Doctor Faustus* (c. 1604), which famously "perform[s] / The form of Faustus' fortunes, good or bad" (Prologue, ll. 7–8) – and that were commissioned – *Fortune's Tennis* (1600) – for the venue's opening seasons.[13] As the visual centrepiece of the composite *Spanish Tragedy*, the unfortunate pine, which Hieronimo had earlier associated with tragedy, thus has a complex material relation to the theatre in which the play was mounted. Like *Friar Bacon and Friar Bungay*'s tree prop, this wooden object is a synecdoche for the playhouse and, as such, vectors early modern discourses pertaining to the theatre industry. On the back of an Ovidian allusion, which is an elegiac account of clear-cutting woodlands for mercantile use, the tree's destruction at the Fortune proves, as we shall see, *both* environmentally wasteful *and* commercially productive. As does the detail of the sawpit in *The Merry Wives of Windsor*, the emblem of a felled tree in the composite *Spanish Tragedy* opens for us a vista onto the devastation that was carried out in English woodlands so that timbers could be transported to a northern suburb of London for the construction of the new Fortune playhouse. The composite play marks the disappearance of (English) woodlands as an unfortunate eco-political loss; and we may regard that loss as necessary for supplying fresh timber for the theatre and for the performance in it of a revenge tragedy whose plot pivots on (the fall of) a stage tree. No wood, no Fortune.

The Idolatrous Tree in the Painter's Part

We begin the process of exploring the tree prop's rich meanings roughly halfway through the "Painters part" when the artist Bazardo enters Hieronimo's garden in this new scene in the play's third act (l. 78). We do so in the spirit of the small scholarly tradition of the Additions that attends to the discourses of representation that Bazardo introduces into the revised play.[14] In elaborating here some details of the Fourth Addition, we elaborate not only the idolatrous valences of Hieronimo's conference with the painter, but also realize that the author(s) of the Additions composed this scene with an eye towards the play's horrific ending.

In the Fourth Addition, Hieronimo quizzes Bazardo about the limits and powers of his art: can it, the aggrieved Hieronimo inquires, reverse time by five years to return father, mother, and son back to a happier state (ll. 115–23)? Can Bazardo "paint," Hieronimo further presses, "this tree" upon which his son was murdered in act two and accompany it with a "doleful cry" (ll. 125–6)? Can the painter's art be "stretch[ed]" (l. 133) so that the murderers resemble Judas (l. 134), and can it then "bring ... forth" Hieronimo in his "shirt" (l. 136) as he was just before he discovered a "youth, run through and through with villains' swords, hanging upon this tree" (ll. 128–30)? And, finally, can Bazardo portray Hieronimo's "distracted countenance" at the instant of recognition (l. 143) and effectively transform a painting into a sort of moving picture? As the vibrant details of the commission indicate, Hieronimo would see, feel, and hear in the painting the "winds blowing, the bells tolling, the owl shrieking, the toads croaking, the minutes jarring, and the clock striking twelve" (ll. 145–7). Suddenly, however, the lively painting, which might be said to have afforded Hieronimo "comfort," if only "painted comfort" (ll. 73–4), calms when a "trance" overwhelms him (l. 157). This stillness marks the moment at which Hieronimo begins to confuse representation with reality: in a delusion produced by an imagined work of art, he beats the painter offstage, mistaking him for "one of the murderers" responsible for Horatio's untimely demise (l. 163). The artist suffers for a crime he never committed and which he never depicted.

Bazardo never seeks Hieronimo's artistic commission in this interpolated scene. Rather, he attends upon Hieronimo in his official capacity as Spain's Knight Marshal, for Bazardo desires "Justice" (l. 82) on behalf of his *own* "murdered son" (l. 91). He selects, however, an inauspicious moment to approach the judicial officer, for he salutes Hieronimo after "midnight" (l. 2) at the precise "place," near "the very tree," where "Horatio died" (ll. 60–1). Hieronimo comes to this "hideous" spot (l. 103), at this ominous hour because, as he informs his servants, he was unable to "behold [his] son Horatio" in "every crevice of each wall," "on each tree," in "every brake," in the "bushes," "in the water," and, finally, "up" in "heaven" (ll. 17–21). Having scoured high and low, in the cosmos as well as in every sublunary nook, for a trace of his dead son, Hieronimo returns, at the start of the Fourth Addition, to the location where Horatio's body was last seen – on the tree. In his madness, Hieronimo may have forgotten where he has stored his son's body, which upon discovering he vowed "not [to] entomb" until he has exacted revenge (2.5.54). In the Fourth Addition's landscape, then, Hieronimo is in a heightened state of lunacy:[15] much like Demetrius in *A Midsummer Night's Dream*, he is mad, or "wood within this wood" (2.1.192).

The inventory of places that Hieronimo details in this report of his frantic search for Horatio recalls the cadences of the Book of Exodus (20:4). In the Authorized Version's wording, this Old Testament verse proscribes the sin of idolatry: "Thou shalt not make vnto thee any grauen Image, or any likenesse *of anything* that is in heauen aboue, or that is in the earth beneath, or that is in the water vnder the earth" [emphasis in original]. For Huston Diehl, Hieronimo exhibits an idolatrous attachment to Horatio's body and bloodied handkerchief at the end of *The Spanish Tragedy* (122),[16] and this interpolated scene anticipates his improper devotion there. It does so, in the formulation of Eric Griffin, because the Fourth Addition "amplifie[s] Hieronimo's idolatrous devotion to his fallen son" in its allusions to a superstitious worship that are loaded with "heavy irony" ("Nationalism" 351, 354). Griffin identifies in the scene a number of such instances – most notably, Hieronimo's reference to a "lie" that is as "massy" or as Mass-like "as the earth" (ll. 94–5). To Griffin's findings, we could adduce the chatter near the start of scene about the use of torches, which Hieronimo's servants have lit, but which he would have put out and instead relit "at the mid of noon" (l. 28). To "burn daylight" (l. 30), which is how one of the servants restates Hieronimo's command, reworks a passage from "An Homilie Against perill of Idolatrie, and superfluous decking of Churches" that condemns the ceremonial use of candles: it was "euer a prouerbe of foolishness," the Elizabethan homily reads, "to light a candle at noone time" (50–1). Margaret Aston has linked the homiletic passage to Queen Elizabeth's rebuke of churchmen who carried torches at the opening of Parliament in 1559: "Away with those torches, for we see very well" (297). Hieronimo's account of his search for Horatio is thus steeped in Elizabethan controversies about the nature of idolatry.[17] The Fourth Addition marks Hieronimo's actions as especially suspect since he seeks his son's body in some form (material and then representational) at the proverbial witching hour. Such nighttime stage business in the vicinity of a tree proves more kin to the "gloomy woods" in *Titus Andronicus* that were "buil[t]" by "nature" so that "the gods" can "delight in tragedies" (4.1.53, 58–9) than to the fairy revels in Little Park that close *The Merry Wives of Windsor*.

The Fourth Addition frames the conversation that Hieronimo has with Bazardo with these idolatrous references. In so doing, the scene suggests that the second painting (the first is a family portrait) that Hieronimo describes to his midnight guest is not immune to the taint of superstition. It is all the more significant, then, that in the broadest details of its design this second painting explicitly recalls a narrative from the New Testament that also featured a son's death on a rood – Jesus's Passion. This narrative was a staple subject of art in the medieval era, and in many of the period's paintings, poems, and plays the rood was depicted as a tree. In the York play of *The Crucifixion*, for instance, the device to which the bumbling soldiers nail the actor's body is consistently referred to as "tree" (ll. 42, 74).[18] The composite *Spanish Tragedy* echoes this tradition when, in the Fourth Addition, it casts Horatio as the Son: the painted murderers, Hieronimo insists, must have "beards" like the turncoat Judas (l. 134),[19] and Horatio should hang, and then be cut down, from a tree that the play later designates as pine – the material out of which the cross upon which Jesus was crucified was thought to have been made.[20] The painting that Hieronimo wants Bazardo to make for him is a perverse rendering of *imitatio Christi*.

By aligning Horatio and Jesus, the "Painters part" also appears plotted to anticipate the startling presentation of Horatio's body in the final moments of *The Spanish Tragedy*. There, after Hieronimo has exacted revenge in a bloody play-within-a-play, he unveils his son's body as well as Horatio's blood-stained handkerchief to members of the noble audience, directing them, priestlike, to "behold" these elevated objects in a parody of Eucharistic ritual (4.4.88, 122).[21] Without the aid of the painter's art at play's end, Hieronimo finally manages to make an icon out of his son, mounting him as if on a crucifix – a tree of popery, as we observed in chapter 2 – during an amateur theatrical, a household passion play.

In a marketing strategy that from our vantage can only seem a cruel joke inspired, in part, by the figure Hieronimo cuts in the Fourth Addition,[22] the frontispiece to the 1615 edition of the composite *Spanish Tragedy* likewise produces an icon out of Horatio's dead body. Layering in a single frame two scenes from Kyd's text (act two, scenes four and five), the illustration focuses on Horatio's murder, not on his father's triumphant and equally spectacular revenge at play's end. "Alas it is my son Horatio," is all that this static father figure manages to say in the banderole or speech ribbon as he discovers Horatio hanging from the "tree," which is depicted

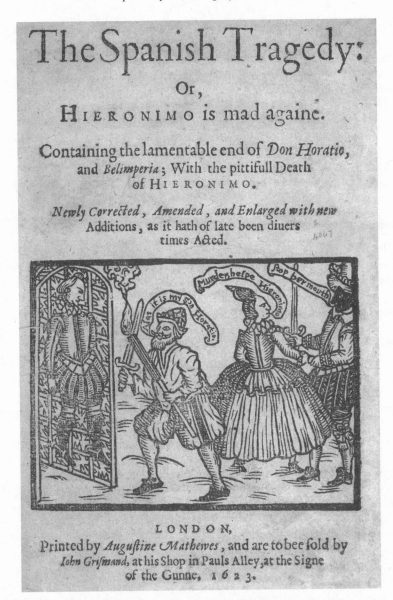

Figure 3.1 Title page to Thomas Kyd, *The Spanish Tragedy: Or, Hieronimo is mad againe* (London, 1623). This item is reproduced by permission of The Huntington Library, San Marino, California.

as a trellis-like stage prop. Although the illustration does not afford the Fourth Addition's Hieronimo the moving picture he desired, it succeeds in making an arresting image out of Horatio's murder by uncannily capturing the iconographic impulse motivating the maddened father in the interpolated scene. As do the memorable frontispieces to *Doctor Faustus* (1616) and to *Friar Bacon and Friar Bungay* (1630), this seventeenth-century visual addition to the revised play has come to function, retroactively, as a mnemonic for Kyd's *Spanish Tragedy*.[23] In so doing, it also enshrines in print the trellis-like stage prop that is one of the composite play's leading players, the tree around which an "accursed tragedy" (3.7.41) and a "murderous spectacle" (2.5.9) unfold.

The Gardener's Part: Planting Horatio

The strong emphasis that criticism on the Fourth Addition places on the painter's art has had the effect of diverting scholarly attention away from the other form of art this interpolated scene dilates upon – the gardener's – and, by extension, from its relation to Bazardo's image-making. In exploring this set of images, which Hieronimo invokes before the painter appears onstage, we delve to the root of Hieronimo's immoderate grief as the Fourth Addition presents it: a genealogy or family tree cut short before it could fully prosper.[24] In so doing, we also observe how the composite play aggregates some of the various allusions that make the tree so richly meaningful. By this logic, the Passion-like painting that Hieronimo seeks to commission while standing next to the tree on which Horatio was murdered proves a horrifying genealogical icon that testifies to his family's thwarted hope for a firmly planted lineage. In effect, Hieronimo appropriates the biblical story to elaborate the disappointment of his own social aspiration, which originates in the tree itself.

Before Bazardo arrives in the garden in the Fourth Addition, Hieronimo encounters his wife Isabella and his servants there, all of whom express worry that his midnight exploits will only serve to "increase" his "sorrow" (l. 55). Hieronimo attempts to allay their fears, claiming that he is indeed "very merry, very merry" (1. 58). Isabella disbelieves him, since he is, as she is quick to remind him, in "the place" and standing next to "the very tree, / Where my Horatio died" (ll. 60–1). Calling attention to the tree and pointedly designating Horatio as her (instead of their) son, Isabella rattles Hieronimo's mirthful pretense. To counterweigh Isabella's maternal claim, Hieronimo recounts his singular relation to the tree, which also articulates his singular relation to his murdered son. He launches into a genealogical history framed by his recollection of planting this tree himself and by Horatio's unfortunate demise on it. Gesturing towards the stage prop, perhaps even re-presenting through mime his verbal description of the tree's history, Hieronimo tells an origin story that appears nowhere else in the composite play:

> This was the tree, I set it of a kernel,
> And when our hot Spain could not let it grow,
> But that the infant and the human sap
> Began to wither, duly twice a morning
> Would I be sprinkling it with fountain water. (ll. 63–7)

The play's professional judge casts himself here as a devoted amateur arborist, performing the kind of day labour that would have been carried out by hired manual workers on early modern English estates.[25] So assiduous is Hieronimo in his care of this "kernel" that he succeeds in offsetting the "wither[ing]" effects of an inhospitable climate ("our hot Spain") with a twice-daily regimen of baptismal "sprinkling" that revivifies the parched sapling. In this "vegetable mythography,"[26] Hieronimo narrates a deep emotional investment and a lengthy commitment to the seed's uncertain growth. If Hieronimo administers his judicial duties with the zeal and patience he accorded the fledgling tree, then it is little wonder that he is so celebrated by Spain's populace: "There's not any advocate in Spain / That can prevail, or will take half the pain / That he will, in pursuit of equity" (3.13.52–4), the First Citizen reports just after the Fourth Addition has concluded. It is perhaps little surprise, then, that Hieronimo successfully "plead[s] for young Horatio's right" before the Spanish monarch when Horatio's role in taking captive the Portuguese prince Balthazar is cast in doubt (1.2.169).

Hieronimo's reputation in law and his advocacy of Horatio at court illuminate the paternalism of his act of arboriculture, indicating that he works on behalf of the underdog in both professional and domestic spheres. His recollection of green-thumbed accomplishment in the Fourth Addition further suggests that he approaches his role as *pater* with the same duty that he exhibits in other contexts. Indeed, the conjunction of "infant ... and the human sap" in his description of the vital liquid coursing through the plant figures the "kernel" as his own seed – as it does in *The Winter's Tale* (1.2.161) – and the beleaguered plant as an *infans* for whom Hieronimo has "hope[d] but well" since "his tender infancy" (1.2.117–18). The bodies of the tree and of Horatio thus consistently entail one another in the play; the attention that "Master[]" Hieronimo pays to one is consideration that he pays to the other (Fourth Addition, l. 77).[27] The tree with the "human" sap *is* Horatio,[28] and so both the plant and the son, whose mature body the composite *Spanish Tragedy* casts as an elm tree moments before the murder (2.4.45), constitute Hieronimo's family tree.

By this logic, the maturation of the kernel charts "woodman" Horatio's growth. But as Hieronimo proceeds to narrate the family tree's history, its fatal undoing is a form of metastatic development. He says to his wife Isabella about the tree:

At last it grew, and grew, and bore and bore,
Till at length
It grew a gallows, and did bear our son.
It bore thy fruit and mine: O wicked, wicked plant. (ll. 68–71)

Hieronimo's use of "grew" and "bore" (and "bear") captures at a verbal level the tree's disproportionate increase. This repetition ("grew, and grew, and bore and bore") reaches such prodigious heights that it buckles under its own weight, a collapse registered in the metrical foreshortening of the poetic line, "Till at length." But the family tree doesn't fall to the earth just yet in the composite *Spanish Tragedy*; instead, Hieronimo regards it as having transformed from a vital genealogical icon into an instrument of public execution – the gallows.[29] In Hieronimo's telling, the family tree rapidly metamorphoses into the object upon which the audience had earlier watched the family's sole heir expire.[30]

In its emphasis on wild, deadly heights, the horrifying conclusion to the origin story that Hieronimo rehearses has been crafted to echo an earlier moment of aristocratic trespass in the play's second act. Like the townspeople of Shakespeare's Windsor, but in a genuinely lethal key, Lorenzo and Balthazar – two of the play's aristocrats – enter Hieronimo's garden in disguise to murder Horatio, whom they have deemed an "Ambitious villain" whose "boldness grows" (2.2.41). They string him from the tree, and Lorenzo stabs him "thus, and thus," bestowing upon Horatio what he perversely calls "the fruits of love" (2.4.55).[31] Having dispatched his victim, Lorenzo then glosses the method of execution that they have selected: "Although his life were still ambitious proud, / Yet is he at the highest now he is dead" (2.4.60–1). By invoking a vegetable figure and by linking a superlative ("highest") with a phrase ("ambitious proud") whose redundancy seems purposively designed to overstress the extraordinariness of Horatio's courtly aspirations, Lorenzo sets up the imagery that

Hieronimo elaborates in the Fourth Addition. But unlike the actual death sequence, the Fourth Addition figures Horatio's death as the tree's monstrous birth.[32] Indeed, the "bearings" of Hieronimo's speech convey a reproductive sense: the gallows, Hieronimo laments to Isabella, "did bear our son. / It bore thy fruit and mine." In suggesting an image of stillbirth, the Fourth Addition prompts audiences to recall the stage business of Horatio's death and, perhaps, to reimagine the rope employed in it to hang him as an asphyxiating umbilical "cord" (3.13.175). The Fourth Addition's arboricultural discourse casts as monstrous the social coordinates named in the scene of Horatio's murder and, in so doing, looks forward to Isabella's suicide, which explicitly links Horatio's death to bodily organs associated with nurturance and reproduction: a mother's breast and her womb.

In light of the relation between the tree and Horatio that this narrative forges, as well as its closing emphasis on a genealogically premature death, the start of Hieronimo's history – the setting of the kernel – may also memorialize a birth. In this reading, Hieronimo plants the family tree to celebrate the auspicious event that initiates and should perpetuate his genealogy: the nativity of Horatio. This conclusion is less far-fetched – and has considerable implications – when we survey arboricultural rituals practiced (or claimed to have been) by members of the early modern English aristocracy. Keith Thomas observes that trees "had become an indispensable part of the scenery of upper-class life" during the sixteenth and seventeenth centuries (209), and woodlands thus functioned as ecologies of lineage or, in Andrew Marvell's apt formulation, as the "pedigrees" of England's "ancient stocks" or great families (ll. 489, 491). According to Thomas, at Althorp in Northamptonshire one can still locate stones that mark the planting of oak trees by "successive" members of the Spencer family; the earliest known example of such genealogical planting in England can be dated to 1567 (202). Although composed as much as fifty years later, Ben Jonson's country house poem "To Penshurst" records a more portentous instance of oak planting that is reported to have taken place on 30 November 1554,[33] thirteen years before the planting at Althorp. The occasion, Jonson recounts, was the birth of Philip Sidney, the eldest son of Sir Henry Sidney and nephew of Robert Dudley, the Earl of Leicester: "That taller tree, which of a nut was set / At his great birth, where all the muses met" (ll. 13–14).[34] When Hieronimo sets and then assiduously cares for the kernel in the backstory he narrates in the composite *Spanish Tragedy*, he enroots a powerful fantasy of genealogy, one more appropriate to England's most (recently) powerful families. By establishing an "organic relation to the soil," which, as Jean E. Feerick has shown,

was understood in the period to be the coterminous with the body of the
aristocracy ("Groveling" 243), Hieronimo has, in effect, styled himself as
more noble than he actually is.[35]

Thus, Hieronimo's recollection in the Fourth Addition proves as much
a birth notice for Horatio as it does an obituary for him. Its conclusion,
moreover, rewrites its beginning in that the father no longer bears sole responsibility for Horatio's upbringing; Hieronimo now implicates Isabella
as co-partner in the act of generation and in the genealogical loss – "It bore
thy fruit and mine." Isabella atones for her part in the family tree's ruin
when she later destroys it and then targets her reproductive organs. But
before we look to the tree's obliteration in act four, scene two we should
detail more fully why the family tree grows so lethally in the exact place
that it does. It arrests genealogy there because Hieronimo "set it of a kernel" in the first place. For this high-ranking civil servant keeps a pleasure
garden inspired not only by the kind cultivated on aristocratic estates in
early modern England, but also one informed by the imagery of Vergilian
epic. Both contexts help illuminate the far-ranging scope of the ambition
encapsulated in the kernel Hieronimo planted.

The Vergilian Treehouse: The Epic Architectures
of Hieronimo's Ambition

When the murderers secure Horatio up on the tree's branches, they taunt
him, we recall, by aligning his present height with his habitual self-conceit
("still ambitious proud"), a charge that applies both to Horatio's claim on
a vanquished Balthazar, whom he took into custody during the war, and
to his illicit affair with Bel-imperia, the Spanish Duke's daughter. As Frank
Whigham has observed about such fatal moments in the play, "The destruction of ambitious inferiors reaffirms the insecure superior's potency"
(50).[36] From a perspective less paranoid about collapsed social boundaries
than Lorenzo's, Horatio's successes in love and war testify to his worthi-
ness, to be sure; but in the context of a composite *Spanish Tragedy*, which
foregrounds Hieronimo's social pretensions in the Fourth Addition,
Horatio's triumphs could also be regarded as manifestations of an inherited, deep-seeded trait: ambition.[37] In his reading of Kyd's play, Christopher Crosbie captures precisely this sense of multigenerational social
aspiration when he dubs Hieronimo's family "an ambitious household"
(3). Crosbie comprehends this household both demographically (father,
son, and mother) and architecturally: he links the garden where Hieroni-

mo's son perishes to aesthetic gardens that were kept on the estates of Elizabethan aristocrats to designate elite distinction and that well-off members
of the middling sort had begun to plant on their own lands during the late
sixteenth century to flaunt their disposable income and to indicate their
proximity to social superiors (18–19).[38] (Shakespeare's Fords and Pages, it
is worth remarking, do not seem to possess such spaces.) Like others of its
kind, Hieronimo's pleasure garden is "an extension of the public dimensions of [his] household as well as a more intimate sphere" (Coch 98). It
proves horticultural shorthand in the play both for his family's growing
ambition and for a green version of Renaissance self-fashioning, wherein
the household and its intimates collectively define the aspirational self.
The cultivation of this self in the early modern garden was quite literal
indeed (Bushnell, *Green* 12–16; Munroe 6).

   If Hieronimo's pleasure garden signals his household's ambition in spatial terms, then the kernel he planted there compresses the grand reach of
this aspiration. Locating the household's ambition in the growth of the
most symbolically potent plant in the garden – the family tree – enables us
to observe again how the early seventeenth-century *Spanish Tragedy* layers the tree's meanings: it reconfigures the father's care of the tree as an act
of social emulation that the play punishes when, in the Fourth Addition,
Hieronimo imagines the tree that bears Horatio's dead body transformed
into a gallows. In fabricating this memory of execution, Hieronimo describes a process of manufacture that occludes the labour required to fashion a gallows: a living tree metamorphoses itself into an object that would
have been assembled from pieces of wood and demonstrates the indistinction outlined in the introduction between vital and dead wood, between
tree and wood product.[39] Hieronimo did not set the kernel, of course,
so that it could develop into an instrument of death. The gallows that it
becomes, however, keys us into another wooden object that Hieronimo
hoped to plant in a figurative sense when he tended his garden: a timber-
framed house.

   The Fourth Addition affords a glimpse of the household that Hieronimo
cultivates, although it comes into focus at a moment of devastation. While
conversing with Bazardo, Hieronimo envisions the manner in which he
will discover his son on the Passion-like painting he would own, and, in
so doing, depicts his household in epic terms:

   And looking upon him by the advantage of my torch, find it to be my son
   Horatio. There you may show a passion, there you may show a passion.

Draw me like old Priam of Troy, crying 'The house is a-fire, the house is
a-fire as the torch over my head!'" (ll. 150–4)

Such instructions indicate, on the one hand, that Hieronimo further con-
torts the imagery of the Passion in the composite *Spanish Tragedy*. The
shift from an upper-case to a lower-case consonant transfers "passion"
from a murdered Son to a maddened father, elevating Hieronimo above
his worldly station because it yokes him to Jesus. In their invocation of
The Aeneid, these instructions, on the other hand, perhaps ward off – and
certainly complicate – this dubious identification (the avenging father as
Jesus) by associating Hieronimo with Priam, a classical model of pater-
nal grief. Although, as Eugene D. Hill details ("Senecan and Vergilian"
143–52), there are other instances of Vergilian allusion in the composite
play, especially to Aeneas's journey through the underworld in Book VI
of the epic, this reference to Troy's monarch not only hails from an earlier
part of *The Aeneid* (Book II), but also harkens back to a prior and bleaker
moment in the genealogy of empire.[40] Indeed, Hieronimo's epic persona
in the garden proves a particularly unpromising medium of *translatio imperii*, for shortly after Priam surveys the architectural fallout of the Greek
invasion, Pyrrhus decapitates him.

The allusion's foreboding notwithstanding, it also works to disclose
the far-reaching scope of the chief judge's genealogical self-conceit, figuring the ambitious household as no smaller than the famed city. In effect,
the change from Jesus to Priam does not demote Hieronimo so much as
confirm his bloated self-perception. In dubbing himself Troy's king, Hieronimo imaginatively outranks the play's murderous aristocrats who il-
licitly entered his pleasure garden – his Troy. In so doing, he also recasts
them as an invading army that, in Marlowe's well-known phrase from
Doctor Faustus, "burnt the topless towers of Ilium" (scene 13, l. 91). Hieronimo, however, makes no mention of Troy's legendary walls of stone
in the Fourth Addition. Instead, he laments the loss of a solitary wooden
edifice that is a synecdoche for the city: "The house is a-fire, the house
is a-fire." Hieronimo utters this phrase, whose repetitious cadences resemble the "grew and grew, and bore and bore" of the tree's origin story,
as the flame of his torch illuminates in the painting – maybe even ignites
– Horatio's dead (and highly placed) body. The fatal coupling of son and
plant, then, would seem to be the antecedent of "house," intimating that
both collectively and individually, Horatio and the tree comprise the raw
material out of which Hieronimo builds his family's household. Tellingly,
the magnified scope of this construction is at odds with the measurable

size of "Horatio's house," which, according to the Spanish monarch at
the start of the play, is too "small" to accommodate "all" of Balthazar's
"train" (1.2.187).

Appearing only two scenes before the Fourth Addition in the composite *Spanish Tragedy*, the Third Addition more explicitly casts Horatio in
architectural terms when Hieronimo refers to his dead son as the "very
arm that did hold up our house" (l. 32). Here, "arm," which is also me-
tonymy for Horatio's martial prowess, functions as if it were a wooden
beam or column that supports the elevation ("up") of the entire ("our")
household.[41] Hieronimo further elaborates the wooden architectures of
his son's body in this interpolated scene when he laments the uneven maturation process in terms drawn from the carpenter's craft: "whereas a son,
/ The more he grows in stature and in years, / The more unsquared, unbevelled he appears" (ll. 20–2). In the Third Addition, then, "woodman"
Horatio proves the strong but not invulnerable and perfected feature reinforcing the tree-household Hieronimo grows. When this arm buckles,
Hieronimo's ambitious household topples. It comes as no surprise, then,
that Vergil figures Troy's downfall as the fall of a tree – an elm or an "aun-
cient oke," depending on the sixteenth-century translation.[42]

After the lethal layering of Horatio and the plant, whose consequence is the obliteration of the household's ambitions for upward mobility, Hieronimo plots (and defers) revenge against the murderers and
the aristocratic worldview that they vigorously policed in his garden.[43]
Hieronimo's wife Isabella will also enact vengeance, but not against the
Iberian royal families; instead she targets the multivalent icon of her
household's social pretensions, the tree growing in the garden. But before we (finally) attend to her felling of this tree, we should look to the
composite *Spanish Tragedy*'s Fifth Addition, where Hieronimo updates
his self-identification as a monarch. In this scene, Hieronimo boasts to
the Portuguese ruler, whose son Balthazar is one of the casualties of the
play-within-a-play, "I tell thee Viceroy, this day I have seen revenge, /
And in that sight am grown a prouder monarch / Than ever sat under
the crown of Spain" (ll. 9–11). Echoing the aristocrats' verbal abuse of
Horatio ("still ambitious proud"), Hieronimo claims that witnessing
successful vengeance renders him "prouder" than any Spanish monarch.
This royal company includes, of course, the monarch whose "whole suc-
ceeding hope" he has just cut short (4.4.203). Whereas he had garnered a
"share" in Spain's "victory" over Portugal by virtue of Horatio's military
success (1.2.125), Hieronimo here compels the monarch to share in his
family's genealogical fate.[44]

Reiterating the verb ("grew") he used in the Third Addition to imagine
Horatio's uneven architectural maturation and employed in the Fourth
Addition to describe the family tree's unrestrained development, Hieronimo invokes "grown" in the Fifth Addition to characterize his new emi-
nence as a "sovereign subject"[45] – or, rather, as a royal plant. That kings
and trees both wear crowns enhances his bold self-presentation as a tree
that has grown murderous by the end of the composite *Spanish Tragedy*.
But we may say that Hieronimo can only enjoy this crowning achieve-
ment because Isabella has already felled the family tree growing in the
garden. He can usurp such sovereign force only after the tree – one half
the material out of which he erects his ambitious household – has been
chopped down.

Isabella's Revenge: Eradicating the Tree

The tree prop makes its final appearance in act four, scene two of the composite *Spanish Tragedy*, a scene that also marks the first appearance of
Isabella since the Fourth Addition. Here, the fates of Hieronimo's wife
and of the family tree converge: a frenzied Isabella "revenge[s]" herself
"upon this place," laying waste to all the vegetation in the pleasure garden, but especially the tree, before she mortally wounds herself (4.2.4, 37).
She assaults "this garden-plot," she announces, because "neither piety nor
pity moves / The King to justice or compassion" (4.2.2–3, 12). Her rationale is somewhat faulty, however: the King remains (inexplicably) oblivi-
ous to news of Horatio's death (3.12.83–4) until Hieronimo reveals his
son's body in the play-within-a-play's gruesome finale two scenes later
(4.4.88–152). Isabella is as uninformed about how far word of her son's
death has travelled at court as she is about her husband's revenge plot. Set
against her husband's theatricals, Isabella's garden-variety vengeance pales
in comparison. At worst, it is misguided in its aims and superfluous to the
play's plot: as she concedes, her revenge is "to no end" (4.2.34). At best,
it proves a "symbolic prologue" to Hieronimo's more elaborate and more
satisfactory method for retribution (Wineke 65).[46]
    Attention to the relation between the events of the Fourth Addition
and those of act four, scene two, however, can help us to comprehend
more fully the structural logic of the composite play. It is as if the Fourth
Addition was composed in such a way that act four, scene two proves a
pointed reversal of the interpolated scene's events and themes. Isabella's
actions thus appear as a powerful, if belated and futile, attempt to eradicate
her husband's iconic emblem of "green desire." In destroying the garden's

vegetation, she also literally weeds out the ambition that her husband cultivated and that, in Hieronimo's telling, was responsible for her son's death. In so doing, she enumerates the violent strokes to which she subjects the tree as she carries them out. Her play-by-play commentary neatly undoes the labour Hieronimo had invested to keep the sapling healthy so many years ago:

> Down with these branches and these loathsome boughs
> Of this unfortunate and fatal pine:
> Down with them, Isabella, rent them up
> And burn the roots from whence the rest is sprung. (4.2.6–9)

Isabella's "rent[ing] ... up" of the tree's branches, for instance, echoes and then reverses the "bring[ing] ... up" that Hieronimo supervised in the Fourth Addition (l. 78). Indeed, "up" in Isabella's speech all but means "Down," that plunging word that she twice employs to mark the doom of those limbs from which her "ambitious" and "proud" son had earlier depended. In light of these socially charged directional vectors, Isabella's revenge appears to operate in the service of class conservatism, for it seems to achieve, however unwittingly, a ratification of the social order that Hieronimo tampered with when the kernel that he planted first took root.

At the close of act four, scene two, after she has spoiled the garden's vegetation, Isabella reprises a central concern of the Fourth Addition – parenthood – and effectively rearranges its gendered coordinates as Hieronimo had explicated them to her in the interpolated scene. In her final onstage moments, she modifies Hieronimo's rewriting of his own exclusive involvement in the planting of the kernel ("It bore thy fruit and mine") by claiming sole responsibility for her son – an entitlement, we recall, she had articulated in the Fourth Addition when she pointed to "the very tree, / Where my Horatio died" (ll. 60–1). Isabella predicts that, one day, "passengers" will "look[] at" the pleasure garden she made "Fruitless" and will regard it as a bleak monument to Horatio, whom they will call "the son of Isabel" (4.2.14, 20–2). She pries Hieronimo and Horatio apart so successfully because she analogizes the family tree to her (formerly fruitful) reproductive capacities: "And as I curse this tree from further fruit, / So shall my womb be cursed for [Horatio's] sake" (4.2.35–6). In its alignment of tree and womb, Isabella's scourge also forges a link between the "fruit" that each has already borne – namely, Horatio.[47] She once again removes Hieronimo from the parental equation and crowns herself the unique genealogical source of Horatio and, by extension, of both the family tree and the ambitious household. While destroying herself, she even invokes an activity – nursing – that her husband's routine of plant-watering approximates: "And with this weapon will I wound the breast," she exclaims, "The hapless breast that gave Horatio suck" (4.2.37–8). In yet another inversion of her husband's rhetoric in the Fourth Addition, Isabella reveals that the nurturing of Horatio had always fallen under her care, and for his upbringing she kills herself after she fells the tree. By such logic, the ambitious household's *mater* appoints herself the agent responsible for her family's social overreaching and for the correction of that pretension.

As acts of social restoration, however, Isabella's pruning and her fiery eradication of the tree, as well as her suicide, are ultimately ineffectual. Destroying the tree may rid the pleasure garden of the last living traces of the household's family tree – the tree itself – but her actions cannot curb the epic momentum driving the ambition encapsulated in its seed.[48] Hieronimo, after all, will figure himself as a usurping monarch at the sight of completed revenge near the end of the composite play.

Timber! The Emblem of the Felled Pine

Isabella's destruction of the tree in act four, scene two proves an exercise in "woe-begone" despair and futility (4.3.26). Her acts of socio-political restoration in the garden, which take shape as an assault directed in the first instance against botanical life, find no usefulness for the tree that's been cut down, and they doom the soil to a future of unwholesomeness and sterility. The pile of wood and branches that her violence creates will not be employed to repair the frame of an existing household or a place of worship, to reinforce a new household with a beam, or even to construct a gallows. Although it is a scholarly commonplace to regard her destruction of the tree as improvident, my point here is that it is especially so because, by the start of the seventeenth century in early modern England, firewood and timber were fast becoming luxury goods.

In the introduction we observed the economic factors that made wood and timber an unlikely extravagance during the period. In chapter 1 we had occasion to look at an account by a contemporary of Kyd's – Thomas Harriot – that highlights "the want of wood and deerenesse thereof in England," and in chapter 2 we explored legal efforts undertaken in late-Elizabethan England that aimed to preserve (but not necessarily to renew) woodlands. Within twenty-five years of the publication of these statutes and colonial brochures, when the composite *Spanish Tragedy* had been reprinted in 1610 for a third time, Arthur Standish sounds a more pessimistic note about the scarcity of wood in his pamphlet *The Commons Complaint* (1611). He informs readers, "there is not Timber left in this Kingdome at this instant onely to repaire the buildings thereof an other age, much lesse to build withall" (1). Standish dubs his era the "destroying age," for, in his estimation, the "generall destruction and waste of wood made" in England is "more within twenty or thirty last yeares then in any hundred yeares before" (A2ᵛ, 1). In the sequel to this pamphlet Standish forecasts that "the Kingdome by no meanes can be maintained another age" without "a speedy generall Planting and Preseruing" of trees (*New* 5). In a preface to this publication's second edition, James I echoes this sentiment when he advocates for the implementing of "some proiects for the increasing of Woods" (*New* A2ʳ).[49] Since 1611, Standish had been prognosticating about the doom that would ensue for England should these projects fail to take root: "no wood no Kingdome" (*Commons* 2). This aphoristic statement regards England's forests and woods as if they were imperilled genealogical and political assets, or "posterities," which is a term that Michael Drayton employs in *Poly-Olbion* (1612) to name some of England's "greatest Groues" (E4ʳ).[50] As Robert Markley observes about Marvell's seventeenth-century country house poetry, the "fictions of an endlessly exploitable nature and a stable and always prosperous England are mutually reinforcing" ("Gulfes" 98). When the monarch's trees fall, eco-political disorder necessarily ensues.

During the early seventeenth century, Isabella's tree felling can be said to participate, broadly, in the dissemination of such rhetoric about resource depletion. Through its history of performance, revival, and extensive publication, the composite *Spanish Tragedy* had the potential for amplifying notes of worry about disappearing woodlands, rising lumber prices, and the looming threat of an eco-political collapse that pamphlets like Standish's recorded and, of course, helped to produce in discourse. Its scene of tree felling concentrates such anxiety insofar as it vivifies onstage a classical emblem of "eco-apocalypse."[51] Isabella introduces this emblem into the play when she destroys the tree her husband had planted and classifies the target of her rage as a "pine" (4.2.7), a designation indebted to the genealogical account of the world's devolution that the inaugural book of Ovid's *Metamorphoses* chronicles. There, the razing of a pine forest indexes the permanent loss of the Golden Age's hallmark features, ecological pristineness and political harmony.

In Arthur Golding's mid-sixteenth-century translation of Ovid, we learn that the "lofty pine-tree was not hewen from mountains, where it stood, / In seeking strange and foreign lands to rove upon the flood" dur-

ing the golden epoch where, among other things, "truth and right" remained "unforced and unconstrained" (ll. 104–6; 109–10). But during the
"wicked" Iron Age (l. 145), the goddess of justice, Astraea, fled the earth
(ll. 169–70), and these mountains were denuded of their trees: "The ship-
man hoist his sails to wind whose names he did not know; / And ships that
erst in tops of hills and mountains had ygrow / Did leap and dance on the
uncouth waves" (ll. 149–51). From the Golden Age, where a "lofty pine-
tree" represents in synecdoche a mountainside forest, to the Iron Age,
where that forest now appears in the guise of "ships" that formerly grew
on the mountainside, the advancement of exploration (navigation) and the
degeneration of sociopolitical stability (the loss of Astraea) are coincident.
In the span between these ages, woodland devastation and the use of wood
products measure sociopolitical changes, and the negative and positive effects of such shifts are imagined in typical Ovidian manner – that is, magically, as if without the logger's labour and the shipwright's skill.[52] Ovid's
chronology inspires the composite Spanish Tragedy, then, in at least three
ways: Hieronimo's depiction of the family tree that transforms into the
gallows exemplifies an Ovidian logic of effortless construction with wood;
Isabella's ruination of a pine tree, which Hieronimo had loaded with epic
genealogical weight, forecasts sociopolitical catastrophe; and the destruction of the play's single tree corresponds to the deforestation of an entire
woodland. In the felled tree in Hieronimo's pleasure garden, we can begin
to behold the fate of England's forests during what Standish, in a nod to
Ovid, names the "destroying age."

A rewriting of Ovid's Metamorphoses, Ben Jonson's masque The Gold-
en Age Restored confirms the availability of plant life – but only implicitly
the pine tree – to emblematize the eco-political legacy of the Iron Age to
seventeenth-century England. Performed at the Jacobean court in 1615,
the same year that the composite Spanish Tragedy was republished with
a frontispiece of Hieronimo discovering Horatio's body, this masque features Astraea, the émigrée goddess from Ovid, and Golden Age, both of
whom return to earth after Pallas disperses the antimasque presided over
by Iron Age. At the close of a dance celebrating the return of Astraea and
Golden Age, the three female figures envisage a change that will soon be
discernible in "all things" (l. 148):

ASTRAEA: But when they [all things] have enjoyed awhile
The age's quickening power –
GOLDEN AGE: That every thought a seed doth bring,
And every look a plant doth spring,

And every breath a flower –
PALLAS: Then earth unplowed shall yield her crop. (ll. 149–54)

The rejuvenation of the Golden Age requires that signature aspects of Iron Age life – here, a dearth of plants, which presumably includes Ovid's pine forest – be restored to their former vitality. Yet the replanting entails no human exertion: in a nifty homage to Ovid's theory of labour, every thought will conceive a seed, every look will engender a plant, and every breath will bring forth a flower in this neo-Golden Age. At the end of the masque Astraea names such universal regeneration a "second birth" (l. 213). Like Hieronimo, she commemorates the delivery of the world from the grips of the Iron Age by planting a genealogical tree: "My silver feet, like roots, are wreathed / Into the ground, my wings are sheathed, / And I cannot away" (ll. 210–12). Her "region" becomes England's pleasure garden (l. 220), and she its new tree of justice and good governance.

Jonson's masque is, as Robert N. Watson observes, a fantasy of "liberating regression to garden and wilderness" that trades in nostalgia for an irrecoverable eco-political loss (6).[53] Much recent commentary on the status of the Golden Age in seventeenth-century letters regards nostalgia as the distinctive affective register for an early modern engagement with Ovid's genealogical scheme.[54] Such affect could structure colonialist pursuits in foreign locales, as it does in Shakespeare's *Tempest*, where the old counsellor Gonzalo imagines that his plantation on the island would "excel the Golden Age" (2.1.168).[55] And it could provide a blueprint for response to Standish's pamphlets. According to Arthur Hopton, an early reader and supporter of Standish's publications, the application of Standish's project for replanting England with trees "Will bring againe a golden age to vs" (qtd. in Standish, *New*).[56]

My aim is not to cast doubt on such readings and nostalgic responses so much as to highlight that allusions to this forever-lost era also sometimes convey (consciously or not) anxious expectation about the eco-political condition of England's woodlands. In the introduction I called such affect a darker shade of green. Although Standish's pamphlets and the composite *Spanish Tragedy* would seem at first glance to have little in common – neither shares the same publisher or genre, and only Standish's texts endorse without reservation the planting of trees in an effort to offset ecological loss – each in its own way presents the woodlands of turn-of-the-seventeenth-century England through the lens of such colouring. In different registers, they express the dire consequence of deforestation, suggesting that, without standing trees, England's eco-political durability is tenuous.

In this bleak context, the imminent ascendancy of "little England" on the world stage (1.4.160) that much scholarship has detected as the aspiring subtext of Kyd's sixteenth-century play appears to be less guaranteed.[57]

The "Trees" of the Fortune

In encapsulating the devastation of English woodlands in the emblem of a felled tree, the composite *Spanish Tragedy*, like Greene's *Friar Bacon and Friar Bungay* and Shakespeare's *The Merry Wives of Windsor*, also affords "inside" commentary on the material conditions of playing in London's theatres at the turn of the seventeenth century. Such winks and nods become particularly apparent to us when the revised play moved, as if spirited by means of *translatio studii*, to the Admiral's Men's new theatre. Even if the Additions, as Roslyn L. Knutson contends, were authored anonymously in 1597, the entire eco-inflected playbook was shipped across the Thames from the Rose to the Fortune playhouse within years of a rival troupe ferrying its theatre's constitutive wood and timber across the river in the other direction. Performed at the Fortune in 1601–2, the composite *Spanish Tragedy*, which in Knutson's account may have been further revised for these occasions, generates site-specific and literally topical meaning about the business of playing unimaginable when it was staged in original (or revised) form at the Rose. In the spectacular destruction of a pine tree in this novel theatre, the eco-history of the Fortune playhouse comes into view.

As our explorations of Greene's and Shakespeare's plays have outlined, the tree stage prop can articulate a relation to the wooden walls of the theatre in which it was mounted and, in Shakespeare's case, to the woodland ecology whence the theatre's timber and wood were extracted. The composite *Spanish Tragedy*'s pine tree similarly functions as a figure for the new playhouse where it takes centre stage and around which the murderers, according to Hieronimo, are "actors" in a "tragedy" (3.7.41). Indeed, in the composite *Spanish Tragedy*'s performance in the early years of the seventeenth century, further evidence for such a reading stems from a textual holdover that the walls of the Fortune playhouse infuse with new significance. This holdover frames my investigation in the chapter: "Down with these branches and these loathsome boughs / Of this unfortunate and fatal pine" (4.2.6–7). Christened after Dame Fortune, the Admiral's Men's novel venue imbues Isabella's violence with the punning force of an inside-joke that testifies to a set of circumstances that nearly thwarted the rise of the Fortune and Henslowe's ambitions for the "playhousehold." When spoken in 1601–2 and accompanied by Isabella's destructive actions,[58] this passage wittily heralds the triumph of the Fortune – an assemblage of theatrical trees – over a campaign that sought to forestall the playhouse's opening. Since the theatre had recently begun to admit customers, the emblematic pine tree can fall and, as Hieronimo says of "all tragedians," "in a minute start[] up again, / Revive to please to-morrow's audience" (4.4.78, 81–2). Like stage tragedians (and even like the more comical Falstaff), the fatal tree will stand up and fall down once again.

In an introductory note to the contract for the Fortune in her documentary history of Henslowe's dealings, Carol Chillington Rutter includes, as an afterthought, a comment that describes the conditions of playing in the Admiral's Men at the turn of the seventeenth century. She observes, "The new playhouse was to be called the Fortune, hopefully, no doubt" (175). We could regard the playhouse's name as articulating a wish for more fortunate financial circumstances at the new venue than those that had obtained at the Rose since February 1599, when the housekeepers of the Chamberlain's Men leased a plot of ground on the Bankside. After enduring a season of competition from neighbour-rivals who staged fare like *Julius Caesar* and *Hamlet*, Henslowe decided to transport his company to a venue on the other side of the Thames. The master carpenter for the project was Peter Street, who was responsible for dismantling the Theatre and re-erecting its timbers in 1599, and the contract for the Fortune that Street negotiated with Henslowe and Edward Alleyn makes it clear that the Globe loomed large in the imagination of the commissioning party. In some cases, it was to serve as a model for constructing the Fortune. In the contract Street agrees to employ his first-hand knowledge of the Globe's measurements and to duplicate them exactly at the Fortune. There are provisions for "suche like streares Conveyances & divisions without & within as are made & Contryved in and to the late erected Plaiehowse On the Banck … Called the Globe," and for the "Stadge to be in all other proporcions Contryved and fashioned like vnto the Stadge of the saide Plaiehowse Called the Globe." In other cases, Street was instructed to outdo his work at the Globe. The wood and timber he used would not, for instance, be second-hand. Scholars have estimated that the new venue cost between £520 and £880; the contract implies that no small portion of this cost would be disbursed for materials and labour for building the playhouse. The contract records that the building materials included "good stronge and sufficyent newe oken bourdes," "newe deale [fir or pine] bourdes," and "good stronge and substancyall newe Tymber and other necessarie stuff." With freshly lumbered wood, Street

will construct the "saide howse and other thinges beforemencio*n*ed … ac-
cordinge to the manner and fashion of the saide howse Called the Globe
Saveinge only that all the princypall and maine postes of the saide fframe
and Stadge forwarde shalbe square and wrought pal*asterwise* [like pilas-
ters] with carved propor*c*ions Called Satiers [satyrs] to be placed & sett on
the Topp of every of the same postes," and saving that "the saide fframe
in every poynte for Scantling*es* [be] lardger and bigger in assize Then the
Scantlinges [measurements of thickness and breadth] of the Timber of the
said newe erected howse, Called the Globe" [emphasis in original] (qtd. in
Rutter 175–7). Such material extravagance, ornate decoration, and architectural innovation – a rectangular, not a rounded superstructure – aimed,
in sum, to give the wheel of the Admiral's Men's fortunes a positive spin.[59]
In ways that recall the grandness of Hieronimo's architectural aspirations,
the Fortune proves an ambitiously designed playhouse, at least on paper.
If the Additions were composed after this project's completion in 1601–2,
then perhaps the maturing playhouse, like "woodman" Horatio in the
Third Addition, appeared slightly "more unsquared" and "unbevelled"
than it had once been (l. 22).

It may well be that the name of the Fortune was intended to herald the
hoped-for success of the Admiral's Men on the other side of the Thames.
But when the venue opened it doors, the positive valence of its name may
also have functioned to proclaim triumph over those groups that had
shown ill will towards the playhouse by advocating for its closure before
construction was completed. There was, in short, significant pushback by
the City and the Privy Council to the plan to build a theatre on Golding Lane that would outstrip the Globe in opulence and, presumably, in
attracting crowds. At the likely request of his servant Edward Alleyn,
Charles Howard, Earl of Nottingham, issued a warrant dated 12 January 1599/1600 that anticipated such public outcry against the theatre and
aimed to allay it. (It may be that Howard's warrant responds to undocu-
mented threats to thwart the completion of the playhouse's construction.)
Howard calls on the Queen's officials in the county of Middlesex to "per-
mitt and suffer my saide Servant [Alleyn] to proceede in theffecting and
finishinge of the saide Newhowse, w*i*thout anie yor lett or molestac*i*on
towarde*s* him or any of his woorkmen" [emphasis in original] (qtd. in
Rutter 177–8). On 9 March 1600, which surely coincides with the toil that
Street and his carpenters were carrying out on the Fortune's superstructure in the English countryside, the Privy Council ordered justices of the
peace in Middlesex to ensure that "the foresaid intended Buildinge … be
staied, and yf any be begone, to see the same quite defaced." According to

this Privy Council minute, to permit the playhouse's construction would amount to "an offence, and scandall," in no small part because it would countervail a "spetiall direction" from the Council, likely the injunction issued in 1597 discussed in previous chapters, "to pluck downe" theatres already standing and "to see them defaced" (qtd. in Rutter 182–4). The March order did not go uncontested, and on 22 June 1600, a month before work at the site of the playhouse was slated for completion, the Privy Council reversed its position and allowed the Admiral's Men's new venue. The wheel of Fortune finally had a favourable turn, but the general "misgouerment" of theatres across London prompted the Council to declare in this minute that all other playhouses, excluding the Globe, be closed (qtd. in Rutter 190–3).

In the next section we'll turn to the impact of this stipulation on London's other theatres, but we would do well to consider first the surprising readings of the tree prop's destruction that this theatrical history helps us to articulate. Staged in a venue with a history as changeable as the Fortune's, the scene of destruction in Hieronimo's pleasure garden could tout the success of the playhouse against its adversaries. Isabella's assault against the "unfortunate" emblem – the tree prop – of the theatre confirms the playhouse's good luck: although the scene pulls down the prop, its production in this playhouse requires that the trees of theatre not be cut down. The scene, in effect, displays what antitheatrical opponents wanted to have happen to this "idol of the revels," which is Ben Jonson's phrase for the Fortune playhouse. And yet, as we have observed, the play restages this desire over and over again in revival and thus never fully realizes it. By this logic, Isabella appears a misguided agent of antitheatrical violence whose efforts to "pluck downe," "deface[]," and set ablaze a figure for the Fortune ultimately prove futile and self-defeating.[60] The scene, after all, closes with her suicide.

By means of an Ovidian allusion, the tree prop's felling can also function as counterpart to the sawpit in *The Merry Wives of Windsor*. It can gesture towards the English countryside where the Fortune's timbers were felled, fashioned into a rectangular frame, and then disassembled before being transported to London. Isabella emerges, by this logic, as a shadow for the workmen who undertook this enormous labour. Especially in March 1600, when the fate of Alleyn and Henslowe's project was most uncertain, such labour in England's woodlands must have seemed a potential waste of sturdy, substantial, and costly timber. But it would prove not to be so. In the context of such theatrical history, Isabella's uneconomical actions become infused with new purpose and so remind us that, although Ovid's

chronology records an act of massive deforestation, it also specifies that
clear-cutting was supervised in the forests for express commercial ends,
such as the building of a ship – a wooden space that is, as we shall see in the
next chapter, as massive as a playhouse. In a composite *Spanish Tragedy*,
then, the tree's fall betokens both the collapse of Hieronimo's Troy and the
establishment of the Fortune's theatrical empire.

Curtains for the Rose

With the opening of the Fortune in 1600, another theatrical woodland became enrooted around London. If the relocation of the Theatre was an act
of recycling, then the erection of the Fortune harkened back to the kind of
fantasy explored in the introduction in which English trees were lumbered
to build a new theatrical woodland that then, in performance, staged an
uncanny vision of the spot from which the theatre's materials had been
extracted. As we observed in the previous section, however, the success
of the Fortune sometimes seemed as if it depended on the loss of other
theatres. Documents pertaining to the construction of the Fortune, after
all, both implied and predicted the destruction of other playhouses. The
Earl of Nottingham, for example, commences his 12 January 1599/1600
warrant in support of Alleyn and Henslowe's venture by noting that the
"Howse which he [Alleyn] and his Companye haue nowe, on the Banck"
is unsuitable because it is in a state of "dangerous decaye" and "stand-
eth verie noysome for resorte of people in the wynter time" [emphasis in
original] (qtd. in Rutter 177–8). Never named outright, the Rose is this
dilapidated playhouse. Its portrayal in the warrant seems designed to lead
to two conclusions: first, the depiction justifies the expense Alleyn and
Henslowe have incurred for the Fortune because the decayed timbers of
the Rose appear unfit for recycling; second, it intimates that when the
Admiral's Men's repertory debuts at the Fortune, the doors of the wilted
Rose will close. Appearing only three months after Nottingham's warrant,
on 8 April 1600, a Privy Council order defending the building of the new
venue linked the "decaye" of the Rose to the prospect of the Fortune, and
then instructed that work at the construction site should not be hindered
"because an other howse is pulled downe, in stead of yt" (qtd. in Rutter 184–6). The Privy Council here makes plain a professed adherence to
the status quo: statistically, no new theatre was erected when the Globe
appeared on the Bankside and so no increase in the number of theatres
should accompany the rise of the Fortune. Indeed, on 22 June 1600, about
a month before the Fortune was slated for completion, the Privy Council

showed further support for the Alleyn-Henslowe venture by insisting, in-explicably in light of the previous notices about the Rose, that the Curtain "is either to be ruyned and plucked downe or to be putt to some other good vse" (qtd. in Rutter 190–3). At the same time, the council ordered that only two playhouses – the Globe and the Fortune – remain opera-tional at the start of the new century. In effect, the council was remoulding its injunction from 1597 that called for the demolition of all playhouses. Such zero-sum rhetoric for building new venues shifts into a call for the "deforestation" of almost all playhouses. By this logic, the impact of these two pockets of theatrical woodlands – the Fortune and the Globe – would indeed have proven unfortunate and fatal for the wider expanse of theatri-cal "trees" around London.

Despite the Privy Council's claim in 1600 that a playhouse "is pulled downe" to offset the construction of the Fortune, no old theatre, of course, was dismantled at this time. Of the Curtain, the Rose, and the Swan, which were three playhouses built during the sixteenth century that were still standing on the Bankside as debate about the Fortune whirled, it was Henslowe's old venture that was the first to close its doors. "Diana's rose," as Greene's *Friar Bacon and Friar Bungay* had celebrated this theatre, was disassembled in 1606, and we cannot be certain that its wood and timbers were "putt to some other good vse." In Hieronimo's lament for the death of his son in a seventeenth-century *Spanish Tragedy*, we may hear an ex-pression of loss for the old playhouse. Gazing on his son's decaying body, Hieronimo grieves for a "Sweet lovely rose, ill plucked before [its] time" (2.5.46).[61] By 1610, when the revised play had its third print run, the mur-der of "woodman" Horatio in Hieronimo's pleasure garden and Isabella's subsequent destruction of the tree could also capture the fate of the Rose. With the Rose having been plucked, the theatrical woodlands in London's suburbs began to recede.

4

"There's wood enough within": *The Tempest*'s Logs and the Resources of Shakespeare's Globe

At the sound of a thunderclap, Caliban throws down the "burden of wood" he has hauled onstage in act two, scene two of Shakespeare's *Tempest*. Having done so, he launches into a speech act that has come to distinguish him in postcolonial criticism and literature: "All the infections that the sun sucks up / From bogs, fens, flats, on Prospero fall, and make him / By inch-meal a disease!" (2.2.1–3). Such bravura skill in employing Prospero's "language" (1.2.366) has made Caliban, as Jonathan Goldberg observes, "a byword for anticolonial riposte" (*Tempest* ix).[1] But what should we make of the logs that Caliban discards before he curses? In pursuing this question, this chapter designates the woods of *The Tempest*'s island, which Caliban's bundle of logs emblematizes, as overlooked "stuff / As dreams are made on" (4.1.156–7). They are the vital matter of *The Tempest*'s eco-fantasies of colonialist extraction and theatrical production.[2]

Caliban's logs are, of course, not trees. Rather, in their lumbered form, they point to the prior existence of some measure of woodland on the island.[3] But although Prospero reminds Ariel that the spirit was once confined in a "cloven pine" before threatening to sequester him in the "knotty entrails" of "an oak" (1.2.279, 296–7) and although Ariel later informs Prospero that under the spell of magical paralysis, the shipwrecked aristocrats cannot "budge" from their spot near "the lime-grove which weather-fends" Prospero's "cell" (5.1.10–11), the play presents hardly any trees on the island. Unlike the other dramas that *Wooden Os* considers, *The Tempest* does not call prolonged attention to a single and noteworthy onstage tree. It features no tree prop like those that take centre stage in *Friar Bacon and Friar Bungay* and the revised *Spanish Tragedy*, and although it may conscript a stage post to play the role of "this lime" tree (4.1.193) in the way that *The Merry Wives of Windsor* does,[4] the duration of such performance is fleeting. And yet *The Tempest* loads Caliban's logs, of which there are reported to be "Some thousands" on the island (3.1.10), with the rich range of meaning associated with these earlier stage trees, and infuses them with new significance. The play bundles in this pile of logs matters of survival, dependency, and incarceration on the island, resource extraction in an age of energy insecurity, the eco-politics and erotic coordinates of power in a fictive colonialist locale, and the potential for theatre to conjure and to unmask that power. Caliban's burden thus signals the extensive reach of lumber in and beyond the virtual world of Shakespeare's play, and attention to its polyvalence amounts to picking up the sticks that Caliban drops. That scant scholarly consideration has been paid to the deforesting of *The Tempest*'s woodlands stems perhaps from all the curiosity that the play attracts to its magical and natural wonders and from the fact that Caliban does not retrieve the logs.[5]

The preceding chapter examined the literature on resource scarcity that Arthur Standish penned to emphasize, in part, the eco-wastefulness of the stage tree's obliteration in the revised *Spanish Tragedy*. Here we should note that the performance of Shakespeare's *Tempest* and the publication of Standish's *Commons Complaint* are coincident: both date from 1611. *The Tempest*, of course, is not a direct response to the dire eco-political collapse that Standish imagines for England ("no wood no Kingdome"), but by keeping in mind such temporal proximity we can heed Meredith Anne Skura's call to explore the play's complex relation to the discourse of colonialism in light of the "particular historical situation" that obtained then in England, rather than to colonialist discourse's more modern iterations (293).[6] The eco-keystone to this relation is a supply of wood: whereas Prospero houses a pile of logs earmarked for "mak[ing] ... fire" and for other employments on the island (1.2.314), Standish fears that England will suffer an unbearable catastrophe without an intensive program of planting trees. In this context, the island's logs emerge as a solution to the shortage of wood and timber that Standish and others claimed to be besetting England and as a theatrical representation of the resource that could be transported home from overseas enterprises to alleviate the shortage.

Standish, we recall, does not advocate a venture abroad to offset a looming eco-political collapse. But since the publication of Thomas Harriot's treatise on Virginia in 1588, English propagandists had cast the New World "discovered" across the Atlantic as an abundant storehouse of natural resources whose instrumentalization would not only benefit English consumers, but would also free its merchants from a diplomatically complicated traffic in bulk goods with continental suppliers. By 1611, when

Shakespeare's island play debuted and Standish's pamphlet was garnering him favour in the Jacobean court, a host of news reports, sermons, and poems had been circulating in England to drum up support for financing and manning resettlement at Jamestown. Even though, as scholars attempting to reorient the New World readings of *The Tempest* have insisted, Shakespeare's logged island is, strictly speaking, located nowhere near the colony in Virginia,[7] the play does in its staging of useable timber invoke the Virginian tissue of the "textual palimpsest" that Barbara Fuchs sees as articulating its "condensed layers of colonialist ideology" (45, 46).[8] One crucial ecological "figure of the New World," to borrow a phrase from John Gillies,[9] that *The Tempest* evokes on its island is the former woodland to which its logs point.

The grand scope of the stockpiled logs, Falstaffian in their magnitude, as well as the absence of the logger's labour on the island, also tarnishes the Golden Age fantasy about which the counsellor Gonzalo muses in the play. The Ovidian coordinates of Gonzalo's colonialist fantasy, especially as they pertain to the promotional treatises and bureaucratic reports circulating in the English press about the sustainability of the Jamestown settlement in Virginia, comprise this chapter's opening sections. But since Prospero announces no plan to take the wood back with him to sell on continental markets, the substantial logging on the island might prompt us to wonder what the magus actually does with all that wood. In his very first words in the play, Caliban seems aware that his efforts are in excess of Prospero's need: "There's wood enough within" (1.2.317), he responds from offstage to Prospero's summoning. In the diegetic register, this "within" presumably points to the cell, or to the "primitive architecture,"[10] where Prospero and Miranda reside and where logs sufficient to carry out the day's tasks are located. In a metatheatrical key, Caliban's deictic may refer to the backstage of Shakespeare's Globe,[11] whence the actor playing Caliban projects his line, or to the playhouse's walls, both of which hold plenty of wood and timber "within."

Caliban's possible gesture to the theatrical superstructure accords with the strand of *Tempest* criticism that comprehends the play's "most salient sources" to reside in the domestic sphere (Bruster, "Local" 257). Frances E. Dolan sees in the play's multiple conspiracies a meditation on the household crime of petty treason ("Subordinate['s]"), and both Douglas Bruster ("Local") and Daniel Vitkus regard the play's tense master-servant dynamics in terms of the relations that obtained between actors and theatre impresarios in early modern "playhouseholds." By stressing wood in his inaugural lines, Caliban perhaps hints at a "project,"[12] which is the play's preferred term for Prospero's plots and schemes (2.1.295; 5.1.1; Epilogue l. 12), that the magus might be planning for the logs he has stockpiled: the building of a theatre. In conspiring with the Neapolitan servants Stefano and Trinculo to oust Prospero, Caliban mentions that his former master has "brave utensils ... / Which when he has a *house* he'll deck withal" [emphasis added] (3.2.91–2). The future tense of Caliban's report ("he'll") intimates that, at this point in the play, the construction of the island's playhouse is still a work in progress. As this chapter's closing section demonstrates, such building follows a literary model of colonialism set forth in classical epic and contrasts with the on-the-ground practice in the Virginia colony, where a permanent venue for theatre was not set up until the early eighteenth century. By evoking another potential use for wood and timber on the island, *The Tempest* counters the antitheatrical tone of the promotional literature associated with Virginia's resettlement in the early 1600s and discloses the role of theatre in maintaining power over people and the natural world alike in colonialist discourse and practice.

The Tempest's Logs: A Brief Literary History

We begin our exploration of the colonialist layers condensed in *The Tempest*'s logs a scene before Caliban appears onstage with them. The sound of Caliban's burden hitting the stage floor in act two, scene two retroactively punctures the utopian vision that the Neapolitan counsellor Gonzalo elaborated in act two, scene one. Washed ashore after the storm, Gonzalo deems it best to apply "plaster" to the "sore" (2.1.137–8) that King Alonso endures – the presumed death of his heir Ferdinand in the shipwreck – and so he chats with the marooned aristocrats about the island's environment. Yet Gonzalo's longest speeches in this sequence have been comprehended less as the prattle of a man aiming to lift his monarch's spirits than as an impromptu program for colonization. As David Scott Kastan observes, the opening gesture of Gonzalo's first speech features an English word "coined for *old* world domination" in Ireland that had come to be "applied to the new world" by the close of the sixteenth century [emphasis in original] (273). "Had I *plantation* of this isle" and "were the king on't" [emphasis added] (2.1.143, 145), Gonzalo famously conjectures,

> I'th commonwealth I would by contraries
> Execute all things. For no kind of traffic
> Would I admit, no name of magistrate;
> Letters should not be known; riches, poverty,

And use of service, none; contract, succession,
Bourn, bound of land, tilth, vineyard, none;
No use of metal, corn, or wine, or oil;
No occupation, all men idle, all:
And women too – but innocent and pure;
No sovereignty – (2.1.147–56)

* * * * * * *

All things in common nature should produce
Without sweat or endeavour. Treason, felony,
Sword, pike, knife, gun, or need of any engine,
Would I not have; but nature should bring forth
Of it own kind all foison, all abundance,
To feed my innocent people. (2.1.159–64)

Caliban's arrival with the logs a scene later indicates that "sweat or endeavour" – the exertions of resource extraction – have been transpiring
literally under the cover of Gonzalo's daydream. The display of slavery's
presence on the island in act two, scene two is evidence against Gonzalo's
musings that is as damning as are the logical inconsistencies of "Gonzalo's
paradox" (H. Levin 126) – no "sovereignty" but the king's, for instance
– that Antonio and Sebastian delight in mocking (2.1.156–8). Were Gonzalo's program for plantation to take effect on the island, the colonialist
economy already present there, the material proof of which is Caliban's
logs, would need to be superseded or altogether undone.

Although *The Tempest* does not permit Caliban and Gonzalo to occupy the stage jointly until the final act and even then does not script
dialogue between them, it is nonetheless apt to persist in regarding Gonzalo's musings about plantation through Caliban's work on the island.
Scholars interested in tracking Shakespeare's literary borrowings suggest
to us a further connection between counsellor and slave.[13] Editors of the
play routinely note that Gonzalo lifts his vision of utopia almost verbatim
from Montaigne's essay "Of the Caniballes," which John Florio translated
into English in 1603.[14] There, Shakespeare would have read the French
essayist's report of a Brazilian "nation ... that hath no kinde of traffike,
no knowledge of Letters, no intelligence of numbers, no name of magistrate, nor of politike superioritie; no use of service, of riches or of pov-
ertie; no contracts, no successions, no partitions, no occupation but idle;
no respect of kinred, but common, no apparell but naturall, no manuring
of lands, no uses of wine, corne, or mettle. The very words that import
lying, falshood, treason, dissimulations, covetousnes, envie, detraction,

and pardon, were never heard of amongst them" (220). *The Tempest*, then, parcels out its debt to Florio's Montaigne across these two characters: the essayist's words come out of Gonzalo's mouth in the form of poetry, and the title of the essay christens Caliban, an appellation that, as Peter Hulme demonstrated some time ago, is "an anagram of the earlier form 'canibal.'" The latter term, Hulme also shows, is a potent philological legacy of European contact with the New World ("Hurricanes" 58–9).

This intertextual account provides a literary history for both Caliban's name and for Gonzalo's plantation. But the passage quoted from Montaigne's essay has little to offer by way of explanation for the specificity of Caliban's log-carrying labour. The passage's framing, however, identifies a classical intertext that can help account for the pile of wood: Ovid's *Metamorphoses*.[15] In introducing the account of the Brazilian cannibals, Montaigne observes, "for me seemeth that what in those nations we see by experience, doth not only exceed all the pictures wherewith licentious Poesie hath proudly imbellished the golden age, and all her quaint inventions to faine a happy condition of man, but also the conception and desire of Philosophy" (220). For Gonzalo, too, life on his imaginary plantation would "excel the Golden Age" (2.1.168). Although both Montaigne and Gonzalo invoke the Golden Age of "licentious" Ovid to mark its descriptive insufficiency, each nonetheless "channels" Ovid's narration and treats it as a stylistic resource (Harris, *Marvellous* 39). For Ovid's account, like Montaigne's quasi-anthropological report and Gonzalo's utopian reverie, is structured by negation. In Arthur Golding's version of the Golden Age, for example, "There was no fear of punishment; there was no threatening law," and "No muck nor tillage was bestowed on lean and barren land / To make the corn of better head and ranker for to stand" (ll. 105, 125–6). And as we observed in the previous chapter, "The lofty pine-tree was not hewn from mountains, where it stood, / In seeking strange and foreign lands to rove upon the flood" during this antique era (ll. 109–10). Tellingly, although the island's "grass" "looks" "lush and lusty" and "green" to him (2.1.53–4), Gonzalo records no trace of a significant eco-hallmark of the Golden Age: a virgin forest. My suggestion is that this hallmark appears in altered form as Caliban's burden of logs, a sign perhaps that the Golden Age has already run its course on *The Tempest*'s island. "If," as Harry Levin observes, the Golden Age "were attainable, then by definition it would no longer be golden" (112).

In the next section we'll examine in greater detail the colonialist relation between early seventeenth-century reports promoting the Virginia Company and the figure of the Golden Age in *The Tempest*. But before doing so we should note that *The Tempest*'s woods do not seem to be lumbered to build Iron Age ships. Prospero and the island's occupants, as we shall see, put the logs to other employments, and ships, it turns out, are already present in the play: they bookend *The Tempest*'s action, from the storm in act one, scene one to Prospero's request for "Gentle breath" to "fill" his "sails" in the Epilogue (ll. 11–12).[16] The scene featuring Gonzalo and the mocking aristocrats also includes an exchange whose conceit is unimaginable without the maritime mobility that post–Golden Age seafaring afforded:

> ANTONIO: What impossible matter will he [Gonzalo] make easy next?
> SEBASTIAN: I think he will carry this island home in his pocket, and give it his son for an apple.
> ANTONIO: And sowing the kernels of it in the sea, bring forth more islands.
> (2.1.87–91)

In a proleptic way, the aristocrats undercut Gonzalo's reverie by infusing his relation to the island with genealogical aspiration (like Hieronimo's tree planting) and a colonialist agenda.[17] Sebastian reduces the island to (the size of) an apple, and Antonio casts a homeward-bound Gonzalo as a sower of its kernels.[18] A series of islands sprout therefrom, and each island, according to the conversation's biblical "pomo-logic," is a tree whose fruit would engender an enticing diaspora of wood(is)lands ripe for future harvesting. The dispersal and growth of this new archipelago would seem to replant the Golden Age seed by seed in the open waters: this "forest on the sea" is not a fleet of ships, but rather an oceanic woodland. But discovering a living fruit tree on *The Tempest*'s island, especially on those parts that Gonzalo surveys, may be an "impossible matter" indeed, since not until the end of the play does the counsellor meet Caliban, who prides himself on knowing "every fertile inch o'th' island" (2.2.140). No fruit passes between them in this moment.

The Golden Age of Virginia and *The Tempest*'s Trees

As we observed in chapter 3, the prefatory materials to Arthur Standish's literature on the timber shortage affirm that only the intensive replanting of England "Will bring againe a golden age to vs." This is a future-oriented solution to the problem of resource scarcity, and it seeks to remedy that crisis on home turf and thus to return England to a presumed eco-condition marked by abundance. In the years leading up to the publication of

Standish's calls for the reform of English woodland management, colonialist propaganda put forward a more immediate option for reattaining the Golden Age that depended on the efforts of different English planters: "*Coloni*," or "tillers of the earth, and stewards of fertilitie," in Virginia [emphasis in original] (*Trve Declaration* 15). In an essay on colonial settlement, Francis Bacon observes, the "Planting of countries is like the planting of woods" (104). But in the early seventeenth-century propaganda campaign about Virginia, a major attraction to the transatlantic plantation of people is the felling of, and the potential uses for, its "golden" woods.

As early as 1584, natives of the land the English called Virginia were reported to be "most gentle, loving and faithful, void of all guile and treason, and such as live after the manner of the golden age" (*first voyage* 274). After "Scepticall Humorists" (Price F3^r) and "mockers" (Crashaw E2^v) disparaged the Jamestown settlement in the wake of its near disaster in the first decade of the seventeenth century,[19] propagandists began to encourage reinvestment in the colony, and one of the more potent figures used to sell the enterprise was "the ecology of the golden age" (H. Levin 67). For instance, in "Ode to the Virginian Voyage," Michael Drayton explicitly links Virginia's trees – "The cedar reaching hie" and "The cypresse, pine, / And usefull sassafras" – to "the Golden Age" which "Still natures lawes doth give" (ll. 33, 35–6, 37–8). As they had in Harriot's late sixteenth-century account, Virginia's trees, some of which are estimated to be a thousand years old (Crashaw D3^v), emerge in the larger campaign in which Drayton's ode participates as a quick fix for the effects of woodland scarcity in England.[20] Indeed, one pamphlet's depiction of the "plentie of woods (the wants of England)" rehearses in the space of a paragraph the inventory of Virginia's commodities that Harriot had detailed (*Nova* 11–12). But unlike the poem affixed to Standish's pamphlet, Drayton's poem and its fellows in this publicity campaign pair such abundance with allusions to the Golden Age to indicate that this lost era is no longer a *topos* of nostalgia: it not only exists in the present moment across the Atlantic[21] but also promises to secure the stability of England's eco-political future. By this logic, there is little excuse to wait for the Golden Age to take root once again in England, because it's there for the plundering in Virginia.

In *Nova Britannia* (1609) there is no shortage of pressing economic and ecological reasons for explaining why England should seize the opportunity to refortify the Virginia plantation. According to its author,

First, if we consider what strength of shipping may be raysed and maintained thence, in furnishing our owne wants of sundrie kindes, and the wants of

other Nations too, in such needfull things arising thence which can hardly
now be obtained from any other part of the world, as planck and tymber
for shipping, with Deale and Wainscot, pipestaues and clabbord, with store
of Sope ashes, whereof there grow the best woods to make them in great
abundance, all which we may there haue, the wood for the cutting, and the
Ashes for the burning, which though they be grosse commodities, yet no
Marchandize is better requested [.] ... And from thence we may haue Iron
and Copper also in great quantitie, about which the expence and waste of
woode, as also for building of Shippes, will be no hurt, but great seruice to
that countrey; the great superfluity whereof, the continuall cutting downe, in
manie hundred yeares, will not be able to ouercome, whereby will likewise
grow a greater benefite to this land, in preseruing our woodes and tymber at
home, so infinitely and without measure, vpon these occasions cutte downe,
and falne to such a sicknesse and wasting consumption, as all the physick in
England cannot cure. (16)

A Trve Declaration Of The estate of the Colonie in Virginia (1610) more
explicitly identifies the geopolitical incentives for the project: "The merchant knoweth, that through the troubles in Poland & Muscouy, (whose
eternall warres are like the Antipathy of the Dragon & Elephants) all their
traffique for Mastes, Deales, Pitch, Tarre, Flax, Hempe, and Cordage, are
euery day more and more indangered, and the woods of those countires
are almost exhausted. All which are to be had in Virginia with farre lesse
charge, and farre more safety." As does *Nova Britannia*, *A Trve Declaration* touts the relief to the stressed woodlands across Europe – and
especially in England – that settlement in Virginia could afford. "When
therefore our mils of Iron," its author continues, "and excesse of building,
haue already turned our greatest woods into pasture and champion, within
these few years; neither the scattered Forrests of England, nor the diminished Groues of Ireland, will supply the defect of our Nauy. When in Virginia there is nothing wanting, but onely mens labours, to furnish both
Prince, State and merchant, without charge or difficulty" (23, 25). In these
treatises, the panacea for England's exhausted woodlands and for Europe's
weakened market in wood product will be Virginia's abundance of trees.
    Such eco-well-being at home perforce depends upon the transplanting
of specific skilled labourers to the colony. First among the ranks of desirable craftsmen listed in *Nova Britannia* are "Carpenters, Ship-wrights,
Masons, [and] Sawyers" (21).[22] These workmen could lumber the New
World woods, build up and fortify the settlement with hedges and fenc-
es,[23] and transport staple goods back home. In a nod to such provisions for

employing a skilled workforce in the colony, Thomas Heywood's myth-inspired play *The Golden Age* (1611) depicts Saturn carrying onstage "*models of ships, and buildings, bow and arrowes, &c.*" as props that herald the end of the play's title. Addressing the play's audience, Saturn could just as well be debriefing the colony's craftsmen: "I have deuis'd you formes for tooles / To square out timber, and performe the Art / Of Architecture" (11–12). In this propaganda, there is no place for Gonzalo's insistent vision of leisure on the plantation: "all men idle, all" (2.1.154).

In prescribing colonial plantation and extraction as if they were curatives for England's woodlands, *A Trve Declaration* also unfolds a brutal logic of serial instrumentalization. The driving force of this logic is the sign that, in Ovid's Golden Age, betokens epochal closure: a maritime search, first in Ireland and now in Virginia, for trees to build English ships that, in Golding's Ovid, would then "rove upon the flood."[24] In *A Trve Declaration* the ecological plentitude of Virginia indeed merits comparison to "Vtopian, and legendarie fables" like the Golden Age (14), and the fulfillment of the colony's eco-promise, which *Nova Britannia* may refer to as "a golden dreame" (12),[25] would be realized in the timber and other "grosse" goods that woodworkers could fashion for sale in European markets. In such rhetoric, the destruction of woodlands proves desirable, expedient, and seemingly repeatable across space and time. In this context, *The Tempest*'s pile of logs abets a colonialist imagination eager to remedy a resource crisis at home: just over there, offstage and within reach, it emblematizes the anticipated result of woodland extraction in Virginia.

And yet *The Tempest* does not translate to the stage the colonialist figures employed in the Virginia campaign in consistent or straightforward ways. Its Europeans, for instance, are castaways, not "single-minded colonial invader[s]" (Skura 310) or commercial agents intent on returning home with supplies of saleable lumber and other wood-based commodities.[26] For Steve Mentz, *The Tempest* distinguishes itself from Shakespeare's other romances insofar as its "ecological fantasy" pivots on "Prospero's close connection to and mastery of the powers of nature" ("Shipwreck" 179 n. 20): it is not a drama about human modesty in the face of an unforgiving landscape, since its most potent natural phenomenon – the sea storm in act one, scene one – retroactively proves to be an example of the magician's "art" (1.2.1). Attention to the history of such art on the island brings into view a further instance of the aslant relation between the play and the trees of the Virginia archive: the curious matter of the labour required to fell and lumber the island's woodlands. The play depicts two men bearing logs and one woman (Miranda) who offers to "bear ... logs the while"

(3.1.24), but shows no agent(s) swinging the axe and cutting down the trees. Such exploitation of "mens labours" is both the absent counterpart of and yet the prerequisite for the manual carriage of logs reported and staged in the play. The sawyer's "occupation," to borrow Gonzalo's term, thus proves as mystified on *The Tempest*'s island as it is in Ovid's account of the Golden Age's devolution into the Iron Age, at which moment "ships that erst in tops of hills and mountains had ygrow / Did leap and dance on uncouth waves" (ll. 150–1). This Ovidian account of shipbuilding, as we saw in chapter 3, euphemizes the hard labour carried out on hills and mountaintops; my suggestion is that it also helpfully glosses the destructive power of Prospero's "art." Prospero, for example, associates the execution of his magic with the species of tree that Ovid imagines as leaping and dancing on the waters: the pine. "It was mine art," he reminds Ariel, "When I arrived and heard thee, that made gape / The pine and let thee out" (1.2.293–5). We could speculate that the blast that released Ariel from the imprisonment of his "wooden wals"[27] also splintered the standing pine into a pile of useable wood. The sonic effect produced by such an explosion anticipates the Mariners' exclamations during the sea storm: "We split, we split!" (1.1.55).

But surely one pine tree, however massive, does not divide into some thousand logs. While abjuring his "so potent art" and "rough magic" in a speech that recalls Ovid's Medea (5.1.50),[28] Prospero claims that his obliteration of the pine tree was no one-off. He recounts that he "rifted Jove's stout oak / With his own bolt" and "by the spurs [roots] plucked up / The pine and cedar" (5.1.45–6, 47–8). Prospero's elaboration of Medea's more generic boast in Golding's translation of Ovid's Book 7 ("Whole woods and forests I remove" [l. 273]) suggests not only that his magical threat and his abjuration of magic have been tailored to resemble one another, but also that a possible effect of his (reported) exercises of magic on oaks, pines, and cedars is all the wood that Caliban and Ferdinand haul in the play. With the flick of a "stick" (1.2.476), which could refer either to a wand like those that the magicians brandish in *Friar Bacon and Friar Bungay* or to a walking "staff" (5.1.54), Prospero could have magically knocked down and divided innumerable trees in the prehistory of the play or still be doing so on the island while other characters occupy the stage.[29] But it little matters when Prospero fells trees. The more significant fact is that in doing so, he artfully eliminates the labour of the woodworkers that the Virginia pamphlets designate as key to the colony's re-establishment and makes obsolete the iron tools that would be needed to chop and lumber wood. He is a magical lumberjack.

Three (Possible) Uses for *The Tempest*'s Logs: Energy, Murder, and Trothplight

Bundled in Ovidian and New World allusion and split by Prospero's "so potent art," *The Tempest*'s logs prove, initially at least, homely stage objects that would have been invaluable for survival in early seventeenth-century England and Virginia, for they supply the most mundane of needs. According to Prospero, he and Miranda depend upon Caliban, who "does make our fire, / Fetch in our wood, and serves in offices / That profit us" (1.2.314–16). These additional offices, in Caliban's own terms, include "mak[ing]" "dams ... for fish," "scrap[ing] trenchering," or wooden dinnerware, and "wash[ing] dish" (2.2.171, 174). Caliban is, as Julia Reinhard Lupton remarks, "the creature at the heart of an economy governed by the necessities of life" (10). "We cannot miss him" (1.2.314),[30] Prospero admits to Miranda well before he more famously – and publicly – "Acknowledge[s]" Caliban as his "thing of darkness" (5.1.278–9). And, of course, all these essential offices, the execution of which permits the aristocrats to tend to more socially decorous matters,[31] require that creature Caliban handle wood. The logs that he throws down at the start of act two, scene two are thus the material substrate without which bare subsistence for the exiled Europeans would be impossible, and Prospero mobilizes them routinely in the exercise of power over Caliban: "If thou neglect'st or dost unwillingly / What I command, I'll rack thee with old cramps, / Fill all thy bones with aches, [and] make thee roar" (1.2.371–3).[32] Emblematized by the logs, energy – both physical and social – circulates in this play in an economy that another character dubs "wooden slavery" (3.1.62).

Once Caliban drops the logs, which could remain onstage for further scenes, they accrue two new layers of meaning that invert and eroticize, respectively, their status as a source of life-sustaining energy. One layer emerges when we trace Caliban's subsequent action in the play. During his next stage appearance he explains to Stefano and Trinculo that he and the island's subjected "sprit[s]" (including Ariel?) "all do hate" Prospero "rootedly" (3.2.89–90). Together, the trio hatches a plan to assassinate Prospero. Caliban's plot elaborates in a lethal key the wordplay on roots: he proposes that after he has "first seized [Prospero's] books," Stefano should "brain" a napping Prospero "or with a log / Batter his skull, or paunch him with a stake, / Or cut his weasand [throat] with thy knife" (3.2.83–6). If the logs remain onstage for the duration of the intervening sequence, which is act three, scene one, then Caliban could pick one up during this speech in act three, scene two and physically rehearse, with wooden prop in hand, the murderous acts requiring "a log" and wooden "stake." In Caliban's hands, the log can both support and threaten Prospero's livelihood.

Whatever choice the actor playing Caliban makes while delivering these lines, none of the conspirators bears a log or sharpened wooden instrument in Prospero's cell. Indeed, they show up empty-handed: they have lost in a stinky "pool" their "bottles" (4.1.207), handmade wooden drinking vessels from which they have been guzzling alcohol. Before long, Stefano and Trinculo are distracted from their bloody purpose by the magical materialization of a "wardrobe" of "*glistening apparel*" (stage direction, 4.1.221) on "this lime" tree (4.1.193), whose staging may require the stringing of a "line" of rope between two wooden stage posts / trees and from which the clothing depends. The bedraggled Europeans proceed to pluck with delight individual articles of clothing from the tree's "branches" – or, more likely, the string – as if they were golden apples; they then order Caliban to "carry" the garments away for them (4.1.249).[33] But to Caliban, these glittery robes prove flimsy substitutes for the bulk of a deadly log, or perhaps for an emboldening swig of liquor: they are, as he terms them, "but trash" (4.1.222). Thus stopped in their tracks, these would-be-assassins are quickly hounded offstage by a pack of magical dogs that Prospero summons (4.1.252–7), and the fantasy of employing a log to murder the island's master evaporates.

The sense of eroticism associated with the logs comes into view in act three, scene one, and so it makes good dramaturgical sense for the stagehands not to sweep the sticks into the tiring house after Caliban drops them in act two, scene two. According to the stage direction, Ferdinand, the marooned nobleman who offers to make Miranda "The Queen of Naples" soon after having made her acquaintance (1.2.453), arrives, according to the inaugural stage direction in act three, scene one, "*bearing a log.*" Ferdinand, whom Prospero had already dubbed "a Caliban" (1.2.484), could stumble upon the burden that his rebellious predecessor had discarded and see in them a prompt for more work. Like Caliban, Ferdinand performs this "mean task" (3.1.4) "Upon a sore injunction" (3.1.11): Prospero enlists him in "wooden slavery" for the untoward affection he has shown Miranda and, in so doing, may repeat history, since Caliban's position on the island similarly altered after he "didst seek to violate / The honour" of Miranda (1.2.350–1). But in switching from the arms of Caliban to Ferdinand, the logs differentiate, rather than affiliate, their successive carriers.[34] In the first instance, there seems to be more of them for

Ferdinand to haul. Whereas Caliban employs sufficiency as a measure of his work ("There's wood enough within" [1.2.317]), Ferdinand can barely estimate the number of sticks – "Some thousands" – that he "must remove" (3.1.9–10). Moreover, Ferdinand does not contemplate a murder in which the log features as a lethal weapon. He instead paints himself "a patient log-man" (3.1.67) for Miranda's sake: "The mistress which I serve quickens what's dead, / And makes my labours pleasures" (3.1.6–7). In Ferdinand's arms, then, the logs have been sapped of their hearth-and-home value and transformed into the nearly incalculable material of an erotic test,[35] which Prospero later dubs "my trials of thy love" (4.1.6) – presumably, Ferdinand's love *for* Miranda.

Neither Prospero's "trials" nor Ferdinand's pleasurable endurance in them has room for Miranda as an erotic agent.[36] But in the log-carrying sequence, she boldly inserts her person into the details of the erotic transaction that Prospero supervises. Against her father's "hest" and "precepts," for instance, she "prattle[s] / Something too wildly" with the enslaved European and lets slip her name (3.1.37, 57–8). Such disobedience is, in retrospect, less surprising when we recall that before she reveals her name she breaks decorum by offering to do Ferdinand's work for him. "If you'll sit down," Miranda urges, "I'll bear your logs the while. Pray give me that; / I'll carry it to the pile" (3.1.23–5). When Ferdinand declines the respite that she generously proffers him,[37] Miranda reassures him that her labour would constitute no "dishonour" (3.1.27):

> It would become me
> As well as it does you; and I should do it
> With much more ease, for my good will is to it,
> And yours it is against. (3.1. 28–31)

Stubbornness, self-assurance, and a sense of gender equity are perhaps not the traits that we traditionally identify with Miranda, who more famously exhibits compassion at the sight of the shipwreck (1.2.5–6), disgust in her interaction with Caliban (1.2.354–65), and "wonder" at the vision of the "brave new world" (5.1.184, 186). Yet during this intimate exchange all three overlooked aspects of her character shine, and they do so specifically over a bundle of the island's logs. Although the playtext does not indicate whether Ferdinand indeed hands "that" log over to the as-yet-unnamed Miranda or whether she snatches it from him despite his protestation, it is clever dramaturgy for the scene's erotic charge to develop – or smoulder – around the sticks. "Heavens rain grace / On that which breeds between 'em," Prospero says as he secretly observes their warming conversation (3.1.75–6). His words articulate a blessing, but they also call for water. As if on command, Miranda weeps (3.1.76), but the tears do not dampen the excitement. Rather, they incite Miranda to speak to Ferdinand her boldest line in the play: "I am your wife, if you will marry me" (3.1.83).

The couple would thus seem to lay the matter of the logs to rest by sealing this marriage proposal. "Here's my hand," Ferdinand initiates (3.1.90); "And mine, with my heart in't," Miranda responds (3.1.91). But Ferdinand's parting gesture – "A thousand thousand" "farewell[s]" (3.1.91, 92) – reintroduces in a linguistic register the wood that has been the scene's central vector of erotic energy: it echoes his estimation of the logs that he has been enjoined to carry ("Some thousands") and that Miranda is willing to haul on his behalf. By the close of the scene, a log – a "heart" of wood – and not only hands could conjoin physically the lovers as they pledge their troth.[38] Indeed, in an earlier era such a "contract of true love" (4.1.84, 133) required the lovers who were party to it to swear a binding oath upon a stick.[39] A variant of this tradition appears in *Pericles* (1607–8), which the Oxford editors "reconstructed": they added to the play lines derived from the prose of Shakespeare's collaborator, George Wilkins. There, King Simonides pretends to dislike the union of his daughter Thaisa and the romance's eponymous hero on the grounds that the match is socially inapt, while taking great pleasure in the proposed marriage and, presumably, in his Prospero-like creation of erotic roadblocks. This is the King's feigned rationale for keeping the couple apart:

> Equals to equals, good to good is joined.
> This not being so, the bavin of your mind
> In rashness kindled must again be quenched
> Or purchase our displeasure. (scene nine, ll. 88–91)

A "bavin" is a piece of fuelwood, and its use here to signify the kindling of erotic desire is the figurative counterpart of *The Tempest*'s perhaps more literal reliance on firewood in the courtship of Miranda and Ferdinand. As in *The Tempest*, the clasping of the lovers' hands in *Pericles* follows hard upon the allusion to bavins. Simonides grabs a hand from the offending lovers and, just as he's about to impose some sore punishment on them, he surprises them by joining them as "man and wife" (scene nine, l. 105); in quick succession, he then unclasps the hands of the stunned couple before finally giving his blessing to the marriage. During this manic sequence, Simonides proves a more hands-on manager of his daughter's desire than does Prospero, but it is important to recall that unbeknownst to Ferdinand and Miranda, Prospero looks on as the desire of the young lovers heats up around a pile of logs in act three, scene one. It is as if he were watching – and shaping from behind the scenes – an erotic interlude whose staging depends upon and re-energizes the meaning of the firewood.

Later in *The Tempest*, Prospero calls for two magical spectacles in the vein of *Friar Bacon and Friar Bungay*. During the playlette staged to commemorate the couple's engagement, the revival of one possible use for *The Tempest*'s logs – murder – notoriously disrupts the performance. In the moment when Prospero remembers Caliban's assassination plot, the threat posed by a disgruntled slave halts a show whose fabric, as we shall observe, is no insubstantial amount of wood. But the threat is hardly the three-alarm fire that Prospero makes it out to be.

Prospero's Masques of Wood

In an effort to suggest that wood is the material substrate of the spectacles that Prospero mounts on the island, it is worth noticing that the logs drop out of sight in act three. The play's first log carrier, Caliban arrives at Prospero's cell in act four, scene one, although both he and his co-conspirators do not bring with them – or employ there – a blunt wooden instrument to kill Prospero, as had been proposed in act three, scene two. Instead, the trio discovers and becomes distracted by a lime tree outfitted with fine clothes. In another plot, a betrothed couple departs the stage in act three, scene one, vowing to marry one another over a heap of bavins, and yet Ferdinand doesn't seem inclined to return to work. When the lovers reappear, Prospero "makes amends" for having "too austerely punished" Ferdinand (4.1.1–2); no one speaks further about the logs. This timeline highlights that the logs are emblematically and physically indispensable to the action of the play's first half, but then they quickly disappear, except perhaps for their restoration to "life" in the lime tree / stage post. But my sense is that all the logs do not vanish into thin air like *Friar Bacon and Friar Bungay*'s golden tree. Nor have they been consigned to the dustbin of island history. Rather, *The Tempest* repurposes them to supply Prospero's spectacular enterprises – the "vanit[ies] of [his] art" (4.1.41). By this logic, the logs are hidden in plain view, transformed into and reassembled as the theatrical "stuff / As dreams are made on" (4.1.156–7) by the force of the woodworking magician's art.

The shows that Prospero mounts in act three, scene three and act four, scene one, as Stephen Orgel has detailed (49–69), approximate the structure of the Jacobean court masque. Prospero's "high charms work"

(3.3.88), for instance, to produce an anti-masque that taunts a famished cohort of European nobles whom he calls, in an aside, "worse than devils" (3.3.36). For their benefit he conjures a "living drollery" (3.3.21), in which Ariel "Perform[s]" "the figure of this harpy" (3.3.83–4) and in which, according to the stage direction, a banqueting table *"vanishes"* under the cover of the creature's wings when the aristocrats try to "feed" on the "viands" that it bears (3.3.41, 49).[40] By the close of this spectacle, the "desperate" Italians (3.3.104), all of whom Prospero has "knit up / In their distractions" (3.3.89–90), disperse in "fits" of "ecstasy" (3.3.91, 108), as the "monstrous" figures populating an anti-masque would do (3.3.31). In the next scene, Prospero stages an antidote to the fright fest: "revels" performed in honour of Ferdinand and Miranda's proposed union (4.1.148). In this other "trick" (4.1.37), "actors" (4.1.148) representing Ceres, Iris, Juno, and a host of "temperate nymphs" (4.1.132) and "sunburned sickelmen" (4.1.134) gather to elaborate themes – "joys," "blessings," "Earth's increase, and foison plenty" (4.1.108–10) – that offset the punishing hunger and recrimination of the earlier sequence. Counter-balancing each other in theme and tone, but also both invoking the crucial eco-matter of subsistence, Prospero's Jacobean masques dominate *The Tempest*'s middle sections and, superficially at least, reroute the play's interest in wood-based energy (erotic and otherwise) to an equally vital requirement for survival: food.[41]

Yet the presence of the banqueting table upon which the feast rests provides evidence that Prospero's vengeful anti-masque cannot do without some measure of wood. To the masque's immediate audience, the banquet appears a renewed and solid sign "of hope" (3.3.11): although they hesitate after the attendant spirits vanish (3.3.40–52), the castaways nonetheless approach the table as if it could be touched. That it disappears under the harpy's wings just prior to contact does not confirm its status as an "insubstantial pageant" (4.1.155), which is Prospero's term for the spectacle celebrating the betrothal.[42] For merciless persecution,[43] which is this anti-masque's aim, would be better realized in the presentation of a real – not a fake – wooden table and feast. In the moments during which the harpy berates the company for having "supplant[ed] good Prospero" (3.3.70), this theatre of cruelty stuns the Europeans so much that they turn into stocks no less wooden than the banqueting table. According to Gonzalo, the harpy's words leave the Neapolitan monarch in a "strange stare" (3.3.95), while, as we have observed, Prospero takes glee in the fact that his "enemies" have been "all knit up / In their distractions" (3.3.89–90). Such language echoes Prospero's browbeating of Ariel near the beginning of the play. Prospero reminds the spirit that he extracted him from "a cloven pine" tree, from which he "didst vent ... groans / As fast as [wooden] mill-wheels strike" upon water (1.2.279, 282–3), before threatening to "rend an oak, / And peg [Ariel] in [the tree's] knotty entrails till / Thou has howled away twelve winters" if the spirit persists in his overhasty desire for "liberty" (1.2.246, 296–8).[44] Accompanied by groans and howls ("O, it is monstrous, monstrous!" [3.3.95]), the "knit" posture of the Europeans vivifies the threat of being cramped inside an oak or a pine.

Such posture also anticipates the subjection of the aristocrats near the end of the play, where they are reported to be "distracted" "prisoners" incarcerated "In the lime-grove which weather-fends [Prospero's] cell" (5.1.9–10, 12). Prospero's naughty foes have thus had their bodies cast into the shape of knotty wood: with arms folded ("knit"), the monarch and courtiers are puppets in a drollery or, better still, are temporarily transformed into wooden chess pieces that Prospero has Ariel direct in "troops ... 'bout the isle" in spiteful sport (1.2.221). "Sweet lord, you play me false" (5.1.174), Miranda accuses Ferdinand as they are revealed to be playing a chess match in a discovery scene that also borrows from the conventions of court masque. Like father-in-law, like son-in-law: both men play – in the full theatrical sense of the term – false at chess, "wrangl[ing]" for a "kingdom[]" (5.1.177) by manipulating "woodmen" on the game board.

Prospero inaugurates the masque commemorating Ferdinand and Miranda's engagement in act four, scene one in a way that likewise transforms its audience into wooden figures "all knit up" in stillness. "No tongue, all eyes! Be silent" (4.1.59); he will further urge a talkative Ferdinand to "Hush, and be mute" during the masque (4.1.126). With its audience arrested in wonder, the second spectacle concerns food, as had the anti-masque, but here a banqueting table does not taunt onlookers. Instead, "Ceres, [the] most bounteous lady," who supervises "rich leas [arable lands] / Of wheat, rye, barley, vetches, oats, and peas" (4.1.60–1) advances from her regions "To come and sport" (4.1.74) with Juno and "to celebrate" "A contract of true love" "And some donation freely to estate / On the blest lovers" (4.1.84–6). "Ceres' blessing" (4.1.117), which promises a winterless year and the lack of "Scarcity and want" (4.1.116), is a "vision" (4.1.118) very much in the vein of Gonzalo's plantation reverie. As Harry Berger, Jr comments, the wedding masque constitutes "a brief withdrawal into the golden age, Gonzalo's dream as magical theater" (175).

The use of "foison" to describe the abundance that both counsellor and goddess conjure confirms in a linguistic register Berger, Jr's insight about the masque's intratextual source (2.1.163; 4.1.110). And yet Ceres's vision differs from Gonzalo's utopia: he would have "vineyard, none" (2.1.152), while Ceres reigns over a land where is situated a "pole-clipped vineyard" that has "Vines with clust'ring bunches growing" (4.1.68, 112). Such pointed disparity between the set pieces nonetheless suggests from different angles that in each instance, the eco-hallmark of Ovid's Golden Age – the virgin forest – is absent. Whereas the bundle of lumber on the island indexes the end of the Golden Age in Gonzalo's musings, the unmitigated success of agriculture and viticulture in Ceres's benediction glosses over the clear-cutting of woods and the enclosing of land that would be required for these georgic practices. Ceres may claim possession over "bosky acres" that span the length of the rainbow (4.1.81), but shrubs and thickets are not old-growth forest. Moreover, unlike the thickly wooded peaks in Ovid's narration, the "mountains" under the goddess's purview afford only "turfy" – that is, grassy – meals for "nibbling sheep" (4.1.62). These rock formations have been stripped, perhaps supplying some timber for fashioning the poles around which the grapevines wind and for erecting the "twillèd" hedges of enclosure (4.1.64).[45]

In juxtaposing Gonzalo's plantation reverie in act two, scene one with the arrival of Caliban and his burden of logs in act two, scene two, *The Tempest*'s dramatic structure, as we observed, illuminates in an ironic key a possible location for the trees missing from the counsellor's neo-Ovidian plantation. The wedding masque employs to similar effect a metatheatrical nod that is at the argumentative heart of *Wooden Os*: the deictic gesture to the woodenness of the theatre. And it does so three times. The goddess Iris summons Ceres to "this grass-plot, in this very place / To come and sport" with Juno (4.1.73–4), and later calls the nymphs to "this green land" (4.1.130). Ceres, for her part, inquires for more details as to why Juno bids her "to this short-grassed green" (4.1.83). Editors gloss the attention the goddesses call to "this" green spot as a cue for the actor to motion towards a green carpet[46] or to the green rushes covering the stage's floorboards.[47] Whatever the precise referent, there is also in these lines an allusion to the moment in *A Midsummer Night's Dream* in which the amateur players gather in the Athenian woods and designate "a marvellous convenient place for our rehearsal": "This green plot shall be our stage, this hawthorn brake our tiring-house" (3.1.3–4). Such gestures bring dead wood back to virtual life by transforming the theatre into the living materials out of which it was once fashioned.

Iris's "grass-plot" marks only a slight change on Quince's makeshift "stage," but the Shakespearean intertext works to an entirely different end in *The Tempest*. Unlike *Midsummer*, the romance does not conscript the theatre's frame to reafforest woodlands and vivify a dramatic setting for the wedding masque: none of the goddesses and none of Prospero's invited guests comment on "these woods" encompassing the space where the spectacle unfolds. Rather, the masque employs the deictic gesture to highlight the trace of the trees cut down to make possible the theatre company's staging of Ceres's "most majestic vision" (4.1.118). Felled and presumably put to employment, the trees in the unnarrated prehistory of the landscape in Ceres's blessing could figure an imaginary source for Shakespeare's early seventeenth-century theatre, the name of which Prospero invokes when he likens the masque's "fabric" to "the great globe itself" (4.1.151, 153).[48] So too, I argue, do the logs, whose onstage presence deflates the utopianism of the counterpart to Ceres's blessing – Gonzalo's neo-Ovidian plantation fantasy. They are also logs of theatre.

Like the tree props and the post(s)-performing- tree(s) that we have explored, the logs hauled by Caliban and Ferdinand are, in light of their retrospective link to Ceres's blessing, a figure for Shakespeare's theatre. Not seen onstage as logs as late as act three, scene two, they are the material without which the spectacles of act three, scene three and act four, scene one would be impossible. Prospero protests too much when he dubs the pageant "insubstantial" and its fabric "baseless" (4.1.151, 155), but he is uncannily perceptive when, after a "*hollow, and confused noise*" ends the wedding masque abruptly (stage direction near 4.1.142),[49] he says that the globe "shall dissolve" eventually (4.1.154). Prospero's masques of wood, then, signal a fourth possible use for *The Tempest*'s logs: they comprise the material stuff of theatrical performance. Indeed, the offstage pile, which numbers in Ferdinand's estimation to "Some thousands" (3.1.10), captures the scale of timber and wood that was required to erect and to outfit a playhouse (and a ship, as in act one, scene one) in early modern London.

Shakespeare's Globe, Prospero's "House," and Theatre in Virginia

Shakespeare's Globe, in short, is coextensive with the "grass-plot" on which Prospero stages the wedding masque: during this spectacle and presumably during the anti-masque too, Prospero's magic is Shakespeare's theatre. In light of all the surplus wood hauled and stacked "within" in *The Tempest*, we may further construe Ferdinand's labour as the building on the island of a multi-tiered theatre whose contours line up with the playing space in which the King's Men mount Shakespeare's play – "the great globe itself" (4.1.153). While conspiring with Stefano and Trinculo, Caliban intimates that his wood-bearing "offices" (1.2.315) may also

have included work on such an edifice and, in so doing, may also afford
the enormous pile of logs a name. Prospero "has brave utensils," Caliban
reports, "for so he calls them, / Which when he has a house he'll deck
withal" (3.2.91–2). For Geraldo U. de Sousa, the house, which is marked
both as out of Prospero's grasp ("when") in Caliban's report and distinct
in the play from his living quarters or "cell" (1.2.20, 39, 350; 4.1.161, 182,
195, 215; 5.1.10, 84, 295, 305), points towards a "lost home in Italy," the
dynastic seat that Prospero will reclaim by bringing the usurping Europeans under his control (451). Attuned to the metatheatricality of the
island's economy of labour, Douglas Bruster offers an equally plausible
gloss for the term. In a note, he observes, "Prospero's 'house' is thus like
a playhouse in containing the 'trumpery' and 'glistering apparel' – i.e.
costumes – central to the business of playing in early modern London"
("Local" 274 n. 19). Bruster refers here not primarily to Caliban's use of
"house," but rather to a command that Prospero issues to Ariel after the
wedding masque comes to a stop: "The trumpery in my house, go bring it
hither / For stale to catch these thieves" (4.1.186–7). The two invocations
of "house" span the hatching of the plot to assassinate Prospero and its
botched execution, and the second instance suggests that construction is
no longer incomplete. Between these moments, of course, are the masques
whose magic – Shakespeare's theatrical artifice – would seem to finish a
task that Prospero's domestic labourers had been (unwittingly?) carrying
out:[50] the framing of a theatrical house for enacting a revenge tragedy and
a new comedy in the style of the court masque.[51] In an ironic twist, Ferdinand and maybe Miranda have a hand in erecting the stage on which the
revels marking their engagement are performed.[52]

   In supervising the erection of a theatre on the island and staging spectacles there, Prospero presents himself as if he were a both a playwright
and a theatre impresario in charge of the day-to-day operations of a "playhousehold."[53] But unlike the gestures towards the eco-history of theatre
building in *The Merry Wives of Windsor* and the revised *Spanish Tragedy*,
the allusions to Prospero's playhouse in 1611 do not correspond to the
erection of a new wooden O in London. From 1600, when the Fortune
playhouse was framed in a northern suburb, to 1614, when Henslowe
opened the Hope on the Bankside, no new public theatre welcomed customers, excepting perhaps the Red Bull. In an untimely way, we could
comprehend the invocation of the great globe's dissolution during a recorded performance of *The Tempest* at court in 1613 as accruing to itself
a fresh topical resonance,[54] since a fire destroyed the playhouse's "vertuous fabrique" that year and was sumptuously rebuilt.[55] In keeping with

this chapter's interest in early seventeenth-century colonial discourse, we may explore another resonance for the erection of Prospero's "house": the place of the stage in the promotional literature on the Virginia colony. In so doing, the colonialist figure of the New World becomes useful again for apprehending *The Tempest*'s logs. But in this reading, the pile of logs, offstage and "within," comes into view as a theatrical venue. Prospero's playhouse, to borrow a phrase from John Pitcher's essay on *The Tempest*'s Vergilian influences, is "a theatre of the future" (*hic alta theatris / fundamenta locant alii* and *scaenis decora apta futuris*) whose antecedent is ancient – and colonial – Carthage.[56]

At first sight in Vergil's epic, the city ruled by "widow" Dido (2.1.75), as Gonzalo identifies her, is comprehended as "new *Carthage*," where craftsmen work to "rere so hie" "hugy walls" [emphasis in original] (*whole .XII. B1*). Such bustle and business, as David Scott Wilson-Okamura observes, conjured for early modern English advocates of empire the image of "the ideal colony" (724). Such industry could be cited, as it is in *A Trve Declaration Of The estate of the Colonie in Virginia*, as precedent for the English enterprise in Virginia: "The Phenicians first inhabiting *Carthage*, *Vtica*, and *Thebes*" are summoned along with a host of "diuine, humane, externall, and domesticall, examples" to urge England on its imperial course and "not [to] make shipwracke of our intentions, concerning *Virginia*" [emphasis in original] (4).[57] Of especial relevance to *The Tempest*'s wedding revels, which Heather James wittily dubs "Prospero's Vergilian Masque" (190–1), is an architectural feature emergent in the Carthaginian landscape that Aeneas notices while surveying the city in the epic's inaugural book – "a stately place" (*theatris*) that Moorish builders "had found" or established "for the games and plaies" (*.xiii. Bookes* n.p.).[58] If the claim that *The Tempest* constructs a theatre in acts one to three is at all persuasive, then Prospero would seem to have consulted his Vergil very carefully. Dido-like, he directs a labour force on the island to raise a modern theatre in the English vernacular tradition, since its materials have been lumbered from the island's woodlands and not quarried from rocks (*rupibus*) as they are in Vergil's epic. It is as if *The Tempest* stages Jacobean masques in a wooden "house" that proves the successor to Dido's colonial theatre in northern Africa.[59]

From the depiction of Vergil's Carthage, Shakespeare adopts the insight that colonial settlement, however unintended and temporary it may be, requires a "stately" theatre for staging diversions. Although the extent to which Prospero's magical shows produce lasting change in its audience has long been a matter of debate,[60] there can be no question about the power of theatre in early seventeenth-century Jamestown. The Carthage that Aeneas sees upon his arrival was an exemplary model of colonialism in the Virginia context, but a replica of Dido's theatrical complex, of Shakespeare's Globe, or even of Prospero's "house" was not built in the resettled colony. We may attribute this variance in the genealogy of colonies, real and fictive, leading from Carthage to Virginia, to the antipathy to the institution of public theatre evidenced in the promotional literature on Virginia. A sermon printed in 1610, for instance, lists "the Diuell, Papists, and Players" as the "three great enemies" of the Virginia enterprise. Shortly thereafter, the preacher explicates the "Two causes why the Players maligne this action": "First, for that they are so multiplied here, that one cannot liue by another, and they see that wee send of all trades to *Virginea*, but will send no *Players*, which if wee would doe, they that remaine would gaine the more at home. Secondly, … because wee resolue to suffer no *Idle persons in Virginea*, which course if it were taken in *England*, they know they might turne to new occupations" [emphasis in original] (Crashaw H, H4^r). Included at the end of *For The Colony in Virginea Britannia. Lawes Diuine, Morall and Martiall, &c.* (1612), a prayer intended to be recited twice daily also inveighs against "Papists & players." Annexed to this draconian guidebook that regulates the colonists' time, this prayer further harangues such "scum and dregs of the earth": "they that be filthy, let the[m] be filthy still, & let such swine still wallow in their mire, but let not ye rod of the wicked fal vpon the lot of the righteous, let not them put forth their hands to such vanity, but let them that feare thee, reioyce & be glad in thee, & let them know, that it is thou O Lord, that raignest in England, & vnto the ends of the world" (67–8). As Stephen Greenblatt has remarked in the context of this prayer, which marks English planters as "the righteous," "Even if the content of a play seemed acceptable, the mode of entertainment itself was the enemy of the colonial plantation" (*Shakespearean* 158).

By such logic, which is familiar to us from the sermons, petitions, and treatises issued against commercial theatre that we've examined in preceding chapters, the colony in Virginia is, officially, an antitheatrical venture whose survival depends upon the weeding out of idleness and the decision to transplant tradesmen, like carpenters, masons, sawyers, and shipwrights, who would be immediately advantageous to Jamestown rather than to stock the settlement with players. To build a theatre, then, would be a waste of valuable manpower and would put to impractical use a significant number of Virginian trees.[61] Doing so would erect in a clearing an enormous wooden idol (a term that can punningly describe a playhouse in English antitheatrical literature) that would seduce day labourers away from the authorized double aim for the colonialist project. According to a sermon that William Crashaw preached around 1610, one aim is the eradication of "abominable Idolatry and superstition" in a native population that has come under the corrosive influence of Catholicism, so many Calibans whom continental Europeans have taught to "kiss the book" (2.2.122), which, literally in the play, is the wooden vessel that contains Stefano's Spanish wine and, more figuratively, is the Bible.[62] The second aim is the "plantation of a Church of English christians" in the place of such idol worship (C3ʳ, K2ʳ). Watching a play in a New World wooden O runs the risk of erasing a primary religious mark distinguishing English settlers from their Spanish counterparts and from indigenous peoples, for this exercise in idleness turns the English missionary into a celebrant at "*Venus Pallace* and *Sathans Synagogue*" [emphasis in original] (J.G. 57). The "woods" of theatre, in short, were not transported across the waters of the Atlantic in a way reminiscent of the movement of the Theatre's timbers across the Thames or the literary translation of empire from Vergil's Carthage to Shakespeare's England.

In a curious way, then, the topography of seventeenth-century Virginia resembled London's cityscape before the erection of the Theatre in 1576: neither space had a permanent playhouse.[63] Indeed, no such venue would welcome patrons in colonial Virginia until 1716, the earliest date when William Levingston could have opened "the first theatre in the British continental colonies" on a plot of ground near the (aptly named) Palace Green in Williamsburg (Land 359, 362), the city that superseded Jamestown as Virginia's capital in the late 1690s. At the end of *The Tempest* (one of two Shakespeare plays printed for the first time in the American colonies in 1761),[64] Prospero's playhouse might stand abandoned as had done the Theatre in very late sixteenth-century London. It is "vnfrequented" by the play's Europeans – Ariel and Caliban stay onshore – "in darke silence, and vast solitude."[65] A Shakespearean wooden O, Prospero's "house" is an Old World figure of colonialism that has been transported to *The Tempest*'s "New World" and that the play's "islander[s]" could repurpose to different ends when the Europeans returned home (2.2.33). It is, literally, a wooden "figure of potentiality."[66]

Epilogue: The Afterlives of the Globe

Wooden Os has thus far elaborated the richly interwoven histories of early modern England's woodlands and London's outdoor theatre industry. Its central claim about the theatres dotting the cityscape – that, in an era marked by a perceived scarcity of wood and timber, the cultural imagination typecast playhouses as virtual woodlands where an array of eco-fantasies and nightmares about that shortage could be staged – requires that we see (as many early modern writers and dramatists seem to have done) the English woods inhering in the superstructure of the wooden O. But when the cost pegged to the construction and maintenance of theatres began to exceed their relevance, the long wished-for desire of sixteenth- and seventeenth-century antitheatrical writers was realized: the playhouses were demolished during unstable political and religious times. According to a manuscript dating from the mid-seventeenth century, which the Victorian Shakespeare scholar F.J. Furnivall discovered tucked inside an edition of Stow's *Annales* and which has subsequently been labelled a forgery, the Second Globe playhouse was "pulled downe to the grownd, by Sir Matthew Brand [Brend], On Munday the 15 of April 1644, to make tenements in the roome of it" ("End" 315).[1] (A less dubious legal account that also mentions the erection of tenements at the site of the playhouse places the end of the Second Globe's life at mid-1653.)[2] In the bogus document, which Furnivall included in an article called "The End of Shakespeare's Playhouses" (1882), we also find that Henslowe's Fortune was "pulled downe on the in-side by the Souldiers this 1649" and that his Hope was "pulled downe to make tennementes" in March 1656 (315).[3] Despite its calculation and inaccuracies, this theatrical obituary, which reminds us of the uncertain evidentiary status of early modern English material culture, articulates an eco-fantasy about the playhouses' afterlives.

In the document's logic, London's theatre districts were green no more. Landowners disassembled some playhouses, while members of Cromwell's New Model Army defaced other venues, such as the Fortune and Salisbury Court. We could enlist theatres that fell at the hands of soldiers as counterparts to the forests and trees that were damaged during the mid-seventeenth century by a range of "antiauthoritarian" figures and radical Protestant movements because they were emblems of royal culture.[4] And yet there is no mention of wood, timber, or theatrical trees in the forged account of the Fortune's demise or of Salisbury Court's end. The wood-enness of theatre is likewise absent in the reports of the Second Globe's demolition and the destruction of the Hope's interior. Matters related to urban densification are implicitly more important in this terse account. Since more space ("roome") is required to house a growing population, landowners converted the ground on which these "playhouseholds" were situated to "make tennementes," abetted in their actions no doubt by the fervour of mid-century antitheatricalism and religious reform. Furnivall's document, then, tells in reverse a version of the story about woodland clearance that we observed in the Prologue: whereas in More's *Utopia* the island's living woods were brought closer to cities and rivers where they could be put to a variety of ends, here a telltale sign of city life – the timbered tenement – has encroached upon and cleared out the virtual woodlands dotting London's suburbs.

But perhaps it is not entirely the case that the eco-materials of theatre have vanished into thin air. One possible construal of the report of the Hope's destruction – it was "pulled downe to make tennementes" – suggests that the tenements put up at the site may have been culled and refashioned from the wood and timber that had been "pulled downe" there. At the property upon which the Second Globe had been repurposed, so too might the theatre's constitutive wood and timber have been recycled there "to make" a complex of buildings. To reuse the theatre's material fabric in this way fuses two early seventeenth-century proposals for the Curtain playhouse, which we noted in our discussion of the 22 June 1600 Privy Council minute in chapter 3: "either to be ruyned and plucked downe or to be putt to some other good vse" (qtd. in Rutter 190–3). Such possible reuse also puts a new spin on an old trick that the Burbages had performed in 1598–9 when they transported the wood and timber of the Theatre across the Thames to make the First Globe. The eco-material history of Shakespeare's playhouse(s) thus comes into view as a series of ligneous transformations, from woodlands and then proto-theatre in the countryside, into the Theatre, into the Globe and from the woodlands and proto-theatre in the countryside (again) into the Second Globe and finally perhaps into tenements.

Furnivall's antiquarianism, in the end, could be said to attempt to document the palimpsest-like quality of architectural layering in London's (sub)urban environment. He charts (with whatever misinformation) the history of the cityscape, but he could do so only with the aid of written documents and a bibliophile's good (or too convenient) luck. The techniques of modern archaeology, however, have permitted scholars, city planners, and enthusiasts a vision of Shakespeare's theatre unavailable to their ancestors. Having carefully removed the literal strata of urban history from the Bankside, archaeological teams uncovered in the late twentieth century partial remains of the foundations of both Henslowe's Rose and the 1598–9 Globe.[5] Near the site of Shakespeare's theatre, a new Globe was rebuilt, indicating that the gain associated with its construction and maintenance (continue to) exceed its costs. In our age of inconvenient truth, in which fossil fuels supply our energy needs and in which environmental activists warn against the diminishment of the planet's forests, it is as if London has been culturally reafforested again. Indeed, a production of *As You Like It* that I attended in 2009 conscripted the stage's wooden posts to perform, ecomimetically, trees: the black fabric covering the posts was effortlessly whisked away when Rosalind and her companions set foot in Arden. It was a breathtaking moment of eco-wonder.

Although the acting company has added a flourish to early modern stage conventions, there is nonetheless the suggestion that the new wooden O differs hardly at all from its early modern predecessors. According to a playbill for a production of *Doctor Faustus* I saw at Globe 3.0 in 2011, the "techniques used in the reconstruction of the theater were painstakingly accurate. 'Green' oak was cut and fashioned according to 16th-century practice and assembled in two-dimensional bays on the Bankside site; oak laths and staves support lime plaster mixed according to a contemporary recipe and the walls are covered in white lime wash. The roof is made of water reed thatch, based on samples found during the excavation."[6] It would seem that we need, we desire, and we enjoy wood and timber in the polygonal shape of this faux heritage site more than we do carbon sinks or woodland biodiversity.[7] Or, at least, we deem the trees of both to have commensurate cultural value.

Notes

Prologue: Evergreen Fantasies: *Utopia*'s Trees and Early Modern Theatre

1 Thomas More, *A Most pleasant, fruitfull, and wittie worke, of the best state of a publique wealth, and of the new Yle called Vtopia*, N3ᵛ. References to the translation of *Utopia* are from this edition; they appear parenthetically. For More's Latin, I have consulted Thomas More, Utopia: *Latin Text and English Translation* 178–9.

2 For designations of premodern England as a "wooden" age, see Michael Williams, *Deforesting the Earth* 181 and John Perlin, *A Forest Journey* 227, 245. On "the age of wood" more generally, see my "Wooden Slavery."

3 On the importance of wood in other early modern polities, see Karl Appuhn, *A Forest on the Sea*; Conrad Totman, *The Green Archipelago*; and Paul Warde, *Ecology, Economy and State Formation*.

4 On the idea of the "standing reserve," see Martin Heidegger, "The Question Concerning Technology" 17–18. On Heidegger's use of forestry language in this essay, see Greg Garrard, "Heidegger Nazism Ecocriticism" 254.

5 On the outlandish nature of Utopian woodland management, see Harry Berger, Jr, *Second World and Green World* 34.

6 On the sophisticated theorizing that Renaissance authors did on the relation between "the material" and economy, see Douglas Bruster, "The New Materialism in Renaissance Studies" 238.

7 Unless otherwise noted, I take all Shakespeare citations in this book from *The Norton Shakespeare*. They are included parenthetically.

8 On prefabrication at the Fortune theatre, see John Orrell, "Building the Fortune."

9 For an overview of scholarship on the material history of Shakespeare's theatre through the reconstruction of the Globe in London, see Gabriel Egan, "Reconstructions of the Globe."

10 I borrow this language about sixteenth-century efforts in Germany from
    Simon Schama, *Landscape and Memory* 95.
11 My thinking in these pages on the affective and material resonances of "trans-
    port" owes a great debt to Miranda Burgess, "Transport."
12 The term "evergreen" originates in a colonialist context. The *Oxford English
    Dictionary* dates this use to Richard Eden's 1555 translation of Peter Martyr's
    Decades of the Newe World. I accessed this database online on 15 June 2011.

Introduction: Wood, Timber, and Theatre in Early Modern England

 1 On the obfuscation of the gastronomic substrate in More, see Julian Yates,
    "Humanist Habitats." In my reading, the table itself, likely crafted from
    the most solid wood, comes back into view. It's where food is consumed in
    between – and after – Books in *Utopia*; it's also the object around which and
    over which guests at Cardinal Morton's dinner party debate in Book I. Pres-
    ent, but never described, these tables arrange and support social communion.
 2 Lawrence Manley suggests that "the 'solutions' of Book II," among which we
    should number Utopian woodland management, "figuratively analyzed the
    problems they solved." In this case at least, a full explanation of the problem
    does not accompany the solution. See *Literature and Culture* 43. According
    to Halpern, Utopia's "governing logic is that of utility," but, unlike the gold
    molded into chamber pots and slaves' chains, the utility of trees is not de-
    based and then sacrificed during extraordinary circumstances (like war), when
    the pots and chains are liquidated to hire mercenary soldiers. We never know
    what the uses of trees are in *Utopia*. See *The Poetics of Primitive Accumula-
    tion* 144–7, 161.
 3 Thomas More, *A Most pleasant, fruitfull, and wittie worke, of the best state
    of a publique wealth, and of the new Yle called Vtopia* N3^v. References to the
    translation of *Utopia* are from this edition; they appear parenthetically. For
    More's Latin, which I've included parenthetically in these pages, I consulted
    Thomas More, Utopia: *Latin Text and English Translation* 178–9.
 4 "Wood and timber" and "wood" thus amplify and vary More's *ligna*, which
    translates as "wood" or "that which is collected." For these definitions, see
    Robert Pogue Harrison, *Forests* 202.
 5 For an illustrated survey of timber-framed buildings in early modern Eng-
    land, see Hans Jürgen Hansen, ed., *Architecture in Wood* 69–115.
 6 For a detailed survey of shipbuilding in wood from the seventeenth century
    onward, see N.D.G. James, *A History of English Forestry* 139–60.
 7 On softwoods used for masts, see John F. Richards, *The Unending Frontier*
    225.

8 On retrofitting housing and places of worship in wood, see Margaret Aston, *England's Iconoclasts* 331–2 and Maurice Howard, *The Building of Elizabethan and Jacobean England* 61–2, 103–4.

9 On the problems attendant upon writing the history of this catastrophe, see Frances E. Dolan, "Ashes and 'the Archive.'"

10 Such nomenclature for an architectural style seems to have emerged in print during the nineteenth century, as early as 1842 for "half-timbered" and in 1880 for the phrase "Tudor house." For this information, I consulted the on-line *Oxford English Dictionary*.

11 For a general account of the material's indispensability in premodernity, see Harvey Green, *Wood*.

12 On the use of "treen" in the early modern household, see Natasha Korda, *Shakespeare's Domestic Economies* 17.

13 Throughout the course of the sixteenth century, many of these industries began to substitute coal or "sea-coal" for charcoal and firewood because of deforestation and timber shortages. See J.U. Nef, *The Rise of the British Coal Industry* 190–223 and Ken Hiltner, "Early Modern Ecology" 557.

14 On the process of making charcoal and its use in the iron industry, see G. Hammersley, "The Charcoal Iron Industry."

15 John Perlin, *A Forest Journey* 173 and Michael Williams, *Deforesting the Earth* 186.

16 On the coal industry, see John Perlin, *A Forest Journey* 241–3 and John F. Richards, *The Unending Frontier* 227–40.

17 Paul Warde estimates that in 1550 England and Wales "had some 3.2 million cubit metres of firewood *per annum* at their disposal." Although this figure, as Warde himself immediately notes, is an overestimation, he also says it likely increases over the course of the century. See *Energy Consumption in England and Wales, 1560–2004* 38.

18 See also see my "Wooden Slavery."

19 Population demography and crop failures put an especial strain on English resources during the late sixteenth century. By 1600, London had become the third densest city in Europe, housing 200,000 people. On the relation between these statistics and early modern drama, see Jean E. Howard, *Theater of a City*. Throughout the sixteenth and seventeenth centuries, a period that climatologists have dubbed the "Little Ice Age," England endured unseasonably colder and wetter weather and crop failures, particularly during the 1590s. Under such conditions, it is little wonder that a staple good like "wood" became ever more necessary for subsistence and was sold at inflated price rates. On the "Little Ice Age," see H.H. Lamb, *The Changing Climate* 1–20, and on its relation to early modern English literature and cul-

ture, see Robert Markley, "Summer's Lease" and Alvin Snider, "Hard Frost, 1684."

20 The context for this remark is naval shipbuilding, so I perforce employ the remark more expansively. On the ligneous philology of "matter" and "material," see Judith Butler, *Bodies That Matter* 31–2.

21 James I prorogued Parliament in 1608, and when it reconvened in 1609, "wood" – its "better Breeding" and "Preservation," for instance – was debated six times by its members through the summer of 1610. See *Journals of the House of Commons* (1547–1624), vol. 1, 394–5, 405–6, 408, 409, 430, 434.

22 Standish's program for replanting was antedated thirty-four years by William Harrison's call for property owners to plant one in every four acres of land with trees. See "The second Booke, of the hystoricall description of Britaine" 91ᵛ.

23 Although Flinn fails to identify the early modern pamphleteers he derides, he names a trio of historians whom he also considers to be unreliable guides. They are J.U. Nef, *Rise of the British Coal Industry* and A. Clow and N.L. Clow, "The Timber Famine and the Development of Technology."

24 On the discursive production of environmental crises, see Greg Garrard, *Ecocriticism* 105.

25 As the 1581 Elizabethan law discussed above suggests, the iron industry was the main target of political aspersion in the period, as upset neighbours and landowners with vested interests in the shipbuilding industry defended available wooded land from rival users. Flinn's critique of the underlying forces motivating the pamphlets and legislation is apt insofar as shipwrighting and charcoal-making did not employ the same kind (or age) of trees and so were not exactly competitors.

26 Yet on the next page, Williams takes a comparatist's view of the crisis and undermines his narrowest claim about it scope: "Rome at its peak never came anywhere near the timber crisis of England in the later sixteenth century, though northern China during the twelfth century was a serious contestant."

27 Keith Thomas, *Man and the Natural World* 193.

28 Our author signs a prefatory letter to "the Nobilitie, Gentrie, and Yeomanrie of great Britaine" as "R. Ch." Search engines identify him as "Rooke Churche," "R. Churton," and "Robert Chambers." Of the three, the first appeals insofar as the motto that R.C. associates with himself on the title page to *An Olde Thrift*, *Tout pour L'Eglise* ("Very much for the Church"), winks at the *nom de plume*.

29 For an account of the revenue extracted from royal woodlands, see G. Hammersley, "The Crown Woods and Their Exploitation."

30 On the persistence of transportation inadequacies in the generation of local freshwater shortages, see Charles Fishman, *The Big Thirst* 20.

31 On the organizational insufficiencies of transporting wood product, see Oliver Rackham, *Trees and Woodland* 100 and N.D.G. James, *A History of English Forestry* 123–5. On the matter of carriage in a later period, when these internal systems for moving goods and ideas were newly operable, see Miranda Burgess, "Transport."

32 Ken Hiltner argues that Utopian-like measures for transporting lumber were necessary and indeed implemented after the fire of 1666. He perhaps underestimates the expense, labour, and woodland extraction to rebuild London. See "Early Modern Ecology" 561–2.

33 The classic study of the relation between the "liberties" and London's theatres is Steven Mullaney, *The Place of the Stage*.

34 For a review of the complex economic and legal history of the Theatre, see William Ingram, *The Business of Playing* 182–218.

35 On the failure at the Blackfriars and the move to the Globe, see Andrew Gurr, "Money or Audiences" 6.

36 For a bibliographic account of the legal proceedings pertaining to the Theatre, see Herbert Berry, *Shakespeare's Playhouses* 19–44.

37 I borrow this phrase from a letter recounting the fire at the Globe by Sir Henry Wotton, which is included in *The Norton Shakespeare* 3311. On the use of brick in playhouse construction, see Gerald Eades Bentley, *The Jacobean and Caroline Stage*, vol. 6, 154–5.

38 Polygons are not uniform, and neither was the shape of England's theatres. Most were rounded (although not strictly circular), but the Fortune was rectangular. For more on the shapes of theatres, see John Orrell, "The Architecture of the Fortune Playhouse." I do not emphasize distinctions in form because my interest is the theatre's shared material fabric.

39 Andrew Gurr quotes in some detail the contracts for both the Fortune and the Hope. See *The Shakespearean Stage* 137–8, 153.

40 For Gabriel Egan, such modelling establishes a "'living' dynasty of venues." See *Green Shakespeare* 80.

41 The work of Ann Rosalind Jones and Peter Stallybrass in *Renaissance Clothing and the Materials of Memory* on another "material" inflecting the development of the theatre industry – costumes – is my model.

42 On the archival history of both the Red Lion and the playhouse at Newington Butts, see William Ingram, *The Business of Playing* 102–13, 150–81.

43 On the Curtain, see ibid., 219–38.

44 The Swiss traveller Thomas Platter's account of watching *Julius Caesar* at the
   Globe in 1599, from which I quote, is included in *The Norton Shakespeare*
   3301.

45 On the history of the Rose, see Julian Bowsher and Pat Miller, *The Rose and
   the Globe*.

46 On the "magnificent" Swan, see Andrew Gurr, *The Shakespearean Stage*
   131–6.

47 On the Fortune, see John Orrell, "Building the Fortune."

48 For Alexander Leggatt, it is not entirely clear whether the Red Bull Inn was
   converted into a playing space or if it was torn down and replaced with a
   playhouse. See *Jacobean Public Theatre* 20. But Andrew Gurr classifies the
   Red Bull alongside custom-built playhouses like the Fortune. See *The Shakespearean Stage* 120.

49 On the Hope, see Andrew Gurr, *The Shakespearean Stage* 152–4.

50 On the fees negotiated and transacted for the Fortune, see John Orrell,
   "Building the Fortune" 127, 144. Court records dating from later sixteenth-
   century lawsuits associated with the Theatre indicate that its erection and
   provisioning cost was between £500 and £700. See William Ingram, *The Business of Playing* 193.

51 I take all quotations from the Fortune contract from Andrew Gurr, *The
   Shakespearean Stage* 137.

52 On the possible use of paint in "theater décor," see John Orrell, "The Theaters" 110. For evidence of painting at the Swan, see Andrew Gurr, *The
   Shakespearean Stage* 132.

53 On this feature at the Hope, see Andrew Gurr, *The Shakespearean Stage*
   153.

54 As S.P. Cerasano reminds us, the document known today as *Henslowe's
   Diary* contains information that does not pertain to the running of the playhouses. Indeed, until 1580–1, this folio-sized book belonged "to Philip's
   older brother John, who used it to record forestry accounts that related to
   a local iron-mining business where he worked as a clerk and probably also
   as a part-time manager." See S.P. Cerasano, "The Geography of Henslowe's
   Diary" 331. Edmund, the father of the brothers Henslowe, was Master of
   Ashdown Forest, and Queen Mary granted their uncle license to operate an
   iron foundry in Sussex. Might this "family business" be the source of (some
   of) the wood and timber needed for the Rose playhouse? On the Henslowe
   family's connections to the ironmongering industry, see S.P. Cerasano, "The
   Fortune Contract in Reverse" 91.

55 But see Andrew Gurr, "The Bare Island" 35, 37, which suggests that the pre-
   1592 Rose may have already had a stage canopy.

56 For an overview and critique of the subversion/containment thesis, see Louis Montrose, *The Purpose of Playing* 1–16.

57 For Jean-Christophe Agnew, *Worlds Apart* 12, the theatre functions as an economic laboratory; I thus expand his sense of the term.

58 On the theatre as a virtual space, see Henry S. Turner, "Life Science."

59 "Theatre" derives from the Greek *theatron* ("beholding place"). On these etymologies in relation to early modern theatres, see William N. West, *Theatres and Encyclopedias* 46–8. According to Anne Barton, in Roman spectacles of the hunt at the circus, which were known as *silvae*, "the amphitheatre, at enormous expense, was landscaped: provided with trees and rocks, thickets, running streams, and artificial hills, so that the Roman crowd seemed to be looking down at a real forest or, given its protective barriers and circular shape, upon an enclosed park." See *Essays, Mainly Shakespearean* 361. See also John Orrell, "The Theatres" 104.

60 For a survey of Shakespeare's "green" scenes, see Linda Woodbridge, *The Scythe of Saturn* 152–205.

61 For a representative example of this tradition, see Jeanne Addison Roberts, "Shakespeare's Forests and Trees," 110. Such scholarship also informs Corinne J. Saunders, *The Forest of Medieval Romance* 187–203.

62 On the purchase and use of "Tymber" for the creation of a "forest" setting for performance at court, see *Extracts from the Accounts of the Revels at Court, in the Reigns of Queen Elizabeth and King James I* 41. My sense is that tree stage props employed in the public theatre were at least made of the same material.

63 On the use of stage trees to supply a forest setting, see G.F. Reynolds, "'Trees' on the Stage of Shakespeare" and Werner Habicht, "Tree Properties and Tree Scenes in Elizabethan Theater."

64 In calling the theatre a "green world," I invoke the work of Harry Berger, Jr on the imaginative construct known as the "second world," of which the green world is a special subtype. See *Second World and Green World* 111–29. In broad terms, Berger, Jr traces how the counterfactual second world affords a fresh perspective on the "first world" in which readers and viewers reside. Although the beholding of a "new woodland" in the wooden walls of a theatre could indeed be construed as a counterfactual experience for Londoners enduring a shortage of wood and timber, it is also a more complex phenomenon precisely because the theatre and this new woodland share a material substrate. In elaborating this material logic, as I will do below, I have found the work of Jonathan Gil Harris especially helpful.

65 Bruce R. Smith comprehends the wooden theatre as an enormous "sound-making device" upon which actors played. See *The Acoustic World* 207–8.

66 On the theatres as "part of [the] fabric" of Shakespeare's drama, see Tiffany
    Stern, *Making Shakespeare* 11.

67 On the gestic quality of stage speech, see Alan C. Dessen, *Elizabethan Stage
    Conventions* 53–69.

68 On the association of this room "with more general breaches of social
    order," see Andrew Gurr and Mariko Ichikawa, *Staging in Shakespeare's
    Theatres* 2.

69 On the affinities between Morton's ambient poetics and "the imagination of
    Shakespeare and his contemporaries," see Bruce R. Smith, "Shakespeare @ the
    Limits" 112.

70 On the relation between such deictic language and the creation of virtual real-
    ity in the theatre, see Henry S. Turner, "Life Science" 208.

71 I take this phrase from Michael D. Bristol, "Shamelessness in Arden" 279.

72 In the vein of Jeanne Addison Roberts ("Shakespeare's Forests and Trees"),
    Theis also proposes that Shakespeare "encourages an audience to see the
    wood as a mental construct and a product of each character's perspective on
    the world" (*Writing* 38).

73 On the uncanny experience of losing "one's way in a mountain forest," see
    Sigmund Freud, "The 'Uncanny'" 237. On the forest as an uncanny iteration
    of trees, see Timothy Morton, *Ecology Without Nature* 178.

74 I excerpt Simon Forman's diary from *The Norton Shakespeare* 3309–10.

75 On the repertory system, see Roslyn L. Knutson, "The Repertory."

76 This is S.P. Cerasano's phrase for naming where the timbers for the frame of
    the Fortune theatre were extracted. She more narrowly locates this place as
    "probably from forests near Windsor." See "The Fortune Contract in Re-
    verse" 87.

77 On this feature of the theatre's construction, see Irwin Smith, "Theatre into
    Globe."

78 For a detailed account of the "customary practice" for constructing theatres,
    see John Orrell, "Building the Fortune" 130–1.

79 Orrell further suggests here that the frame would have been originally as-
    sembled "in the builder's yard or framing-place," the latter of which could
    still signal the woods.

80 See Gillen D'Arcy Wood, "Introduction: Eco-historicism." Three recent es-
    say collections highlight the critical payoffs of reading early modern literature
    eco-historically and in concert with presentist environmental concerns. See
    Thomas Hallock, Ivo Kamps, and Karen Raber, eds. *Early Modern Ecostud-
    ies*; Lynne Bruckner and Dan Brayton, eds. *Ecocritical Shakespeare*; and Jen-
    nifer Munroe and Rebecca Laroche, eds. *Ecofeminist Approaches to Early
    Modernity*.

81 For eco-historical accounts that identify early modern precursors to modern environmentalist practices and ecocritical habits of thought, see Gabriel Egan, *Green Shakespeare*; Steve Mentz, "Strange Weather in *King Lear*"; Todd A. Borlik, *Ecocriticism and Early Modern Literature*; and Ken Hiltner, *What Else Is Pastoral?* 95–155. For a powerful critique of the hope underpinning so many "green" readings of Shakespeare, see Steve Mentz, "Shakespeare's Beach House."

82 In Simon C. Estok's terms, many of the darker green representations outlined in this study would classify as examples of ecophobia. See *Ecocriticism and Shakespeare* 3–5.

1: "Vanish the tree": *Friar Bacon and Friar Bungay* at the Rose

1 I take all citations from Robert Greene, *Friar Bacon and Friar Bungay*, ed. Daniel Seltzer, and record them parenthetically by scene and line number. The first edition of the play is from 1594, but the editorial tradition typically dates its composition to 1589–90, or after the dispersal of the Spanish Armada. Andrew Gurr suggests that the Lord Strange's Men may have mounted the play at the Theatre in 1589. In 1592, according to Gurr, it was performed at the Rose. Since Gurr places a question mark next to his own supposition about the Theatre and since (to my knowledge) there is no evidence of textual revision, the allusions to the Bankside – and especially the pun on "Rose" – in the play make it no less likely that the play debuted at Henslowe's theatre. See Andrew Gurr, *The Shakespearean Stage* 233.

2 For brief notices of the tree prop's significance, see Kent Cartwright, *Theatre and Humanism* 226; Bryan Reynolds and Henry S. Turner, "From *Homo Academicus* to *Poeta Publicus*" 91; and Brian Walsh, "'Deep Prescience'" 74.

3 The most important accounts of magic and dramaturgy (together and separate) in *Friar Bacon* include William Empson, *Some Versions of Pastoral* 32–4; Barbara Howard Traister, *Heavenly Necromancers*; Kent Cartwright, *Theatre and Humanism*; and Bryan Reynolds and Henry S. Turner, "From *Homo Academicus* to *Poeta Publicus*."

4 On *Friar Bacon*'s general relation to "festive comedy" and the "green world," see Peter Mortenson, "*Friar Bacon and Friar Bungay*" and Joseph Stodder, "Magus and Maiden." On the play's eroticizing of pastoral labour, see Wendy Wall, *Staging Domesticity* 132–4, 142–6.

5 On the "new forms of drama" that antitheatricalism and iconoclasm could generate, see Huston Diehl, *Staging Reform* 64.

6 For a similar depiction of antitheatrical desire as the desire for an extirpation, see Ellen Mackay, *Persecution, Plague, and Fire* 94.

7 On the "impossibility of erasing or preventing a foreign presence in England" that the lines about the brazen head conjures, see Deanne Williams, "*Friar Bacon and Friar Bungay*" 43. On the appeal of, and political drawbacks to, "transnational" relations that would result from dynastic matches like the union between an English prince and a Castilian princess in this play, see Eric Griffin, "'Spain is Portugal / And Portugal is Spain.'"

8 Yet in terms of staple foodstuffs *Friar Bacon* seems merrily sufficient: its England is "a land of plenty in which the mentions of butter and cheese have an almost choric function." See Katharine Wilson, "Transplanting Lillies" 200.

9 I borrow this language from Jean E. Feerick, *Strangers in Blood*, where it appears in a discussion of the western-oriented, imperial lines at the end of Shakespeare's *Cymbeline* (5.6.470–6). Feerick goes on to connect these lines to the early seventeenth-century ventures in Virginia.

10 On the history of this woodcut illustration and its relation to the textual history of Greene's play, see Richard Levin, "Tarlton in *The Famous History of Friar Bacon*."

11 On the brazen head as "an icon of evil ideas and ambitions," see Frank Ardolino, "Severed and Brazen Heads" 173. See also Kevin LaGrandeur, "The Talking Brass Head." For the idea that many early modern tragedies "endorse and even engage in acts of iconoclasm," see Huston Diehl, *Staging Reform* 5.

12 For general comments about Greene's tense relation with the stage, see Charles W. Crupi, *Robert Greene* 20–1 and Arul Kumaran, "'Hereafter suppose me the said Roberto.'"

13 On these iconoclastic acts in the play, see Mark Dahlquist, "Love and Technological Iconoclasm."

14 Despite the attention to Greene's iconoclastic impulses in *Friar Bacon*, there are some scholars who regard *Friar Bacon* as a defence of the "stage" and the "theatre." See, for instance, Kent Cartwright, *Theatre and Humanism* 246 and Robert W. Maslen, "Robert Greene and the Uses of Time" 176.

15 On the magical disputation as "a hyperbolic representation of actual university practice" whose greatest stakes include "reputation, recognition, and reward," see Bryan Reynolds and Henry S. Turner, "From *Homo Academicus* to *Poeta Publicus*" 87–8, 91. See also Bryan Reynolds and Henry S. Turner, "Performative Transversations."

16 It may be no coincidence that another of Greene's plays, *The History of Orlando Furioso* (1594), rewrites its source text – Ariosto's romance – to the extent that, in the adaptation, a furious Orlando does not engage in an act of superhuman forest clearance when he discovers that his beloved has married an enemy. Greene, in other words, has a habit of declining to cut down

"trees" inside the theatre, even when his source material calls for him to do so.

17 Daniel Seltzer makes this connection in his edition of *Friar Bacon*, 41 n. 23.
18 See also Brian Walsh, "'Deep Prescience'" 74.
19 For a great discussion of the purlieus in relation to Milton, see Jeffrey S. Theis, *Writing the Forest in Early Modern England* 269–73.
20 Roy Strong adduces this passage as evidence for the link between flowers and Elizabethan iconography in *The Cult of Elizabeth* 69.
21 On Bacon's prediction and the mood of pageantry in the play, see Peter Mortenson, "*Friar Bacon and Friar Bungay*." On the prediction's chauvinism, see Frank Ardolino, "'Thus Glories England Over All the West.'" For a less optimistic reading of the prediction, see Brian Walsh, "'Deep Prescience'" 64.
22 The title page of the 1594 edition of *Friar Bacon* records that it "was plaid" by the Queen's Men. Andrew Gurr has suggested that Greene's play may have first been mounted by Lord Strange's Men, but as Scott McMillan and Sally-Beth MacLean argue, the existence of two plays by the name *Friar Bacon* until 1936, when the manuscript sequel was published, has caused – and persists in causing – confusion about the ascription of the "first" *Friar Bacon* to the Queen's Men. See *The Queen's Men and Their Plays* 90. The rhetoric of Elizabethan triumphalism in Diana's Rose has, at the very least, a more resounding ring if the Queen's Men articulated it.
23 On the theatre as "an object of representation over whose meaning and value various partisans engaged in heated discursive struggle," see Jean E. Howard, *The Stage and Social Struggle* 22.
24 On the effect that stage representation was feared to have on the real-world object being represented, see Laura Levine, *Men in Women's Clothing*. See also the discussion of antitheatricality in Bryan Reynolds, *Becoming Criminal*.
25 On the characteristic conflations of player and audience and player and playhouse in antitheatrical literature, see Jonathan V. Crewe, "The Theatre of the Idols" 330.
26 Peter Lake observes that the antitheatrical "pamphlet campaign" was "conducted, probably at the behest of powerful elements in the city," which suggests a close affiliation between "hack writers on the make" like Gosson and Munday and London's civic elite who were directing missives to court. See Peter Lake with Michael Questier, *The Antichrist's Lewd Hat* 487.
27 On the popularity of *The Spanish Masquerado*, see Anthony Esler, "Robert Greene and the Spanish Armada."
28 On the history of iconoclasm in early modern England, see John Phillips, *The Reformation of Images* and Margaret Aston, *England's Iconoclasts*. On the

fate of manuscripts taken from abbeys during the English Reformation, see Jennifer Summit, *Memory's Library*.

29 On the communal and national nature of idolatry as it was construed in Elizabethan England, see Mark Dahlquist, "Love and Technological Iconoclasm" 65–6.

30 On the "the idolatrous originall of Stage-playes," see William Prynne, *Histrio-Mastix*, "To the Christian Reader." For more on the charge of idolatry in antitheatrical writings, see Huston Diehl, *Staging Reform* 70–1; Michael O'Connell, *The Idolatrous Eye* 33–4; and Peter Lake with Michael Questier, *The Antichrist's Lewd Hat* 448–54.

31 On this phrase for the green space of Eden, see John Milton, *Paradise Lost* Book IV, l. 141. By the time that Milton calls Paradise a "woody theatre" at the moment that Satan invades it, the open-air venues of the late sixteenth and early seventeenth centuries were closed to customers and replaced by the indoor theatres of the Restoration.

32 On the magic glass's capacity to engender competing perspectives that the audience is prompted to collate, see Barbara Howard Traister, *Heavenly Necromancers* 84.

33 Although scholars generally assume that the prose romance upon which Greene modelled his play dates from the mid-sixteenth century, the earliest survival of it is an edition from 1623. On the relation between the prose and the play texts, see Waldo F. McNeir, "Traditional Elements." I consulted *The Famous History of Frier Bacon* in preparing this chapter.

34 For more on the link between Vandermast and the Holy Roman Empire, see Deanne Williams, *"Friar Bacon and Friar Bungay"* 43–4.

35 The "wooded" sea that Nashe describes here is not unique to England. In 1470, for instance, a Venetian observer of a Turkish fleet dubbed it "a forest on the sea." See Karl Appuhn, *A Forest on the Sea* 6.

36 The sequel exists only in a damaged manuscript, and its modern editor observes, "Greene's authorship is on the whole probable" (xii). The sequel's use of "werlwind" (l. 36) to describe what happened to Vandermast nods to the moment in *Friar Bacon* when the Hostess, whom Bacon has magically fetched from Henley, invokes the same term to name the experience of being whisked to Oxford, as if "in a trance" (2.130, 132).

37 See Peter Stallybrass, "Patriarchal Territories."

38 For more on this forest's role in seventeenth-century literature, see Julie Sanders, "Ecocritical Readings and the Seventeenth-Century Woodland."

39 Albion cites as his source the second volume of *The Victoria History of the Counties of England*, ed. William Page. When I examined an edition of this

volume on Gloucestershire, I could find no reference to the shipwreck that Albion mentions. There we observe that the "tradition" about Dean was "current in the early seventeenth century." See *The Victoria History of the Counties of England: Gloucestershire*, vol. 2, 271. In the version of the legend that Simon Schama tells, the letter was composed in "King Philip's hand." See *Landscape and Memory* 155.

40 Venus possibly refers to Trojan ships as "their wooden walls" (1.1.67) in Marlowe's *Dido, Queen of Carthage*. In Thomas Dekker's *Whore of Babylon*, the figure for Queen Elizabeth, Titania, sets forth a plan to "build about our waters wooden walles" (1.2.64), a design that invokes a fleet of ships. By 1635 Lord Coventry would dub England's "wooden walls ... the best walls of this kingdom" because they are increasingly making English ships "masters of the sea." See N.D.G. James, *A History of English Forestry* 139.

41 On the role of the Armada and Greene's *Spanish Masquerado* in this tradition of anti-Hispanism, see William S. Maltby, *The Black Legend in England* 78–9 and Edmund Valentine Campos, "West of Eden" 268–9.

42 On the use of such catchall terminology, see Robert Greenhalgh Albion, *Forests and Sea Power* 139.

43 On this trade pattern, see J.K. Fedorowicz, *England's Baltic Trade* 90–131.

44 On the English policy of search-and-seizure, see J.K. Fedorowicz, *England's Baltic Trade* 39 and T.H. Lloyd, *England and the German Hanse* 339–40.

45 For an exhaustive account of Spanish forces, see *A true Discourse of the Armie...*, translated by Daniel Archdeacon.

46 On the complexities of such terminology in early modern London, see Alan Stewart, "'Euery Soyle to Mee Is Naturall.'"

47 Insofar as the tree prop encapsulates a range of staple forest goods imported in bulk from foreign lands, it complements the internationalism of the luxury foodstuffs that Bacon transports to Oxford to feast the royal entourage after he has defeated Vandermast. On this magical meal, see Wendy Wall, *Staging Domesticity* 145.

48 On the Hesperides in the colonial imagination of Iberia, see David A. Lupher, *Romans in a New World* 176, 215–18 and Antonello Gerbi, *Nature in the New World* 271–4.

49 Wendy Wall records two instances of England being "connected to" the Hesperides, one of which dates from 1609. See *Staging Domesticity* 143, 255 n. 52.

50 On colonial projection in Harriot's Virginia and for a critique of historiography that misrecognizes such projection as an inevitability, see Jonathan Goldberg, "The History That Will Be."

2: "Come, will this wood take fire?" *The Merry Wives of Windsor* in Shakespeare's Theatres

1 My eco-reading of *The Merry Wives of Windsor* requires that I consult an edition of the play based on the Folio text. As Leah S. Marcus has demonstrated, there are stark differences between the 1602 Quarto and the 1623 Folio versions of *Merry Wives*, the most notable of which is an insistence in the Folio on a Windsor locale that is largely absent in the Quarto. See Leah S. Marcus, "Levelling Shakespeare" 173–7.

2 Scholarship that studies the Folio text for its local occasions overwhelmingly does so to explore the reference in the play's final moments to the Order of the Garter, a crown ceremony convened at Windsor Castle. See, among others, Leslie S. Katz, "*The Merry Wives of Windsor*"; Giorgio Melchiori, *Shakespeare's Garter Plays*; and Maurice Hunt, "The Garter Motto."

3 For an account of the history of gaming and social protest in Windsor Forest, which begins with a reading of social relations in *Merry Wives*, see Daniel C. Beaver, *Hunting and the Politics of Violence* 89–92.

4 For scholarship that regards the humiliation as an instance of ritual practice, particularly the comic sacrifice of the scapegoat, see Northrop Frye, *A Natural Perspective* 58; J.A. Bryant, Jr, "Falstaff and the Renewal of Windsor"; Jeanne Addison Roberts, *Shakespeare's English Comedy* 80–2; and Christiane Gallenca, "Ritual and Folk Custom." For the view that the play is not "properly or primarily a festive comedy" in C.L. Barber's sense of the genre, see Anne Barton, *Essays* 71–2.

5 Even though a number of scholars agree that *Merry Wives* stages the appearance of a Windsor middle (or bourgeois) class, they tend to disagree over the forces that shape it. Touchstone accounts of this social formation in the play include Peter Erickson, "The Order of the Garter"; Rosemary Kegl, *The Rhetoric of Concealment* 77–125; Richard Helgerson, "The Busk Basket"; Wendy Wall, *Staging Domesticity* 94–126; and Will Stockton, *Playing Dirty* 25–43. For a critique of the anachronism of describing the play in such classed terms, see Maurice Hunt, "'Gentleness' and Social Class." For a more general account of the "middling sort," see Theodore B. Leinwand, "Shakespeare and the Middling Sort."

6 On Shakespeare's use of the Actaeon tradition, see John M. Steadman, "Falstaff as Actaeon" and Leonard Barkan, "Diana and Actaeon" 351–2.

7 For different approaches to Falstaff's beastliness here and in the canon more generally, see Hanna Scolnicov, "The Zoomorphic Mask" and Gail Kern Paster, *Humoring the Body* 140–5.

8 For accounts of the material and rhetorical relations between human bodies

and plant forms, see Jean Feerick, "Botanical Shakespeares" and my essay "The Wooden Matter of Human Bodies." For studies of human-tree hybrids whose bodies, like Falstaff's, are suffering physically, see Tzachi Zamir, "Wooden Subjects" and Joseph Campana, "Reading Bleeding Trees."

9 On this *topos* in the literary imagination, see Robert Pogue Harrison, *Forests* and Simon Schama, *Landscape and Memory* 82–7.

10 In addition to the scholarship on domesticity that I engage below, see also Philip D. Collington, "'I Would Thy Husband Were Dead,'" for an account of the play's parodic refunctioning of staple moments in a genre that explores the crimes and repercussions of domestic disorder. For a critique of the scholarship on domesticity on the grounds that it installs marital heteronormativity, see Jonathan Goldberg, "What Do Women Want?"

11 Korda does note that a royal figure – the Fairy Queen – presides over the household theatricals in the final scene of *Merry Wives*, an allusion that "suggests an analogy between the housewife's governance of the domestic sphere and Queen Elizabeth's governance of the state." This insight leads to a discussion of the relation between "domestic and political oeconomy," and the particularities of the Park vanish. See Natasha Korda, *Shakespeare's Domestic Economies* 102–3. The best study of Little Park as part of Windsor Forest is Jeffrey S. Theis, *Writing the Forest*. But whereas Wall and Korda regard the park as a household, Thesis explores its contours as a contested preserve for the monarch's deer. This chapter bridges these two ways of comprehending the park.

12 For a concise account of the play's dating that favours 1597–8, see Stanley Wells and Gary Taylor, *William Shakespeare* 120.

13 For an account of the play that is sensitive to the relation between market conditions and ecological concerns, especially the bad harvests of the late 1590s, see Arthur F. Kinney, "Textual Signs." For a critique of Kinney that casts the distinction between the Folio and the Quarto as a concern with the money economy, see Peter Grav, "Money Changes Everything."

14 Oliver Rackham contends that the attribution of English forests to the Anglo-Saxon era is a "medieval forgery." In his estimation, they are instead a "development" of Anglo-Norman England. See *Trees and Woodland* 152.

15 On John Manwood's career, see Robert Pogue Harrison, *Forests* 70.

16 On the ideological work that Manwood's treatise accomplishes only provisionally and on the fissures that thereby become apparent, see Richard Marienstras, *New Perspectives* 30 and Sean Keilen, *Vulgar Eloquence* 152–3.

17 For an account detailing forest disturbances and rights in an earlier period, see Jean Birrell, "Common Rights in the Medieval Forest."

18 See also Robert Pogue Harrison, *Forests* 69–70, 74–5.

19 For an eco-critique of conservation from a legal viewpoint, see Christopher D. Stone, *Should Trees Have Standing?* 8.

20 On this phenomenon, see Oliver Rackham, *Trees and Woodland* 153.

21 On the competing claims made on the forest, see also Daniel C. Beaver, *Hunting and the Politics of Violence* 8.

22 For descriptions of the pale surrounding a Renaissance park, see Oliver Rackham, *Trees and Woodland* 144 and Keith Thomas, *Man and the Natural World* 201–2.

23 On the complex intricacies of such (transfer of) ownership, see John Manwood, *A Treatise* 16v–20^v, esp. 18^r. Private game preserves, particularly the aristocratic deer park, were ubiquitous features of the Elizabethan landscape, demonstrating the owner's social pre-eminence; on this vogue, see Keith Thomas, *Man and the Natural World* 201–2.

24 In *As You Like It*'s Forest of Arden, Rosalind/Ganymede refers to the oak as "Jove's tree" (3.2.214), suggesting the aptness of Falstaff having invoked this figure's mythological transformations as he nears Herne's Oak.

25 On the use of the stage's floorboards to signal "elemental earth" and its trap-door to mark the pit in the graveyard sequence of *Hamlet*, see Margreta de Grazia, Hamlet *without Hamlet* 37.

26 On the use of sawpits in late medieval and early modern Europe, see also *A History of Technology*, ed. Charles Singer, et al., 391–2.

27 Sawmills were indeed operational in sixteenth- and seventeenth-century Euro-American contexts, but their productivity, of course, did not reach optimal levels until the introduction of steam power and of improved saws. On these improvements, see Michael Williams, *Deforesting the Earth* 246–8.

28 On the "Sawyers Saw," see Randle Holme, *An Accademie of Armory* 365. According to the *Oxford English Dictionary*, the first recorded use of the term "pit-saw" occurs in 1454; the word "sawpit" seems to enter written language half a century beforehand.

29 Determining the "identity" of Herne's Oak and establishing when it fell constituted something of a cottage industry for Victorian enthusiasts of Shakespeare. Queen Victoria's woodcarver, William Perry, for one, published a treatise that aimed to prove that the tree fell naturally in 1863; in doing so, he contested the prevailing theory that the oak was cut down in 1796. See William Perry, *A Treatise on the Identity* ix–x. For more on the Victorians' fascination with Herne's Oak, see Adam Zucker, *The Places of Wit* 25–9.

30 In the 1602 Quarto version of *Merry Wives*, this figure is called "Horne," a small switch in vowel, but one which clearly works to emphasize the horned headdress and, as I mention in the next note, the relevance of the cuckold's

horns. See Leah S. Marcus, "Levelling Shakespeare" 174–5. On the legend's
uniqueness to Shakespeare, see Adam Zucker, *The Places of Wit* 27.

31 On the play's approximation of these rituals, see Anne Parten, "Falstaff's
   Horns" and Rosemary Kegl, *The Rhetoric of Concealment* 102–3.

32 On Falstaff's tree-ness in *Henry IV, Parts One and Two*, see my essay "Grafted to Falstaff."

33 On the manifold meanings of "translation" in *Merry Wives*, especially as they
   bear upon the theme of adultery in the play, see Patricia Parker, *Shakespeare
   from the Margins* 116–48. On the use of Ovid's *Metamorphoses* as one of
   the play's numerous "frustrated intertexts, which *press* on the surface of the
   playtext to be translated into the action only to be rejected by it," see David
   Landreth, "Once More into the Preech" 429. My reading of this scene differs
   from Landreth's in that although I agree that the Ovidian intertext of Jove-
   as-rapist is frustrated, the transformative impulse of Ovidianism does not
   evaporate at the moment of its frustration. It persists in the metamorphosis of
   Falstaff into a tree and then into unappealing animals.

34 On these orthographies for Falstaff's name, see Patricia Parker, *Literary Fat
   Ladies* 21 and Valerie Traub, "Prince Hal's Falstaff" 463. For accounts of "fe-
   maleness" and effeminacy in the final acts of *Merry Wives*, see Nancy Cotton,
   "Castrating (W)itches" and Roger Moss, "Falstaff as a Woman."

35 On the "direct link" in antitheatrical writings between the lust engendered
   inside the playhouse and a vocabulary of fire, see Ellen Mackay, *Persecution,
   Plague, and Fire* 152–4. Here the wives burn out Falstaff's lust, as if their
   amateur theatricals were also a vector of antitheatricalism.

36 Although one of the common terms for syphilis – the pox – does not appear
   in *Merry Wives*, Falstaff invokes it in *Henry IV, Part Two*, where he tellingly
   yokes "lechery" and "pox" to the verb "pinches" (1.2.211–12).

37 On the "central" role that insults have in the process of social formation in
   this play, see Rosemary Kegl, *The Rhetoric of Concealment* 84.

38 For a reading of Mrs Page's lines that suggests that she "wants the crowd to
   disperse to their homes," see Peter Holland, "*The Merry Wives of Windsor*"
   5. There is some ambiguity in her phrase "let us everyone go home" (5.5.218)
   – it lacks a possessive adjective that would precisely identify *whose* home is
   the destination – so the play's insistence on the Pages hosting breakfast and
   dinner offers reasonable evidence for their hosting the community once again.

39 I borrow this language depicting festival bonfires, held usually in June and
   July, from *A Survey of London by John Stow*, ed. Charles Lethbridge Kingsford, 101. Stow further notes that "euery man bestow[s] wood or labour towards" these bonfires. Would Falstaff bestow his own body?

40 See also Carol Thomas Neely, "Constructing Female Sexuality" 214–15 n. 12.

41 On the idea that, in Windsor, "violence" is "socially useful," see Camille
   Wells Slights, *Shakespeare's Comic Commonwealths* 157.

42 I adapt this phrase for the sawpit from Adam Zucker, *The Places of Wit* 30.

43 Both Rosemary Kegl and Jeffrey S. Theis figure the final scene in Little Park
   as a possible trespass that has been committed on crown land to secure gender
   norms and the social order. See Rosemary Kegl, *The Rhetoric of Concealment*
   103 and Jeffrey S. Theis, *Writing the Forest* 143.

44 On punishments that Manwood would mete out to all persons party to such
   a trespass, see Richard Marienstras, *New Perspectives* 28.

45 For an elaboration of this point, see Adam Zucker, *The Places of Wit*
   40–1.

46 Gabriel Egan reminds us that when "ecology" was coined in the nineteenth
   century to name the subfield of biology that concerns relations between living organisms and their environments, its model was "economy" in its older
   sense as household management. See *Green Shakespeare* 45. For more on
   these etymologies, see Diane Kelsey McColley, *Poetry and Ecology* 1. On
   the benefits of fusing "ecology" and "economy" into one discipline, see Raymond Williams, *Culture and Materialism* 84.

47 On the role of the pawnshop in the business of early modern drama, see
   Natasha Korda, "Household Property / Stage Property" and Ann Rosalind
   Jones and Peter Stallybrass, *Renaissance Clothing and the Materials of Mem-
   ory* 181–7.

48 On the legal history of the Theatre, see William Ingram, *The Business of Playing* 182–218. On the failure at the Blackfriars and the move to the Globe, see
   Andrew Gurr, *The Shakespearean Stage* 44–6.

49 On the finer legal points of Burbage's investments in the Blackfriars and the
   Theatre, see Andrew Gurr, "Money or Audiences."

50 For an account of these legal technicalities, see Charles Stanley Ross, "Shakespeare's *Merry Wives*" 153.

51 In an appendix detailing early modern plays and sites of performance, Andrew Gurr entertains the possibility that *Merry Wives* was also mounted at
   the Theatre. See *The Shakespearean Stage* 239.

52 On the evidence for playing at the Curtain and the Swan, see Andrew Gurr,
   "Intertextuality" 190–2. See also Barbara Freedman, "Shakespearean Chronology."

53 In the fifth satire included in *Skialetheia*, D6^r, Edward Guilpin likens a "troubled" man wearing black to this depiction of the Theatre.

54 On matters of language transmission and fantasies of exact reproducibility,
   especially as they are associated with Quickly, see Elizabeth Pittenger, "Dispatch Quickly."

55 On these "housekeepers," see Andrew Gurr, "Money or Audiences" 8.

56 On the lease for the site of the Globe, see Julian Bowsher and Pat Miller, *The Rose and the Globe* 89–90.

57 On the relation between the conveyance of the Theatre's timbers and the legal category "fraudulent conveyance," see Charles Stanley Ross, "Shakespeare's *Merry Wives*" 152–5.

58 Charles Stanley Ross likens Falstaff's conveyance in the laundry basket to the theatre's transportation across the Thames in "Shakespeare's *Merry Wives*" 153.

59 I excerpt Sir Henry Wotton's account of the Globe's burning from *The Norton Shakespeare* 3311. For other contemporary reports of the fire, see E.K. Chambers, *The Elizabethan Stage* 419–23 and Maija Jansson Cole, "A New Account."

60 On the use of brick in playhouse construction, see Gerald Eades Bentley, *The Jacobean and Caroline Stage*, vol. 6, 154–5 and Andrew Gurr, *The Shakespearean Stage* 143.

61 For speculations about the decision to rebuild the Globe and for Shakespeare's apparent non-involvement in this project, see Douglas Bruster, "On a Certain Tendency" 72–3 and Andrew Gurr, "Venues on the Verges."

3: "Down with these branches and these loathsome boughs / Of this unfortunate and fatal pine": The Composite *Spanish Tragedy* at the Fortune

1 I cite all references to Kyd's play by act, scene, and line number. I cite all references to the Additions by line number. I employ J. R. Mulryne's edition of *The Spanish Tragedy*.

2 For a general discussion of authorship, see Philip Edwards, ed., "Introduction," lxii and Lukas Erne, *Beyond* The Spanish Tragedy 119–23. For a study that rules out Jonson's authorship on a statistical analysis of diction, see D.H. Craig, "Authorial Styles." Anne Barton, however, makes the case for Jonson's authorship, doing so by focusing on a variation of one of this chapter's themes – fatherhood, which she dubs a "most Jonsonian concern." See *Ben Jonson, Dramatist* 19.

3 Roslyn L. Knutson, "Influence of the Repertory System" 258. See also her earlier essay "*Henslowe's Diary*." Possible support for dating the printed revisions (the Fourth Addition, at least) comes from a series of ironic reworkings of Hieronimo's encounter with the painter (4.1.138–56 and 5.1.1–42) in John Marston, *Antonio and Mellida*, ed. W. Reavley Gair. Although Gair designates the date limits for the play as October 1599 and March 1600 (24), it still remains the case that in 1602 the revised *Spanish Tragedy* would have had a particular resonance at the Fortune.

4 For sustained accounts of the Additions, see Charles K. Cannon, "The Rela-
tion of the Additions"; Marguerite A. Tassi, "The Player's Passion"; Kevin
Dunn, "'Action, Passion, Motion'" 52–5; Richard Hillman, "Botching the
Soliloquies"; and Eric Griffin, "Nationalism."

5 Although S.F. Johnson suggests that the genealogical bloodbath that con-
cludes Kyd's version of the play may be a possible allusion to the crisis of
Elizabeth's succession, he nonetheless suggests that an audience would "have
rejoiced in this wishful discomfiture of the Spanish enemy." See *The Spanish
Tragedy*" 36. The Armada context of Kyd's play has also spurred scholars to
see in it either pre-Armada anti-Spanish bias or post-Armada jingoism. See
Frank Ardolino, *Apocalypse and Armada* 142–66; Ronald Broude, "Time,
Truth, and Right"; and Eugene D. Hill, "Senecan and Vergilian Perspectives."

6 On the function of the additions, see also Anthony B. Dawson, "Madness
and Meaning" 59–61.

7 Although this formulation in Leah S. Marcus refers to early seventeenth-
century additions to Marlowe's *Doctor Faustus*, I follow Marcus's lead (66) by
applying it to the revised *Spanish Tragedy*.

8 Although the 1602 edition of the play sets Kyd's play and the Additions side
by side, it is likely that the new scenes replaced the earlier ones in performance. See Lukas Erne, *Beyond* The Spanish Tragedy 123–5. All seventeenth-
century editions of *The Spanish Tragedy* foreground the play's status as a new
dramatic patchwork, even when its additions have aged. The title page of the
1602 edition announces that Kyd's play has been "Newly corrected, amend-
ed, and enlarged with new additions of the Painters part, and others, as it hath
of late been diuers times acted." This tag appears nearly verbatim on the title
pages of the 1603, 1610–11, and 1615 printings of the revised play. Omitting
mention of the "Painters part," the title pages of the 1618, 1623, and 1633 editions persist in advertising these by-then thirty-year-old scenes as "new Additions." The book-buying public, then, were enticed by, purchased, and read
the composite play.

9 On the figuration of city founders in classical literature as trees and on the
health of the tree in question as an indicator of stability, see Andreola Rossi,
"*The Aeneid* Revisited" 573–4.

10 On the membership of Hieronimo's household in the middling sort, see
Christopher Crosbie, "*Oeconomia* and the Vegetative Soul." For a psychoanalytic reading of class politics in the play, see Kay Stockholder, "'Yet can he
write.'"

11 I apply this phrase, which Maus uses to describe Don Andrea and Horatio, to
Hieronimo.

12 On Edward Alleyn's return to the Fortune's stage to star in revised versions

of plays he made popular, see Roslyn L. Knutson, "Influence of the Repertory System" 265.

13 On 12 December 1599, Henslowe paid Thomas Dekker for "the eande of fortewnatus," which was performed at court that winter; *Old Fortunatus* was published in 1600. On 6 September 1600, Dekker received further payment for "his boocke called the fortewn tenes." It is unclear whether these (presumably) distinct plays were mounted at the Fortune playhouse, but they do suggest (at least) an investment on Henslowe's part to associate its company with the playhouse's name in print, at court, and possibly on the public stage. See *Henslowe's Diary* 128, 137. On the revisions to Marlowe's play at the turn of the seventeenth century and the status of the B-text of *Doctor Faustus*, see Leah S. Marcus, *Unediting the Renaissance* 44, 55.

14 On the trope of the "speaking picture" (*ut pictura poesis*) in the Fourth Addition, see Donna B. Hamilton, "*The Spanish Tragedy*." On the traditions of *memento mori* and *memento vindictae*, the latter of which "incite[s] the viewer (in this case, the commissioner) to action," in the Fourth Addition, see Marguerite A. Tassi, "The Player's Passion" 91.

15 On the Fourth Addition's enhancement of Hieronimo's madness, see Richard Hillman, "Botching the Soliloquies" 111, 124.

16 For more on the "primal error" of idolatry in Kyd's play, especially as it relates to its allegory of empire, see Eric Griffin, "Ethos" 205.

17 There are, of course, other allusions in the Fourth Addition that cast the religious milieu as differently pagan or folkloric. See, for instance, Hieronimo's recollection of having "stamp[ed] our grandam earth" (l. 19). Whatever form Hieronimo's heterodoxy takes, the important point is that it is heterodox. I highlight its idolatrous aspect because it accords with the Fourth Addition's emphasis on the visual icon.

18 On Hieronimo's tree as the cross at Calvary, see Charles K. Cannon, "The Relation of the Additions" 236. For more general accounts of the rich iconography of the "tree" in religious discourses, see Douglas Davies, "The Evocative Symbolism of Trees" 32–42 and Della Hooke, *Trees in Anglo-Saxon England* 21–57.

19 On the scene's relation to Gethsemane, where Judas betrayed Jesus, see Lisa Hopkins, "What's Hercules to Hamlet?" 122, 126.

20 On the pine tree and the True Cross, see Douglas Davies, "The Evocative Symbolism of Trees" 39. Such designation has its roots in Isaiah 60:13. The composite play's presentation of the tree may also parody the genealogical iconography of the Tree of Jesse – for instance, its depiction of the nursing of the infant Jesus, an act which both Hieronimo and Isabella claim to have done, respectively, on behalf of the tree and Horatio.

21 On this moment as a parody of the Eucharist and of the *Elevatio* ritual on Easter Sunday, see Andrew Sofer, *The Stage Life of Props* 66, 84–7. For more on the relation between Hieronimo's play-within-a-play and sixteenth-century Eucharistic controversies, see Huston Diehl, *Staging Reform* 109–20.

22 For a reading of this title-page illustration that emphasizes its status as a marketing device and notices the relation between its depiction of events and the Fourth Addition, see Diane K. Jakacki, "'Canst paint a doleful cry?'"

23 On the frontispiece's mnemonic function, see Bruce R. Smith, *The Acoustic World* 121–3. For more on the frontispiece to *Doctor Faustus*, see Leah S. Marcus, *Unediting the Renaissance* 47.

24 For an account of blighted genealogy and thwarted dynastic futurity, especially as they are figured in Bel-imperia's plot, see Frank Whigham, *Seizures of the Will* 22–51.

25 It is true that members of the aristocracy and gentry planted seeds in seventeenth-century gardens, but usually they did so for contemplative or scientific purposes, not for the express purpose of social ambition. See Rebecca Bushnell, *Green Desire* 12–34, 84–107.

26 I borrow this phrase from Frank Whigham, *Seizures of the Will* 36, where it describes the ghost Andrea's vegetable-inspired language in the frame of the play.

27 On the relations among gardening, teaching, and fatherhood in early modern treatises on education, see Rebecca W. Bushnell, *A Culture of Teaching* 89.

28 Although she does not discuss the 1602 Additions in any detail, Lisa Hopkins observes that one of the "thematic structure[s]" of the unrevised play is the analogizing of humans to plants. See "What's Hercules to Hamlet?" 119, 122.

29 On the theme of execution in Kyd's play, see James Shapiro, "'Tragedies naturally performed'" and Molly Smith, "The Theater and the Scaffold."

30 For an account of how Hieronimo's genealogical loss structures the contours of his revenge, see James P. Hammersmith, "The Death of Castile."

31 Encoded in Lorenzo's phrase "fruits of love" may be "the hanged man's resultant fruitless ejaculation" – his seed or kernel – and the growth therefrom of the mandrake. See Frank Whigham, *Seizures of the Will* 50. Although Whigham regards "Lorenzo's sadistic pleasures" as the mandrake, we might also relate this man-vegetable hybrid to the language of reproduction in the Fourth Addition.

32 For a brief discussion of paternity and the birth alluded to in this scene, see Tzachi Zamir, "Wooden Subjects" 283. Zamir, however, does not consider this scene's status as an Addition.

33 The Tree Council, a conservation charity in the United Kingdom, estimated

in 2002 that Sidney's Oak or the Bear Oak might actually have preceded the poet's birth by some 500 years.

34 See also Don E. Wayne, *Penshurst* 59, 84.

35 For an account of how Hieronimo, "the representative of a middle stratum [,] appropriates the behavior and values of the court as self-conscious style, as an art which conceals its artfulness: as *sprezzatura* and an exercise of *decorum*," see James R. Siemon, "Sporting Kyd" 561–2. The tree planting recounted in the Fourth Addition would appear a counterpart to the style Siemon detects in Hieronimo's drama, masques, and speech utterances.

36 On the social anxiety that Horatio instigates in the Iberian royals, especially in Lorenzo, see also Katharine Eisaman Maus, *Inwardness and Theater* 35–71. On the "class war" that *The Spanish Tragedy* stages in moments like this one, see Kevin Dunn, "'Action, Passion, Motion'" 41–2.

37 On the "hubris topos" in Kyd's play, especially as it pertains to the Portuguese subplot, see Eric Griffin, "Nationalism" 342–8, esp. 343.

38 On the history of the English aesthetic garden, see also Jennifer Munroe, *Gender and the Garden* 2–3, 8.

39 On the indistinction between dead and living wood in Christian iconography, which has particular relevance to the vision of Horatio on the tree as Christ, see Simon Schama, *Landscape and Memory* 220.

40 Hieronimo puts a (relatively) more positive spin on his classical persona when, as he beats Bazardo offstage in the Fourth Addition, he fashions himself as Achilles: "At the last, sir, bring me to one of the murderers, were he as strong as Hector, thus would I tear and drag him up and down" (ll. 162–4).

41 On the correspondence linking a tree and an architectural column, which dates from at least Greek antiquity, see Robert Pogue Harrison, *Forests* 177–80 and Simon Schama, *Landscape and Memory* 176.

42 On the elm, see *The* Aeneid *of Henry Howard Earl of Surrey*, ed. Florence H. Ridley, 94. On the oak, see Thomas Twyne, trans., *The whole .XII. Bookes of the Aeneidos of Virgill* E4ʳ.

43 For a brilliant account of how the vegetative soul and its capacity for growth comes to describe (thwarted) social ambition and then revenge in this play, see Christopher Crosbie, "*Oeconomia* and the Vegetative Soul."

44 At the close of Kyd's play, Hieronimo "obliterates, in a sumptuously bloody catastrophe, the ideological gap between royal and subjected flesh." See Katharine Eisaman Maus, *Inwardness and Theater* 69. Hieronimo also fashions the Iberian rulers into versions of himself; on this mimetic phenomenon, see Christopher Crosbie, "*Oeconomia* and the Vegetative Soul" 31–2.

45 On this description of Hieronimo, see Kevin Dunn, "'Action, Passion, Motion'" 50.

46 See also Frank Ardolino, *Apocalypse and Armada* 28 and S.F. Johnson, "*The Spanish Tragedy*" 27.
47 On the rich meanings of fruit in relation to Horatio, see Brian Sheerin, "Patronage and Perverse Bestowal" 266–7.
48 Charles K. Cannon argues that in light of the Fourth Addition, act four, scene two works to "depict[] the utter impossibility of ever tearing out the principle of evil from this world." I would substitute social pretension for "evil" in this formulation. See "The Relation of the Additions" 237.
49 On Standish's career and influence in the field of woodland improvement, see Andrew McRae, *God Speed the Plough* 135–6 and John Perlin, *A Forest Journey* 192.
50 For a detailed account of deforestation in Drayton's poem, see Todd A. Borlik, *Ecocriticism and Early Modern Literature* 96–104.
51 On the narrative trope of "eco-apocalypse" in modern environmentalist writing and for more on how such tropes tend to produce in discourse the catastrophe that they describe, see Greg Garrard, *Ecocriticism* 99, 105.
52 For the use of Ovidian deforestation as a hallmark of the colonial imagination, see Rebecca Ann Bach, *Colonial Transformations* 1–4.
53 In a note outlining a psychoanalytic reading of this fantasy, Robert N. Watson adduces Jonson's masque because, in it, Pallas vows that milk will flow freely in the neo-Golden Age. See *Back to Nature* 337 n. 6.
54 On this tendency, see Ken Hiltner, ed., *Renaissance Ecology* 1–2. See also Raymond Williams, *The Country and the City* 35–45.
55 On the Golden Age and New World geography, Harry Levin, *The Myth of the Golden Age* 58–83.
56 This sentiment appears in a poem directly after the dedicatory epistle in the pamphlet's second edition. According to the *Oxford Dictionary of National Biography*, Arthur Hopton was a celebrated seventeenth-century mathematician, maker of almanacs, and surveyor.
57 On the chauvinism of Kyd's play, see Frank Ardolino, *Apocalypse and Armada* 142–66; Ronald Broude, "Time, Truth, and Right"; and Eugene D. Hill, "Senecan and Vergilian Perspectives."
58 Isabella says in act four, scene two that she will burn the tree's roots, and as we saw in the previous chapter, playing with fire inside an early modern theatre could have unfortunate consequences. In an untimely way, such fiery actions – even if never actually staged in the early seventeenth century – could open a vista onto the fire that destroyed the Fortune on 9 December 1621.
59 On the "radical" designs at the Fortune, including the satyr-decorated pillars or "terms," see John Orrell, "The Architecture of the Fortune Playhouse," 15, 23.
60 On fire's status as "the most self-evident expression of an antitheatricalism

intrinsic to performance," see Ellen Mackay, *Persecution, Plague, and Fire* 147.

61 On the recurring trope of the "plucked" human-botanical body in the drama, see Jean E. Feerick, "Groveling with Earth" 233–4.

4: "There's wood enough within": *The Tempest*'s Logs and the Resources of Shakespeare's Globe

1 On the matter of Caliban's language, see also Stephen J. Greenblatt, "Learning to Curse."

2 On the effects of early modern English colonization on "place" as well on indigenous inhabitants, see Ken Hiltner, *What Else Is Pastoral?* 156–73.

3 On this (former) plenty, see L.T. Fitz, "The Vocabulary of the Environment" 45.

4 I hedge in this claim about the lime tree because, although the *Norton Shakespeare* incudes reference to this citrus tree, the Arden edition of the play supplies "line" – or clothesline – instead of "lime." See William Shakespeare, *The Tempest*, eds. Virginia Mason Vaughan and Alden T. Vaughan, 257 n. 193. I follow the *Norton* treatment of the passage.

5 On deforestation in *The Tempest*, see Geraldo U. de Sousa, "Alien Habitats" and Gabriel Egan, *Green Shakespeare* 155–7.

6 The paradigmatic essay on colonialist discourse in the play is Paul Brown, "'This Thing of Darkness I Acknowledge Mine.'" See also Peter Hulme, *Colonial Encounters*.

7 Representative examples of such reorientations include David Scott Kastan, "'The Duke of Milan / And His Brave Son'" and Richard Wilson, "Voyage to Tunis."

8 Peter Hulme, *Colonial Encounters* 108 employs the figure of the palimpsest to articulate the Atlantic and Mediterranean contexts of *The Tempest*'s colonialist discourse. Fuchs explicitly follows Hulme here.

9 For a fishier ecological figure, see Edward M. Test, "*The Tempest*."

10 I borrow this apt phrase from Jeffrey S. Theis, "Primitive Architecture, Temporary Dwelling?" which is an unpublished essay shared with participants in "Shakespeare's Green Scenes," a seminar conducted at the 2011 SAA in Bellevue, WA.

11 Although there are no recorded performances of the play at the Globe, it could still have been mounted there. On this point, see Stephen Orgel, ed., *The Tempest* 64.

12 On the history of this term, see Joan Thirsk, *Economic Policy and Projects*.

13　Important studies of Shakespeare's intertextuality in *The Tempest* include
　　Barbara Fuchs, "Conquering Islands"; Heather James, *Shakespeare's Troy*
　　189–221; and Barbara A. Mowat, "'Knowing I loved my books.'"

14　For a careful reading of the politics of this textual borrowing, see David Nor-
　　brook, "'What Cares These Roarers for the Name of King?'" 27–34.

15　For general accounts of Shakespeare's use of Ovid in *The Tempest*, see John
　　Gillies, "Shakespeare's Virginian Masque" and Sarah Annes Brown, "Ovid,
　　Golding, and *The Tempest*."

16　On the isomorphism and shared materiality of ships and theatres, see Gary
　　Taylor, "*Hamlet* in Africa" 234–5.

17　On these imperial and lineal points, see also Jean E. Feerick, *Strangers in
　　Blood* 116.

18　On this tendency of early modern English literary texts to figure the colonial
　　enterprise as a return trip home, see Jeffrey Knapp, *An Empire Nowhere*.

19　These preachers may have in mind George Chapman, Ben Jonson, and John
　　Marston when they call out humorists, since the drama on which they collab-
　　orated (*Eastward Ho*) features a scene in its third act in which seamen headed
　　to the Virginia colony reveal their greedy motives for the venture.

20　In the propaganda that I survey here only Bacon's "Of Plantations" 104 and
　　Crashaw's sermon, G3ᵛ elaborate the fact that this "quick fix" requires signif-
　　icant time and labour, both of which give the lie to the idea of what Crashaw
　　terms "*present profit*."

21　On Drayton, the promotional literature on Virginia, and the myth of the
　　Golden Age in America, see David McInnis, "The Golden Man."

22　For a similar list of desirable colonists, see also Francis Bacon, "Of Planta-
　　tions" 104.

23　On the building of houses and the enclosing of land for agriculture and gar-
　　dens as the distinctive "sign" of English colonialist practice, see Patricia Seed,
　　Ceremonies of Possession 16–40.

24　On this temporal logic, see Jonathan Gil Harris, *Marvellous Repossessions*
　　39–40.

25　The full passage suggests that the "golden dreame" also encompasses the
　　fantasy of "greedy" investors looking to make "gaine," likely in the form of
　　gold.

26　For more on the play's distance from the colonialist venture, see also David
　　Scott Kastan, "'The Duke of Milan / And His Brave Son'" 275 and Deborah
　　Willis, "Shakespeare's *Tempest*" 256–68.

27　On this phrase's use to describe Fradubio's imprisonment inside a tree, see
　　Edmund Spenser, *The Faerie Queene* Bk. I, Canto II, 42.

28 For a helpful account of the literary borrowing, see Sarah Annes Brown, "Ovid, Golding, and *The Tempest*" 6–10. See also Stephen Orgel, *The Authentic Shakespeare* 183.

29 For a timely reading of deforestation in the play that nonetheless declines to see magic as the force producing all the island's logs, see Gabriel Egan, *Green Shakespeare* 167.

30 The dependence of the Europeans on "native" labour perhaps forges a resemblance between Prospero and the English colonists who infamously refused to fend for their own survival in Virginia. See Peter Hulme, *Colonial Encounters* 128, 296 n. 74.

31 On Prospero's relentless policing and transplanting of a Europeanized social order on the island, see Jean E. Feerick, *Strangers in Blood* 116.

32 For a longer view on the historical tendency to exercise power to secure energy, see my "Wooden Slavery."

33 On the influence of Aeneas's plucking of the golden bough episode on this moment, see Donna B. Hamilton, *Virgil and* The Tempest 88–91.

34 On the relation between character and work in this scene, see William Rockett, "Labor and Virtue."

35 On the Neoplatonism of Ferdinand's base task, see Donna B. Hamilton, *Virgil and* The Tempest 97–8.

36 For illuminating readings of the political and social implications of this agency, see Barbara Ann Sebek, "Peopling, Profiting, and Pleasure" 469–70 and Melissa E. Sanchez, "Seduction and Service."

37 On the "egalitarianism" of Miranda's gesture to carry Ferdinand's logs, see David Schalkwyk, *Shakespeare, Love and Service* 108–9.

38 "Troth," or *treow*, is a homonym in Old English for "tree." On this philology, see Richard Firth Green, *A Crisis of Truth* 10.

39 On contracts and sticks, see Simon Schama, *Landscape and Memory* 153 and Richard Firth Green, *A Crisis of Truth* 51–2.

40 On the Vergilian intertext of the anti-masque's banquet, see John Pitcher, "A Theatre of the Future" 193–6.

41 For a brief exploration of the colonialist dimensions of food in the play, see Peter Hulme, *Colonial Encounters* 131–2.

42 On the disingenuousness of Prospero's evaluation, see David Norbrook, "'What Cares These Roarers for the Name of King?'" 37.

43 For an account of the persecutory intent of plays-within-plays in the tragedies, see Ellen Mackay, *Persecution, Plague, and Fire* 47–78.

44 On the relation between the language of pain and of trees, especially the pine, in this play, see Mary Thomas Crane, *Shakespeare's Brain* 185.

45 For an important discussion of the recognizably English features of the landscape in Ceres's depiction of plenty, see Charlotte Scott, *Shakespeare's Nature*. I thank Charlotte for sharing this unpublished work with me.

46 On the carpet, see Stephen Greenblatt, *The Norton Shakespeare* 3102 n. 5.

47 On the rushes and/or a green fabric, see Stephen Orgel, ed. *The Tempest* 175 n. 83. Orgel further notes the cross-reference to *Midsummer* in this note, but he assigns the passage to Bottom, not to Quince.

48 On the range of early modern meanings for "globe," the point of departure for which is this passage, see Peter Donaldson, "'All which it inherit'" 185–90.

49 The violence of this sound approximates the "confused" actions undertaken by participants of Jacobean masques, who, after the performance had concluded, would duck into the architectural space known as the "void" and demolish the sumptuous banquet prepared precisely for its obliteration. On this ritual, see Patricia Fumerton, *Cultural Aesthetics*.

50 *The Tempest* may echo here the onstage construction of Barabas's "dainty gallery" in *The Jew of Malta*, but, in so doing, also mystifies the carpentry that Marlowe's protagonist performs and supervises (5.5.33).

51 Although, as Stephen Orgel observes, "despite the normal use of theatrical terminology in descriptions of masques – scene, stage, proscenium, etc. – the masquing hall was never referred to as a theater," *The Tempest* perhaps scrambles the distinction by punningly calling its "masquing hall" the Globe. See *The Authentic Shakespeare* 61.

52 On the depiction of Ferdinand's labour as a "rewriting of the building at Carthage ... that do[es] not emphasize the notions of expansion and domination associated with colonization," see Donna B. Hamilton, *Virgil and* The Tempest 102–3. I add the colonialist aspect of this building back into Shakespeare's play.

53 For accounts of Prospero as playwright and theatre impresario, see Peter Hulme, *Colonial Encounters* 115–20 and Daniel Vitkus, "'Meaner Ministers'" 411.

54 On this performance at court, see Stephen Orgel, ed. *The Tempest* 1.

55 I excerpt Sir Henry Wotton's account of the Globe's burning from *The Norton Shakespeare* 3311.

56 I take the Latin quotations from Virgil, *Eclogues, Georgics, Aeneid 1–6* 292. The passage appears in this edition as *Aeneid* 1, ll. 427–9. For a fuller account of how the future is the past in this play, see Jonathan Gil Harris, *Marvellous Repossessions*.

57 Carthage could also figure the colonizing agent in early modern letters. In Florio's Montaigne, Shakespeare would have come across the "testimonie"

of "certain Carthaginians having sailed athwart the *Atlantike* Sea, without the strait of *Gibraltar*, after long time, they at last discovered a great fertill Iland, all replenished with goodly woods" and other salubrious resources. See Montaigne, "Of the Caniballes" 217–18. For other early modern citations of Carthage in both contexts, see Donna B. Hamilton, *Virgil and* The Tempest ix–x and David Scott Wilson-Okamura, "Virgilian Models of Colonization" 717–19.

58 I cite from the 1584 translation because this passage has not been transliterated in the 1573 edition, perhaps because in 1573 there was no equivalent of Dido's "theatre" in early modern London, but there was at least one – the Theatre – since 1576.

59 Set partly on a Greek island, a recent filmic adaptation of the play has its Prospero figure supervise the building of a classicized amphitheater and may thus pick up on the cues to construction in Shakespeare. On this film and its green implications, see Sharon O'Dair, "*The Tempest* as *Tempest*" 171.

60 On Prospero's magic as "the romance equivalent of marital law," see Stephen Greenblatt, *Shakespearean Negotiations* 156. On the "effectless" nature of Prospero's theatre, see Heather James, *Shakespeare's Troy* 196, 216–21.

61 Not all English colonialist ventures exhibited such strident antitheatricalism. John Smith, for instance, claimed to have witnessed a masque produced by native women in Virginia. On this performance, see Rebecca Ann Bach, *Colonial Transformations* 191–219. For further counter-examples, see Claire Sponsler, "Medieval America" and Gary Taylor, "*Hamlet* in Africa" 232. William Sanders's short story "The Undiscovered" is a humorous account of the performance of *Hamlet*, which the dramatist Spearshaker (Shakes Spear) writes and mounts among the Cherokee. The story also sheds light on the eco-politics of theatrical performance insofar as one character (BigKiller) "complain[s] about the waste of timber and labor" required for building the "platform" where the play is staged (31). I thank Daniel Heath Justice for this reference.

62 On the idolatry, Catholicism, and the figure of the "book" in Virginian discourse, see Stephen Greenblatt, *Shakespearean Negotiations* 33 and John Gillies, "The Figure of the New World" 197–8.

63 On the persistence of pre-Reformation performance practice in the New World, see Claire Sponsler, "Medieval America."

64 *King Lear* was the other play. On this publication, see Michael Dobson, "Fairly Brave New World" 193.

65 In the fifth satire included in *Skialetheia*, D6^r, Edward Guilpin likens a "troubled" man wearing black to this depiction of the Theatre.

66 I adapt this apt phrase from Glen A. Love, "Shakespeare's Origin of Species" 138, where it describes Caliban.

Epilogue: The Afterlives of the Globe

1 On the manuscript's status as a forgery, see Herbert Berry, *Shakespeare's Playhouses* 78.
2 For a transcription of this document, see Gerald Eades Bentley, *The Jacobean and Caroline Stage*, vol. 6, 200.
3 Furnivall printed a transcription of this bogus document in the Supplement to *Harrison's* Description of England *in Shakespere's Youth* 221.
4 On such tree felling and sentiment against the royal forest, see Jeffrey S. Theis, *Writing the Forest* 169, 219.
5 See Julian Bowsher and Pat Miller, *The Rose and the Globe*.
6 I quote from the playbill to Christopher Marlowe's *Doctor Faustus*, which I attended on 2 July 2011. Although there is no pagination here, the excerpt occurs in a section called "Rebuilding Shakespeare's Globe." But according to J.R. Mulryne and Margaret Shewring, the "original Globe" has not been "rebuilt." Rather, that project is "an unattainable ideal." See "The Once and Future Globe" 15.
7 For an account of the complex environmental politics of building a replica Elizabethan theatre in Oregon, where forestry continues to be an important industry and an environmental bugbear, see Sharon O'Dair, *Class, Critics, and Shakespeare* 89–114.

Bibliography

Aaron, Melissa D. "The Globe and *Henry V* as Business Document." *Studies in English Literature, 1500–1900* 40.2 (2000): 277–92. http://dx.doi.org/10.2307/1556129.

Agnew, Jean-Christophe. *Worlds Apart: The Market and the Theater in Anglo-American Thought, 1550–1750*. Cambridge: Cambridge UP, 1986. http://dx.doi.org/10.1017/CBO9780511571404.

Albion, Robert Greenhalgh. *Forests and Sea Power: The Timber Problem of the Royal Navy, 1652–1862*. Hamden: Archon, 1965.

Appuhn, Karl. *A Forest on the Sea: Environmental Expertise in Renaissance Venice*. Baltimore: Johns Hopkins UP, 2009.

Archdeacon, Daniel, trans. *A true Discourse of the Armie which the King of Spaine caused to bee assembled in the Haven of Lisbon, in the Kingdome of Portugall, in the yeare 1588. against England*. London, 1588.

Ardolino, Frank. *Apocalypse and Armada in Kyd's* Spanish Tragedy. Kirksville: Truman State UP, 1995.

Ardolino, Frank. "Severed and Brazen Heads: Headhunting in Elizabethan Drama." *Journal of Evolutionary Psychology* 4.3–4 (1983): 169–81.

Ardolino, Frank. "'Thus Glories England Over All the West': Setting as National Encomium in Robert Greene's *Friar Bacon and Friar Bungay*." *Journal of Evolutionary Psychology* 9.3–4 (1988): 218–29.

Aston, Margaret. *England's Iconoclasts: Laws Against Images*. Vol. 1. Oxford: Clarendon, 1988.

Bach, Rebecca Ann. *Colonial Transformations: The Cultural Production of the New Atlantic World, 1580–1640*. New York: Palgrave, 2000.

Bacon, Francis. "Of Plantations." In *Essays of Francis Bacon*, with an introduction by Oliphant Smeaton. London: Dent, 1928. 104–6.

Barkan, Leonard. "Diana and Actaeon: The Myth as Synthesis." *English Literary*

Renaissance 10.3 (1980): 317–59. http://dx.doi.org/10.1111/j.1475-6757.1980 .tb00720.x.

Barton, Anne. *Ben Jonson, Dramatist.* Cambridge: Cambridge UP, 1984. http:// dx.doi.org/10.1017/CBO9780511518836.

Barton, Anne. *Essays, Mainly Shakespearean.* Cambridge: Cambridge UP, 1994.

Bate, Jonathan. *The Song of the Earth.* Cambridge: Harvard UP, 2000.

Beadle, Richard, and Pamela M. King, eds. *The Crucifixion.* In *York Mystery Plays: A Selection in Modern Spelling.* Oxford: Oxford UP, 1995. 211–21.

Beaver, Daniel C. *Hunting and the Politics of Violence before the English Civil War.* Cambridge: Cambridge UP, 2008. http://dx.doi.org/10.1017/ CBO9780511660184.

Bentley, Gerald Eades. *The Jacobean and Caroline Stage.* Vol. 6. Oxford: Clarendon, 1968.

Berger, Harry, Jr. *Second World and Green World: Studies in Renaissance Fiction-Making.* Berkeley: U of California P, 1990.

Berry, Herbert. *Shakespeare's Playhouses.* New York: AMS, 1987.

The Bible. London, 1616. Authorized King James Vers.

Birrell, Jean. "Common Rights in the Medieval Forest: Disputes and Conflicts in the Thirteenth Century." *Past and Present* 117.1 (1987): 22–49.

Borlik, Todd A. *Ecocriticism and Early Modern Literature: Green Pastures.* London: Routledge, 2011.

Borlik, Todd Andrew. "'More than Art': Clockwork Automata, the Extemporizing Actor, and the Brazen Head in *Friar Bacon and Friar Bungay.*" In *The Automaton in English Renaissance Literature.* Ed. Wendy Beth Hyman. Farnham: Ashgate, 2011. 129–44.

Borlik, Todd Andrew. "Mute Timber? Fiscal Forestry and Environmental Stichomythia in the *Old Arcadia.*" Hallock, Kamps, and Raber 31–53.

Bowerbank, Sylvia. *Speaking for Nature: Women and Ecologies of Early Modern England.* Baltimore: Johns Hopkins UP, 2004.

Bowsher, Julian, and Pat Miller. *The Rose and the Globe – Playhouses of Shakespeare's Bankside, Southwark: Excavations 1988–90.* London: Museum of London Archeology, 2009.

Bristol, Michael D. "Shamelessness in Arden: Early Modern Theatre and the Obsolescence of Popular Theatricality." In *Print, Manuscript, Performance: The Changing Relations of the Media in Early Modern England.* Ed. Arthur F. Marotti and Michael D. Bristol. Columbus: Ohio State UP, 2000. 279–306.

Broude, Ronald. "Time, Truth, and Right in *The Spanish Tragedy.*" *Studies in Philology* 68.2 (1971): 130–45.

Brown, Paul. "'This Thing of Darkness I Acknowledge Mine': *The Tempest* and the Discourse of Colonialism." Rpt. in Shakespeare, The Tempest: *A Case Study* 205–29.

Brown, Sarah Annes. "Ovid, Golding, and *The Tempest*." Translation and Literature 3.3 (1994): 3–29. http://dx.doi.org/10.3366/tal.1994.3.3.3.

Bruckner, Lynne, and Dan Brayton, eds. *Ecocritical Shakespeare*. Farnham: Ashgate, 2011.

Bruster, Douglas. *Drama and the Market in the Age of Shakespeare*. Cambridge: Cambridge UP, 1992. http://dx.doi.org/10.1017/CBO9780511553080.

Bruster, Douglas. "Local *Tempest*: Shakespeare and the Work of the Early Modern Playhouse." Murphy 257–75.

Bruster, Douglas. "The New Materialism in Renaissance Studies." In *Material Culture and Cultural Materialisms in the Middle Ages and the Renaissance*. Ed. Curtis Perry. Turnhout: Brepols, 2001. 225–38.

Bruster, Douglas. "On a Certain Tendency in Economic Criticism of Shakespeare." In *Money and the Age of Shakespeare: Essays in New Economic Criticism*. Ed. Linda Woodbridge. New York: Palgrave, 2003. 67–77.

Bryant, J.A., Jr. "Falstaff and the Renewal of Windsor." *PMLA* 89.2 (1974): 296–301. http://dx.doi.org/10.2307/461452.

Burgess, Miranda. "Transport: Mobility, Anxiety, and the Romantic Poetics of Feeling." *Studies in Romanticism* 49.2 (2010): 229–60.

Bushnell, Rebecca W. *A Culture of Teaching: Early Modern Humanism in Theory and Practice*. Ithaca: Cornell UP, 1996.

Bushnell, Rebecca. *Green Desire: Imagining Early Modern English Gardens*. Ithaca: Cornell UP, 2003.

Butler, Judith. *Bodies That Matter: On the Discursive Limits of "Sex"*. New York: Routledge, 1993.

Campana, Joseph. "Reading Bleeding Trees: The Poetics of Other People's Pain in 'The Legend of Holiness.'" In *The Sense of Suffering: Constructions of Physical Pain in Early Modern Culture*. Ed. Jans Frans van Dijkhuizen and Karl A.E. Enenkel. Leiden: Brill, 2009. 347–76.

Campos, Edmund Valentine. "West of Eden: American Gold, Spanish Greed, and the Discourses of English Imperialism." In *Rereading the Black Legend: The Discourses of Religious and Racial Difference in the Renaissance Empires*. Ed. Margaret R. Greer, Walter D. Mignolo, and Maureen Quilligan. Chicago: U of Chicago P, 2007. 247–69.

Cannon, Charles K. "The Relation of the Additions of *The Spanish Tragedy* to the Original Play." *Studies in English Literature, 1500–1900* 2.2 (1962): 229–39. http://dx.doi.org/10.2307/449502.

Capp, Bernard. "Hopton, Arthur (c.1580–1614)." *Oxford Dictionary of National Biography*. Oxford UP, 2004. Web.

Carleton, George. *A Thankfvll Remembrance of Gods Mercie*. London, 1627.

Cartwright, Kent. *Theatre and Humanism: English Drama in the Sixteenth Century*. Cambridge: Cambridge UP, 1999. http://dx.doi.org/10.1017/CBO9780511483479.

Cavendish, Margaret, Duchess of Newcastle. *Poems and Phancies*. London, 1664.

Cerasano, S.P. "The Fortune Contract in Reverse." *Shakespeare Studies* 37 (2009): 79–98.

Cerasano, S.P. "The Geography of Henslowe's Diary." *Shakespeare Quarterly* 56.3 (2005): 328–53. http://dx.doi.org/10.1353/shq.2006.0004.

Chambers, E.K. *The Elizabethan Stage*. Vol. 2. Oxford: Clarendon, 1951.

Chapman, George, Ben Jonson, and John Marston. *Eastward Ho*. Ed. R.W. Van Fossen. Manchester: Manchester UP, 1999.

Clow, A., and N.L. Clow. "The Timber Famine and the Development of Technology." *Annals of Science* 12.2 (1956): 85–102. http://dx.doi.org/10.1080/00033795600200076.

Coch, Christine. "An Arbor of One's Own? Aemilia Lanyer and the Early Modern Garden." *Renaissance and Reformation* 28.2 (2004): 97–118.

Cole, Maija Jansson. "A New Account of the Burning of the Globe." *Shakespeare Quarterly* 32.3 (1981): 352. http://dx.doi.org/10.2307/2870251.

Collington, Philip D. "'I Would Thy Husband Were Dead': *The Merry Wives of Windsor* as Mock Domestic Tragedy." *English Literary Renaissance* 30.2 (2000): 184–212. http://dx.doi.org/10.1111/j.1475-6757.2000.tb01169.x.

Cotton, Nancy. "Castrating (W)itches: Impotence and Magic in *The Merry Wives of Windsor*." *Shakespeare Quarterly* 38.3 (1987): 320–6. http://dx.doi.org/10.2307/2870506.

Cox, John D., and David Scott Kastan, eds. *A New History of Early English Drama*. New York: Columbia UP, 1997.

Craig, D.H. "Authorial Styles and Frequencies of Very Common Words: Jonson, Shakespeare, and the Additions to *The Spanish Tragedy*." *Style* 26.2 (1992): 199–220.

Crane, Mary Thomas. *Shakespeare's Brain: Reading with Cognitive Theory*. Princeton: Princeton UP, 2001.

Crashaw, William. *A Sermon Preached in London before the right honorable the Lord Lawarre*. London, 1610.

Crewe, Jonathan V. "The Theatre of the Idols: Marlowe, Rankins, and Theatrical Images." *Theatre Journal* 36.3 (1984): 321–33. http://dx.doi.org/10.2307/3206950.

Crosbie, Christopher. "*Oeconomia* and the Vegetative Soul: Rethinking Revenge in *The Spanish Tragedy*." *English Literary Renaissance* 38.1 (2008): 3–33. http://dx.doi.org/10.1111/j.1475-6757.2008.00115.x.

Crupi, Charles W. *Robert Greene*. Boston: Twayne, 1986.

Dahlquist, Mark. "Love and Technological Iconoclasm in Robert Greene's *Friar Bacon and Friar Bungay.*" *ELH* 78.1 (2011): 51–77. http://dx.doi.org/10.1353/elh.2011.0007.

Davies, Douglas. "The Evocative Symbolism of Trees." In *The Iconography of Landscape: Essays on the Symbolic Representation, Design and Use of Past Environments*. Ed. Denis Cosgrove and Stephen Daniels. Cambridge: Cambridge UP, 1988. 32–42.

Dawson, Anthony B. "Madness and Meaning: *The Spanish Tragedy.*" *Journal of Dramatic Theory and Criticism* 2.1 (1987): 53–67.

A Declaration Of The Cavses, Which Mooved The chiefe Commanders of the Nauie of her most excellent Maiestie … to take and arrest in the mouth of the Riuer of Lisbone, certaine Shippes of corne and other prouisions of warre bound for the said Citie. London, 1589.

de Grazia, Margreta. *Hamlet without Hamlet*. Cambridge: Cambridge UP, 2007.

Dekker, Thomas. *The Whore of Babylon*. In *The Dramatic Works of Thomas Dekker*. Vol. 2. Ed. Fredson Bowers. Cambridge: Cambridge UP, 1955. 496–584.

Deloney, Thomas. "A new Ballet of the straunge and most cruell Whippes which the Spanyards had prepared to whippe and torment English men and women." In *The Works of Thomas Deloney*. Ed. Francis Oscar Mann. Oxford: Clarendon, 1912. 479–82.

de Sousa, Geraldo U., "Alien Habitats in *The Tempest.*" Murphy 439–61.

Dessen, Alan C. *Elizabethan Stage Conventions and Modern Interpreters*. Cambridge: Cambridge UP, 1984. http://dx.doi.org/10.1017/CBO9780511554179.

Diamond, Jared. *Collapse: How Societies Choose to Fail or Succeed*. New York: Viking, 2005.

Diehl, Huston. *Staging Reform, Reforming the Stage: Protestantism and Popular Theater in Early Modern England*. Ithaca: Cornell UP, 1997.

Dobson, Michael. "Fairly Brave New World: Shakespeare, the American Colonies, and the American Revolution." *Renaissance Drama* 23 (1992): 189–207.

Dolan, Frances E. "Ashes and 'the Archive': The London Fire of 1666, Partisanship, and Proof." *Journal of Medieval and Early Modern Studies* 31.2 (2001): 379–408. http://dx.doi.org/10.1215/10829636-31-2-379.

Dolan, Frances E. "The Subordinate('s) Plot: Petty Treason and the Forms of Domestic Rebellion." *Shakespeare Quarterly* 43.3 (1992): 317–40. http://dx.doi.org/10.2307/2870531.

Dollimore, Jonathan. *Radical Tragedy: Religion, Ideology and Power in the Drama of Shakespeare and His Contemporaries*. Brighton: Harvester P, 1984.

Donaldson, Peter. "'All which it inherit': Shakespeare, Globes and Global Media." *Shakespeare Survey* 52 (1999): 183–200. http://dx.doi.org/10.1017/CCOL0521660742.015.

Donne, John. "The First Anniversary." In *John Donne: The Complete English Poems*. Ed. C.A. Patrides. London: Dent, 1999. 247–64.

Drayton, Michael. "Ode to the Virginian Voyage." In *The Genesis of The United States: A Narrative of the Movement in England, 1605-1616, which Resulted in the Plantation of North America by Englishmen, Disclosing the Contest between England and Spain for the Possession of the Soil now Occupied by the United States of America.* Vol. 1. Ed. Alexander Brown. London: William Heinemann, 1890. 86–7.

Drayton, Michael. *Poly-Olbion*. London, 1612.

Dunn, Kevin. "'Action, Passion, Motion': The Gestural Politics of Counsel in *The Spanish Tragedy.*" *Renaissance Drama* 31 (2002): 27–60.

Edwards, Philip, ed. "Introduction." *The Spanish Tragedy*. By Thomas Kyd. London: Methuen, 1959. xvii–lxviii.

Egan, Gabriel. *Green Shakespeare: From Ecopolitics to Ecocriticism*. London: Routledge, 2006.

Egan, Gabriel. "Reconstructions of the Globe: A Retrospective." *Shakespeare Survey* 52 (1999): 1–16. http://dx.doi.org/10.1017/CCOL0521660742.001.

Empson, William. *Some Versions of Pastoral*. London: Penguin, 1995.

Erickson, Peter. "The Order of the Garter, the Cult of Elizabeth, and Class–Gender Tension in *The Merry Wives of Windsor.*" In *Shakespeare Reproduced: The Text in History and Ideology*. Ed. Jean E. Howard and Marion F. O'Connor. London: Methuen, 1987. 116–40.

Erne, Lukas. *Beyond* The Spanish Tragedy*: A Study of the Works of Thomas Kyd*. Manchester: Manchester UP, 2001.

Esler, Anthony. "Robert Greene and the Spanish Armada." *English Literary History* 32.3 (1965): 314–32. http://dx.doi.org/10.2307/2872164.

Estok, Simon C. *Ecocriticism and Shakespeare: Reading Ecophobia*. New York: Palgrave, 2011. http://dx.doi.org/10.1057/9780230118744.

Evelyn, John. *A Character of England, As it was lately presented in a Letter, to a Noble Man of France*. London, 1659.

Evelyn, John. *Sylva, Or A Discourse of Forest-Trees, And The Propagation of Timber*. In *The Writings of John Evelyn*. Ed. Guy de la Bédoyère. Woodbridge: Boydell, 1995. 318–32.

"evergreen, adj. and n." *Oxford*.

Extracts from the Accounts of the Revels at Court, in the Reigns of Queen Elizabeth and King James I. London, 1842.

The Famous History of Frier Bacon. London, 1679.

Fedorowicz, J.K. *England's Baltic Trade in the Early Seventeenth Century: A*

Study in Anglo-Polish Commercial Diplomacy. Cambridge: Cambridge UP, 1980. http://dx.doi.org/10.1017/CBO9780511896170.

Feerick, Jean. "Botanical Shakespeares: The Racial Logic of Plant Life in *Titus Andronicus.*" *South Central Review* 26.1–2 (2009): 82–102. http://dx.doi .org/10.1353/scr.0.0043.

Feerick, Jean E. "Groveling with Earth in Kyd and Shakespeare's Historical Tragedies." Feerick and Nardizzi 231–52.

Feerick, Jean E. *Strangers in Blood: Relocating Race in the Renaissance*. Toronto: U of Toronto P, 2010.

Feerick, Jean E., and Vin Nardizzi, eds. *The Indistinct Human in Renaissance Literature*. New York: Palgrave, 2012. http://dx.doi.org/10.1057/ 9781137015693.

Field, John. *A godly exhortation, by occasion of the late iudgement of God, shewed at Parris-Garden*. London, 1583.

The first voyage made to the coasts of America, with two barks, captains Mr Philip Amadas, and Mr Arthur Barlowe, who discovered part of the country now called Virginia, An. 1584. Hakluyt 270–5.

Fishman, Charles. *The Big Thirst: The Secret Life and Turbulent Future of Water*. New York: Free, 2011.

Fitz, L.T. "The Vocabulary of the Environment in *The Tempest.*" *Shakespeare Quarterly* 26.1 (1975): 42–7. http://dx.doi.org/10.2307/2869265.

Fleming, Juliet. "How To Look at a Printed Flower." *Word & Image: A Journal of Verbal/Visual Enquiry* 22.2 (2006): 165–87.

Flinn, Michael W. "Timber and the Advance of Technology: A Reconsideration." *Annals of Science* 15.2 (1959): 109–20. http://dx.doi.org/10.1080/ 00033795900200108.

Foakes, R.A. *Illustrations of the English Stage, 1580–1642*. London: Scolar, 1985.

For the Colony in Virginea Britannia. Lawes Diuine, Morall and Martiall, &c. Vol. 3. London: Rpt. in Force, 1612.

Force, Peter, comp. *Tracts and Other Papers, Relating Principally to the Origin, Settlement, and Progress of the Colonies in North America, From the Discovery of the Country to the Year 1776*. 4 Vols. New York: Peter Smith, 1947.

Freedman, Barbara. "Shakespearean Chronology, Ideological Complexity, and Floating Texts: Something Is Rotten in Windsor." *Shakespeare Quarterly* 45.2 (1994): 190–210. http://dx.doi.org/10.2307/2871217.

Freud, Sigmund. "The 'Uncanny.'" In *The Standard Edition of the Complete Psychological Works of Sigmund Freud*. Vol. 17. Ed. James Strachey. London: Hogarth, 1955. 219–52.

Frye, Northrop. *A Natural Perspective: The Development of Shakespearean Comedy and Romance*. New York: Columbia UP, 1965.

Fuchs, Barbara. "Conquering Islands: Contextualizing *The Tempest.*" *Shakespeare Quarterly* 48.1 (1997): 45–62. http://dx.doi.org/10.2307/2871400.

Fuller, Thomas. *The History Of the Worthies Of England.* London, 1662.

Fumerton, Patricia. *Cultural Aesthetics: Renaissance Literature and the Practice of Social Ornament.* Chicago: U of Chicago P, 1991.

Furnivall, F.J. "The End of Shakespeare's Playhouses." *Academy* 547 (28 October 1882): 314–15.

Furnivall, F.J., ed. *Harrison's* Description of England *in Shakespere's Youth.* London: Chatto, 1908–9.

Gallenca, Christiane. "Ritual and Folk Custom in *The Merry Wives of Windsor.*" *Cahiers Elisabethains* 27 (1985): 27–41.

Garrard, Greg. *Ecocriticism.* London: Routledge, 2004.

Garrard, Greg. "Heidegger Nazism Ecocriticism." *ISLE* 17.2 (2010): 251–71.

Gayton, Edmund. *Pleasant Notes upon Don Quixot.* London, 1654.

Gerbi, Antonello. *Nature in the New World: From Christopher Columbus to Gonzalo Fernández de Oviedo.* Trans. Jeremy Moyle. Pittsburgh: U of Pittsburgh P, 1985.

Gilby, Anthony. *A Pleasavnt Dialogve, Betweene a Souldior of Barwicke, and an English Chaplaine.* London, 1581.

Gillies, John. "The Figure of the New World in *The Tempest.*" Hulme and Sherman 180–200.

Gillies, John. "Shakespeare's Virginian Masque." *ELH* 53.4 (1986): 673–707. http://dx.doi.org/10.2307/2873170.

Goldberg, Jonathan. "The History That Will Be." In *Premodern Sexualities*. Ed. Louise Fradenburg and Carla Freccero. New York: Routledge, 1996. 3–21.

Goldberg, Jonathan. *Tempest in the Caribbean.* Minneapolis: U of Minnesota P, 2004.

Goldberg, Jonathan. "What Do Women Want? *The Merry Wives of Windsor.*" *Criticism* 51.3 (2009): 367–83. http://dx.doi.org/10.1353/crt.0.0109.

Gosson, Stephen. *Playes Confuted in five Actions*, with a preface by Arthur Freeman. London, 1972.

Gosson, Stephen. *The S[c]hoole of Abuse.* London, 1579.

Grav, Peter. "Money Changes Everything: Quarto and Folio *The Merry Wives of Windsor* and the Case for Revision." *Comparative Drama* 40.2 (2006): 217–40. http://dx.doi.org/10.1353/cdr.2006.0019.

Green, Harvey. *Wood: Craft, Culture, History.* New York: Viking, 2006.

Green, Richard Firth. *A Crisis of Truth: Literature and Law in Ricardian England.* Philadelphia: U of Pennsylvania P, 1999.

Greenblatt, Stephen J. "Learning to Curse: Aspects of Linguistic Colonialism in the Sixteenth Century." In *First Images of America: The Impact of the New*

World on the Old. Vol. 2. Ed. Fredi Chiappelli. Berkeley: U California P, 1976. 561–80.

Greenblatt, Stephen. *Shakespearean Negotiations: The Circulation of Social Energy in Renaissance England.* Berkeley: U of California P, 1988.

Greene, Robert. *The Defence of Conny Catching.* London, 1592.

Greene, Robert. *Friar Bacon and Friar Bungay.* Ed. Daniel Seltzer. Lincoln: U of Nebraska P, 1963.

Greene, Robert. *The Spanish Masquerado.* London, 1589.

Greg, W.W., ed. *The History of Orlando Furioso.* London: Malone Society Reprints, 1907.

Greg, W.W., ed. *John of Bordeaux, Or The Second Part of Friar Bacon.* London: Malone Society Reprints, 1935.

Griffin, Eric. "Ethos, Empire, and the Valiant Acts of Thomas Kyd's Tragedy of 'the Spains.'" *English Literary Renaissance* 31.2 (2001): 192–229. http://dx.doi.org/10.1111/j.1475-6757.2001.tb01187.x.

Griffin, Eric. "Nationalism, the Black Legend, and the Revised *Spanish Tragedy.*" *English Literary Renaissance* 39.2 (2009): 336–70. http://dx.doi.org/10.1111/j.1475-6757.2009.01050.x.

Griffin, Eric. "'Spain is Portugal / And Portugal is Spain': Transnational Attraction in the Stukeley Plays and *The Spanish Tragedy.*" *Journal for Early Modern Cultural Studies* 10.1 (2010): 95–116. http://dx.doi.org/10.2979/JEM.2010.10.1.95.

Grove, Richard H. *Green Imperialism: Colonial Expansion, Tropical Island Edens and the Origins of Environmentalism, 1600–1860.* Cambridge: Cambridge UP, 1997.

Guilpin, Edward. *Skialetheia; Or, A shadow of Truth, in certain Epigrams and Satyres.* London, 1598.

Gurr, Andrew. "The Bare Island." *Shakespeare Survey* 47 (1994): 24–43.

Gurr, Andrew. "Intertextuality at Windsor." *Shakespeare Quarterly* 38.2 (1987): 189–200. http://dx.doi.org/10.2307/2870560.

Gurr, Andrew. "Money or Audiences: The Impact of Shakespeare's Globe." *Theatre Notebook* 42 (1988): 3–14.

Gurr, Andrew. *The Shakespearean Stage, 1574–1642.* 3rd ed. Cambridge: Cambridge UP, 1997.

Gurr, Andrew. "Venues on the Verges: Theater Government between 1594 and 1614." *Shakespeare Quarterly* 61.4 (2010): 468–89.

Gurr, Andrew, and Mariko Ichikawa. *Staging in Shakespeare's Theatres.* Oxford: Oxford UP, 2000.

Habicht, Werner. "Tree Properties and Tree Scenes in Elizabethan Theater." *Renaissance Drama* 4 (1971): 69–92.

Hakluyt, Richard. *Voyages and Discoveries: The Principal Navigations, Voyages, Traffiques, and Discoveries of the English Nation.* Ed. Jack Beeching. London: Penguin, 1985.

"half-timber, n. and adj." *Oxford.*

Hallock, Thomas, Ivo Kamps, and Karen L. Raber, eds. *Early Modern Ecostudies: From the Florentine Codex to Shakespeare.* New York: Palgrave, 2008.

Halpern, Richard. *The Poetics of Primitive Accumulation: English Renaissance Culture and the Genealogy of Capital.* Ithaca: Cornell UP, 1991.

Hamilton, Donna B. "*The Spanish Tragedy*: A Speaking Picture." *English Literary Renaissance* 4.2 (1974): 203–17. http://dx.doi.org/10.1111/j.1475-6757.1974.tb01298.x.

Hamilton, Donna B. *Virgil and* The Tempest: *The Politics of Imitation.* Columbus: Ohio State UP, 1990.

Hammersley, G. "The Charcoal Iron Industry and Its Fuel, 1540–1750." *The Economic History Review* 26 (Nov. 1973): 593–613.

Hammersley, G. "The Crown Woods and Their Exploitation in the Sixteenth and Seventeenth Centuries." *Bulletin of the Institute of Historical Research* 30 (Nov. 1957): 136–61.

Hammersmith, James P. "The Death of Castile in *The Spanish Tragedy.*" *Renaissance Drama* 16 (1985): 1–16.

Hansen, Hans Jürgen, ed. *Architecture in Wood: A History of Wood Building and Its Techniques in Europe and North America.* Trans. Janet Seligman. London: Faber, 1971.

Harriot, Thomas. *A briefe and true report of the new found land of Virginia.* London, 1588.

Harris, Jonathan Gil. *Marvellous Repossessions:* The Tempest, *Globalization and the Waking Dream of Paradise.* Vancouver: Ronsdale, 2012.

Harris, Jonathan Gil. *Sick Economies: Drama, Mercantilism, and Disease in Shakespeare's England.* Philadelphia: U of Pennsylvania P, 2004.

Harris, Jonathan Gil. *Untimely Matter in the Time of Shakespeare.* Philadelphia: U of Pennsylvania P, 2009.

Harrison, Robert Pogue. *Forests: The Shadow of Civilization.* Chicago: U of Chicago P, 1992.

Harrison, William. "The second Booke, of the hystoricall description of Britaine." *Holinshed* 48ʳ–94ʳ.

Hartlib, Samuel. *His Legacy òf Husbandry.* London, 1655.

Hattaway, Michael. *Elizabethan Popular Theatre: Plays in Performance.* London: Routledge, 1982.

Heidegger, Martin. "The Question Concerning Technology." In *The Question Concerning Technology and Other Essays.* Trans. William Lovitt. New York: Harper Colophon, 1977. 3–35.

Helgerson, Richard. "The Busk Basket, the Witch, and the Queen of Fairies: The Women's World of Shakespeare's Windsor." In *Renaissance Culture and the Everyday*. Ed. Patricia Fumerton and Simon Hunt. Philadelphia: U of Pennsylvania P, 1999. 162–82.

Henslowe, Philip. *Henslowe's Diary*. 2nd ed. Ed. R.A. Foakes. Cambridge: Cambridge UP, 2002.

Heywood, Thomas. *The Golden Age*. In *The Dramatic Works of Thomas Heywood*. Vol. 3. New York: Russell, 1964. 1–79.

Hill, Eugene D. "Senecan and Vergilian Perspectives in *The Spanish Tragedy*." *English Literary Renaissance* 15.2 (1985): 143–65. http://dx.doi.org/10.1111/j.1475-6757.1985.tb00882.x.

Hillman, Richard. "Botching the Soliloquies in *The Spanish Tragedy*: Revisionist Collaboration and the 1602 Additions." In *The Elizabethan Theatre XV*. Ed. C.E. McGee and A.L. Magnusson. Toronto: Meany, 2002. 111–29.

Hiltner, Ken. "Early Modern Ecology." In *A New Companion to English Renaissance Literature and Culture*. Vol. 2. Ed. Michael Hattaway. Malden: Wiley-Blackwell, 2010. 555–68. http://dx.doi.org/10.1002/9781444319019.ch82.

Hiltner, Ken, ed. *Renaissance Ecology: Imagining Eden in Milton's England*. Pittsburgh: Duquesne UP, 2008.

Hiltner, Ken. *What Else Is Pastoral? Renaissance Literature and the Environment*. Ithaca: Cornell UP, 2011.

Holinshed, Raphael. *The First volume of the Chronicles of England, Scotlande, and Irelande*. London, 1577.

Holland, Peter. "*The Merry Wives of Windsor*: The Performance of Community." *Shakespeare Bulletin* 23.2 (2005): 5–18.

Holme, Randle. *An Accademie of Armory, Or, A Store House of Armory and Blazon*. Chester, 1688.

"An Homilie Against perill of Idolatrie, and superfluous decking of Churches." In *The Second Tome of Homilies, Of Svch Matters As Were Promised, And entituled in the former part of Homilies*. London, 1623. Rpt in *Certaine Sermons Or Homilies Appointed to be Read in Churches in the Time of Queen Elizabeth I (1547–1571)*, with an introduction by Mary Ellen Rickey and Thomas R. Stroup. Gainseville: Scholars' Facsimiles & Reprints, 1968. 11–77.

Hooke, Della. *Trees in Anglo-Saxon England: Literature, Lore and Landscape*. Woodbridge: Boydell, 2010.

Hopkins, Lisa. "What's Hercules to Hamlet? The Emblematic Garden in *The Spanish Tragedy* and *Hamlet*." *Hamlet Studies* 21.1–2 (1999): 114–43.

Howard, Jean E. *The Stage and Social Struggle in Early Modern England*. London: Routledge, 1994. http://dx.doi.org/10.4324/9780203359815.

Howard, Jean E. *Theater of a City: The Places of London Comedy, 1598–1642*. Philadelphia: U of Pennsylvania P, 2007.

Howard, Maurice. *The Building of Elizabethan and Jacobean England.* New Haven: Yale UP, 2007.

Hulme, Peter. *Colonial Encounters: Europe and the Native Caribbean, 1492–1797.* London: Routledge, 1992.

Hulme, Peter. "Hurricanes in the Caribbees: The Constitution of the Discourse of English Colonialism." In *1642: Literature and Power in the Seventeenth Century.* Ed. Francis Barker, et al. Essex: U of Essex P, 1981. 55–83.

Hulme, Peter, and William H. Sherman, eds. The Tempest *and Its Travels.* London: Reaktion, 2000.

Hunt, Maurice. "The Garter Motto in *The Merry Wives of Windsor.*" *Studies in English Literature, 1500–1900* 50.2 (2010): 383–406. http://dx.doi.org/10.1353/sel.0.0101.

Hunt, Maurice. "'Gentleness' and Social Class in *The Merry Wives of Windsor.*" *Comparative Drama* 42.4 (2008): 409–32. http://dx.doi.org/10.1353/cdr.0.0031.

Ingram, William. *The Business of Playing: The Beginnings of the Adult Professional Theater in Elizabethan London.* Ithaca: Cornell UP, 1992.

Jakacki, Diane K. "'Canst paint a doleful cry?' Promotion and Performances in the *Spanish Tragedy* Title-Page Illustration." *Early Theatre* 13.1 (2010): 13–36.

James I. "A Speach to the Lords and Commons of the Parliament at White-Hall, On Wednesday the XXI. of March. Anno 1609." In *The Political Works of James I.* Vol. 1, with an introduction by Charles Howard McIlwain. Cambridge: Harvard UP, 1918. 306–25.

James, Heather. *Shakespeare's Troy: Drama, Politics, and the Translation of Empire.* Cambridge: Cambridge UP, 1997.

James, N.D.G. *A History of English Forestry.* Oxford: Basil Blackwell, 1981.

J.G. *A Refvtation of the* Apology for Actors, with a preface by Arthur Freeman. New York: Garland, 1973.

Johnson, S.F. "*The Spanish Tragedy*, or Babylon Revisited." In *Essays on Shakespeare and Elizabethan Drama in Honor of Hardin Craig.* Ed. Richard Hosley. Columbia: U of Missouri P, 1962. 23–36.

Jones, Ann Rosalind, and Peter Stallybrass. *Renaissance Clothing and the Materials of Memory.* Cambridge: Cambridge UP, 2000.

Jonson, Ben. *Bartholomew Fair.* In *Ben Jonson: Three Comedies.* Ed. Michael Jamieson. London: Penguin, 1985. 325–460.

Jonson, Ben. *Ben Jonson: A Critical Edition of the Major Works.* Ed. Ian Donaldson. Oxford: Oxford UP, 1985.

Jonson, Ben. "An Execration upon Vulcan." Jonson, *Ben Jonson: A Critical* 365–70.

Jonson, Ben. *The Golden Age Restored.* In *Ben Jonson: The Complete Masques.* Ed. Stephen Orgel. New Haven: Yale UP, 1969. 224–32.

Jonson, Ben. "To Penshurst." Jonson, *Ben Jonson: A Critical* 282–5.

Journals of the House of Commons (1547–1624). Vol. 1.

Kahn, Coppélia. *Man's Estate: Masculine Identity in Shakespeare*. Berkeley: U of California P, 1981.

Kastan, David Scott. "'The Duke of Milan / And His Brave Son': Old Histories and New in *The Tempest*." Rpt. in Shakespeare, The Tempest: *A Case Study* 268–86.

Katz, Leslie S. "*The Merry Wives of Windsor*: Sharing the Queen's Holiday." *Representations* 51.1 (1995): 77–93. http://dx.doi.org/10.1525/rep.1995.51.1.99p0291y.

Kegl, Rosemary. *The Rhetoric of Concealment: Figuring Gender and Class in Renaissance Literature*. Ithaca: Cornell UP, 1994.

Keilen, Sean. *Vulgar Eloquence: On the Renaissance Invention of English Literature*. New Haven: Yale UP, 2006.

Kinney, Arthur F. "Textual Signs in *The Merry Wives of Windsor*." *Yearbook of English Studies* 23 (1993): 206–34. http://dx.doi.org/10.2307/3507981.

Knapp, Jeffrey. *An Empire Nowhere: England, America, and Literature from Utopia to* The Tempest. Berkeley: U of California P, 1992.

Knutson, Roslyn L. "*Henslowe's Diary* and the Economics of Play Revision for Revival, 1592–1603." *Theatre Research International* 10.1 (1985): 1–18. http://dx.doi.org/10.1017/S0307883300010452.

Knutson, Roslyn L. "Influence of the Repertory System on the Revival and Revision of *The Spanish Tragedy* and *Dr. Faustus*." *English Literary Renaissance* 18.2 (1988): 257–74. http://dx.doi.org/10.1111/j.1475-6757.1988.tb00955.x.

Knutson, Roslyn L. "The Repertory." Cox and Kastan 461–80.

Korda, Natasha. "Household Property / Stage Property: Henslowe as Pawnbroker." *Theatre Journal* 48.2 (1996): 185–95. http://dx.doi.org/10.1353/tj.1996.0024.

Korda, Natasha. *Shakespeare's Domestic Economies: Gender and Property in Early Modern England*. Philadelphia: U of Pennsylvania P, 2002.

Kumaran, Arul. "'Hereafter suppose me the said Roberto': Greene's *Groatsworth of Wit* as an Allegorizing Pamphlet." *Yearly Review* 10 (2001): 29–45.

Kyd, Thomas. *The Spanish Tragedy*. Ed. J.R. Mulryne. London: Black, 1990.

LaGrandeur, Kevin. "The Talking Brass Head as a Symbol of Dangerous Knowledge in *Friar Bacon* and in *Alphonsus, King of Aragon*." *English Studies* 80.5 (1999): 408–22. http://dx.doi.org/10.1080/00138389908599194.

Lake, Peter, with Michael Questier. *The Antichrist's Lewd Hat: Protestants, Papists and Players in Post-Reformation England*. New Haven: Yale UP, 2002.

Lamb, H.H. *The Changing Climate*. London: Methuen, 1966.

Land, Robert H. "The First Williamsburg Theater." *William and Mary Quarterly* 5.3 (1948): 359–74. http://dx.doi.org/10.2307/1923465.

Landreth, David. "Once More into the Preech: The Merry Wives' English Pedagogy." *Shakespeare Quarterly* 55.4 (2004): 420–49. http://dx.doi.org/10.1353/shq.2005.0028.

Leggatt, Alexander. *Jacobean Public Theatre*. London: Routledge, 1992.

Leinwand, Theodore B. "Shakespeare and the Middling Sort." *Shakespeare Quarterly* 44.3 (1993): 284–303. http://dx.doi.org/10.2307/2871420.

Lemon, Robert, ed. "Queen Elizabeth – Volume 125: July 1578." *Calendar of State Papers, Domestic series, of the reigns of Edward VI., Mary, Elizabeth.* Vol. 1. London, 1856.

Lesser, Zachary. *Renaissance Drama and the Politics of Publication: Readings in the English Book Trade*. Cambridge: Cambridge UP, 2004.

Levin, Harry. *The Myth of the Golden Age in the Renaissance*. Bloomington: Indiana UP, 1969.

Levin, Richard. "Tarlton in *The Famous History of Friar Bacon* and *Friar Bacon and Friar Bungay.*" *Medieval and Renaissance Drama in England* 12 (1999): 84–98.

Levine, Laura. *Men in Women's Clothing: Anti-theatricality and Effeminization, 1579–1642*. Cambridge: Cambridge UP, 1994.

Linschoten, John Huighen van. *His Discours of Voyages vnto the Easte & West Indies*. London, 1598.

Lloyd, T.H. *England and the German Hanse, 1157–1611: A Study of their Trade and Commercial Diplomacy*. Cambridge: Cambridge UP, 1991. http://dx.doi.org/10.1017/CBO9780511560279.

Love, Glen A. "Shakespeare's Origin of Species and Darwin's Tempest." *Configurations* 18.1–2 (2010): 121–40. http://dx.doi.org/10.1353/con.2010.0000.

Lupher, David A. *Romans in a New World: Classical Models in Sixteenth-Century Spanish America*. Ann Arbor: U of Michigan P, 2003.

Lupton, Julia Reinhard. "Creature Caliban." *Shakespeare Quarterly* 51.1 (2000): 1–23. http://dx.doi.org/10.2307/2902320.

Mackay, Ellen. *Persecution, Plague, and Fire: Fugitive Histories of the Stage in Early Modern England*. Chicago: U of Chicago P, 2011.

Maltby, William S. *The Black Legend in England: The Development of anti-Spanish Sentiment, 1558–1660*. Durham: Duke UP, 1971.

Manley, Lawrence. *Literature and Culture in Early Modern London*. Cambridge: Cambridge UP, 1997.

Manwood, John. *A Brefe Collection of the Lawes of the Forest*. London, 1592.

Manwood, John. *A Treatise And Discovrse Of the Lawes of the Forrest*. London, 1598.

Marcus, Leah S. "Levelling Shakespeare: Local Customs and Local Texts." *Shakespeare Quarterly* 42.2 (1991): 168–78. http://dx.doi.org/10.2307/2870546.

Marcus, Leah S. *Unediting the Renaissance: Shakespeare, Marlowe, Milton*. London: Routledge, 1996. http://dx.doi.org/10.4324/9780203424445.

Marienstras, Richard. *New Perspectives on the Shakespearean World*. Trans. Janet Lloyd. Cambridge: Cambridge UP, 1985.

Markley, Robert. "'Gulfes, Deserts, Precipices, Stone': Marvell's 'Upon Appleton House' and the Contradictions of 'Nature.'" In *The Country and The City Revisited: England and the Politics of Culture, 1550–1850*. Ed. Gerald Maclean, Donna Landry, and Joseph P. Ward. Cambridge: Cambridge UP, 1999. 89–105.

Markley, Robert. "Summer's Lease: Shakespeare in the Little Ice Age." Hallock, Kamps, and Raber 131-42.

Marlowe, Christopher. *Christopher Marlowe: The Complete Plays*. Ed. Frank Romany and Robert Lindsey. London: Penguin, 2003.

Marlowe, Christopher. *Dido, Queen of Carthage*. Marlowe, *Christopher Marlowe* 1–67.

Marlowe, Christopher. *Doctor Faustus*. Marlowe, *Christopher Marlowe* 341–95.

Marlowe, Christopher. *The Jew of Malta*. Marlowe, *Christopher Marlowe* 241–340.

Marston, John. *Antonio and Mellida*. Ed. W. Reavley Gair. Manchester: Manchester UP, 1991.

Marvell, Andrew. "Upon Appleton House." In *Andrew Marvell: The Complete Poems*. Ed. Elizabeth Story Donno. New York: Penguin, 1981. 75–99.

Marx, Leo. *The Machine in the Garden: Technology and the Pastoral Ideal in America*. Oxford: Oxford UP, 2000.

Maslen, Robert W. "Robert Greene and the Uses of Time." Melnikoff and Gieskes 157–88.

Maus, Katharine Eisaman. *Inwardness and Theater in the English Renaissance*. Chicago: U of Chicago P, 1995.

McCallum, James Dow. "Greene's *Friar Bacon and Friar Bungay*." *Modern Language Notes* 35.4 (1920): 212–7. http://dx.doi.org/10.2307/2915134.

McColley, Diane Kelsey. *Poetry and Ecology in the Age of Milton and Marvell*. Aldershot: Ashgate, 2007.

McInnis, David. "The Golden Man and the Golden Age: The Relationship of English Poets and the New World Reconsidered." *Early Modern Literary Studies* 13.1 (May 2007). Web.

McMillan, Scott, and Sally-Beth MacLean. *The Queen's Men and Their Plays*. Cambridge: Cambridge UP, 1999.

McNeill, J.R. "Woods and Warfare in World History." *Environmental History* 9.3 (2004): 388–410. http://dx.doi.org/10.2307/3985766.

McNeir, Waldo F. "Traditional Elements in the Character of Greene's Friar Bacon." *Studies in Philology* 45.2 (1948): 172–9.

McRae, Andrew. *God Speed the Plough: The Representation of Agrarian England, 1500–1660.* Cambridge: Cambridge UP, 1996.

Melchiori, Giorgio. *Shakespeare's Garter Plays:* Edward III *to* The Merry Wives of Windsor. Newark: U of Delaware P, 1994.

Melnikoff, Kirk, and Edward Gieskes. "Introduction: Re-imagining Robert Greene." Melnikoff and Gieskes 1–24.

Melnikoff, Kirk, and Edward Gieskes, eds. *Writing Robert Greene: Essays on England's First Notorious Professional Playwright.* Aldershot: Ashgate, 2008.

Mentz, Steve. "Shakespeare's Beach House, or The Green and the Blue in *Macbeth.*" *Shakespeare Studies* 39 (2011): 84–93.

Mentz, Steve. "Shipwreck and Ecology: Toward a Structural Theory of Shakespeare and Romance." *The Shakespearean International Yearbook* 8 (2008): 165–82.

Mentz, Steve. "Strange Weather in *King Lear.*" *Shakespeare* 6.2 (2010): 139–52. http://dx.doi.org/10.1080/17450911003790216.

Meteren, Emanuel van. "The miraculous victory achieved by the English fleet, upon the Spanish huge Armada sent in the year 1588, for the invasion of England." Hakluyt 312–26.

Milton, John. *Paradise Lost.* In *John Milton: The Complete Poems.* Ed. John Leonard. London: Penguin, 1998. 119-406.

Montaigne, Michel. "Of the Caniballes." In *The Essayes of Michael Lord of Montaigne Translated by John Florio.* Vol. 1. London: Dent, 1910. 215–29.

Montrose, Louis. *The Purpose of Playing: Shakespeare and the Cultural Politics of the Elizabethan Theatre.* Chicago: U of Chicago P, 1996.

More, Thomas. *A Most pleasant, fruitfull, and wittie worke, of the best state of a publique wealth, and of the new Yle called Vtopia.* Trans. Raphe Robinson. London, 1597.

More, Thomas. Utopia: *Latin Text and English Translation.* Ed. George M. Logan, Robert M. Adams, and Clarence H. Miller. Cambridge: Cambridge UP, 1995.

Mortenson, Peter. "*Friar Bacon and Friar Bungay:* Festive Comedy and 'Three-Form'd Luna'." *English Literary Renaissance* 2.2 (1972): 194–207. http://dx.doi.org/10.1111/j.1475-6757.1972.tb00734.x.

Morton, Timothy. *Ecology without Nature: Rethinking Environmental Aesthetics.* Cambridge: Harvard UP, 2007.

Moss, Roger. "Falstaff as a Woman." *Journal of Dramatic Theory and Criticism* 10.1 (1995): 31–41.

Mowat, Barbara A. "'Knowing I loved my books': Reading *The Tempest* Intertextually." Hulme and Sherman 27–36.

Moxon, Joseph. *Mechanick Exercise: Or, The Doctrine of Handy-Works.* London, 1695.

Mullaney, Steven. "Affective Technologies: Toward an Emotional Logic of the Elizabethan Stage." In *Environment and Embodiment in Early Modern England.* Ed. Mary Floyd-Wilson and Garrett A. Sullivan, Jr. New York: Palgrave, 2007. 71–89.

Mullaney, Steven. *The Place of the Stage: License, Play, and Power in Renaissance England.* Ann Arbor: U of Michigan P, 1998.

Mulryne, J.R., and Margaret Shewring. "The Once and Future Globe." In *Shakespeare's Globe Rebuilt.* Ed. J.R. Mulryne and Margaret Shewring. Cambridge: Cambridge UP, 1997. 15–25.

Munday, Anthony. *A second and third blast of retrait from plaies and Theaters,* with a preface by Arthur Freeman. New York: Garland, 1973.

Munroe, Jennifer. *Gender and the Garden in Early Modern English Literature.* Aldershot: Ashgate, 2008.

Munroe, Jennifer, and Rebecca Laroche, eds. *Ecofeminist Approaches to Early Modernity.* New York: Palgrave, 2011. http://dx.doi.org/10.1057/9781137001900.

Murphy, Patrick M., ed. The Tempest: *Critical Essays.* New York: Routledge, 2001.

Nardizzi, Vin. "Grafted to Falstaff and Compounded with Catherine: Mingling Hal in the Second Tetralogy." In *Queer Renaissance Historiography: Backward Gaze.* Ed. Vin Nardizzi, Stephen Guy-Bray, and Will Stockton. Aldershot: Ashgate, 2009. 149–69.

Nardizzi, Vin. "The Wooden Matter of Human Bodies: Prosthesis and Stump in *A Larum for London.*" Feerick and Nardizzi 119–36.

Nardizzi, Vin. "Wooden Slavery." *PMLA* 126.2 (2011): 313–5.

Nashe, Thomas. *Pierce Penilesse His Svpplication to the Diuell.* London, 1592.

Neely, Carol Thomas. "Constructing Female Sexuality in the Renaissance: Stratford, London, Windsor, Vienna." In *Feminism and Psychoanalysis.* Ed. Richard Feldstein and Judith Roof. Ithaca: Cornell UP, 1989. 209–29.

Nef, J.U. *The Rise of the British Coal Industry.* Vol. 1. London: Archon, 1966.

Norbrook, David. "'What Cares These Roarers for the Name of King?': Language and Utopia in *The Tempest.*" In *The Politics of Tragicomedy: Shakespeare and After.* Ed. Gordon McMullan and Jonathan Hope. London: Routledge, 1992. 21–54.

Northbrooke, John. *A Treatise Against Dicing, Dancing, Plays, and Interludes,* with an introduction by John Payne Collier. London: Shakespeare Society, 1843.

Nova Britannia: Offering Most Excellent fruites by Planting in Virginia. Vol. 1. London: Rpt. in Force, 1609.·

O'Connell, Michael. *The Idolatrous Eye: Iconoclasm and Theater in Early-Modern England.* Oxford: Oxford UP, 2000.

O'Dair, Sharon. *Class, Critics, and Shakespeare: Bottom Lines on the Culture Wars.* Ann Arbor: U of Michigan P, 2000.

O'Dair, Sharon. "*The Tempest* as *Tempest*: Does Paul Mazursky 'Green' William Shakespeare?" *ISLE* 12.2 (2005): 165–78.

Orgel, Stephen. *The Authentic Shakespeare and Other Problems of the Early Modern Stage.* New York: Routledge, 2002.

Orrell, John. "The Architecture of the Fortune Playhouse." *Shakespeare Survey* 47 (1994): 15–28. http://dx.doi.org/10.1017/CCOL0521470846.002.

Orrell, John. "Building the Fortune." *Shakespeare Quarterly* 44.2 (1993): 127–44. http://dx.doi.org/10.2307/2871135.

Orrell, John. "The Theaters." Cox and Kastan 93–112.

Ovid. *Ovid's* Metamorphoses. Ed. Madeleine Forey. Trans. Arthur Golding. Baltimore: Johns Hopkins UP, 2001.

Oxford Online English Dictionaries. Oxford UP, 2012. Web.

Page, William, ed. *The Victoria History of the Counties of England: Gloucestershire.* Vol. 2. London: Archibald Constable, 1907.

Parker, Patricia. *Literary Fat Ladies: Rhetoric, Gender, Property.* London: Methuen, 1987.

Parker, Patricia. *Shakespeare from the Margins: Language, Culture, Context.* Chicago: U of Chicago P, 1996.

Parten, Anne. "Falstaff's Horns: Masculine Inadequacy and Feminine Mirth in *The Merry Wives of Windsor*." *Studies in Philology* 82.2 (1985): 184–99.

Paster, Gail Kern. *Humoring the Body: Emotions and the Shakespearean Stage.* Chicago: U of Chicago P, 2004.

Perlin, John. *A Forest Journey: The Story of Wood and Civilization.* Woodstock: Countryman, 2005.

Perry, William. *A Treatise on the Identity of Herne's Oak: Shewing the Maiden Tree to Have Been the Real One.* London, 1867.

Phillips, John. *The Reformation of Images: Destruction of Art in England, 1535–1660.* Berkeley: U of California P, 1973.

Pickering, Danby. *The Statutes at Large, From the First Year of Queen Mary, To The Thirty-fifth Year of Queen Elizabeth, inclusive.* Vol. 6. Cambridge, 1763.

Pitcher, John. "A Theatre of the Future: *The Aeneid* and *The Tempest*." *Essays in Criticism* XXXIV.3 (1984): 193–215. http://dx.doi.org/10.1093/eic/XXXIV.3.193.

"pit-saw, n." *Oxford.*

Pittenger, Elizabeth. "Dispatch Quickly: The Mechanical Reproduction of Pages." *Shakespeare Quarterly* 42.4 (1991): 389–408. http://dx.doi.org/10.2307/2870460.

Pliny. *The Historie Of The World.* Trans. Philemon Holland. London, 1601.

Price, Daniel. *SAVLS Prohibition Staid. Or The Apprehension, And Examination Of Saule.* London, 1609.

Prynne, William. *Histrio-Mastix: The Players Scourge, Or, Actors Tragedie.* London, 1633.

Quinn, David. "Thomas Harriot and the Problem of America." In *Thomas Harriot: An Elizabethan Man of Science.* Ed. Robert Fox. Aldershot: Ashgate, 2000. 9–27.

Rackham, Oliver. *Trees and Woodland in the British Landscape.* London: Dent, 1981.

R.C. *An Olde Thrift Newly Revived.* London, 1612.

Reynolds, Bryan. *Becoming Criminal: Transversal Performance and Cultural Dissidence in Early Modern England.* Baltimore: Johns Hopkins UP, 2002.

Reynolds, Bryan, and Henry S. Turner. "From *Homo Academicus* to *Poeta Publicus*: Celebrity and Transversal Knowledge in Robert Greene's *Friar Bacon and Friar Bungay* (c. 1589)." Melnikoff and Gieskes 73–93.

Reynolds, Bryan, and Henry S. Turner. "Performative Transversations: Collaborations Through and Beyond Greene's *Friar Bacon and Friar Bungay.*" In *Transversal Enterprises in the Drama of Shakespeare and His Contemporaries.* Ed. Bryan Reynolds. Houndmills: Palgrave, 2006. 240–50. http://dx.doi.org/10.1057/9780230584570.

Reynolds, G.F. "'Trees' on the Stage of Shakespeare." *Modern Philology* 5.2 (1907): 153–68. http://dx.doi.org/10.1086/386737.

Richards, John F. *The Unending Frontier: An Environmental History of the Early Modern World.* Berkeley: U of California P, 2003.

Ridley, Florence H., ed. *The Aeneid of Henry Howard Earl of Surrey.* Berkeley: U of California P, 1963.

Roberts, Jeanne Addison. *Shakespeare's English Comedy*: The Merry Wives of Windsor *in Context.* Lincoln: U of Nebraska P, 1979.

Roberts, Jeanne Addison. "Shakespeare's Forests and Trees." *Southern Humanities Review* 11 (1977): 108–25.

Rockett, William. "Labor and Virtue in *The Tempest.*" *Shakespeare Quarterly* 24.1 (1973): 77–84. http://dx.doi.org/10.2307/2868741.

Rosador, Kurt Tetzeli Von. "The Sacralizing Sign: Religion and Magic in Bale, Greene, and the Early Shakespeare." *Yearbook of English Studies* 23 (1993): 30–45. http://dx.doi.org/10.2307/3507971.

Ross, Charles Stanley. "Shakespeare's *Merry Wives* and the Law of Fraudulent Conveyance." *Renaissance Drama* 25 (1994): 145–69.

Rossi, Andreola. "*The Aeneid* Revisited: The Journey of Pompey in Lucan's *Pharsalia*." *American Journal of Philology* 121.4 (2000): 571–91. http://dx.doi .org/10.1353/ajp.2000.0057.

Rutter, Carol Chillington, ed. *Documents of the Rose Playhouse*. Manchester: Manchester UP, 1984.

Sanchez, Melissa E. "Seduction and Service in *The Tempest*." *Studies in Philology* 105.1 (2008): 50–82. http://dx.doi.org/10.1353/sip.2008.0001.

Sanders, Julie. "Ecocritical Readings and the Seventeenth-Century Woodland: Milton's 'Comus' and the Forest of Dean." *English* 50 (2001): 1–18. http:// dx.doi.org/10.1093/english/50.196.1.

Sanders, William. "The Undiscovered." *Are We Having Fun Yet? American Indian Fantasy Stories*. Rockville: Wildside, 2005. 10–34.

Sandys, George. *Ovid's Metamorphosis Englished, Mythologized, and Represented in Figures*. Ed. Karl K. Hulley and Stanley T. Vandersall. Lincoln: U of Nebraska P, 1970.

Saunders, Corinne J. *The Forest of Medieval Romance: Avernus, Broceliande, Arden*. Cambridge: Brewer, 1993.

"saw pit, n." *Oxford*.

Schalkwyk, David. *Shakespeare, Love and Service*. Cambridge: Cambridge UP, 2008. http://dx.doi.org/10.1017/CBO9780511483936.

Schama, Simon. *Landscape and Memory*. New York: Vintage, 1996.

Scolnicov, Hanna. "The Zoomorphic Mask in Shakespeare." *Assaph* 9 (1993): 63–74.

Scott, Charlotte. *Shakespeare's Nature*. Oxford: Oxford UP, forthcoming.

Scott, James C. *Seeing Like a State: How Certain Schemes to Improve the Human Condition Have Failed*. New Haven: Yale UP, 1999.

Sebek, Barbara Ann. "Peopling, Profiting, and Pleasure in *The Tempest*." Murphy 463–81.

Seed, Patricia. *Ceremonies of Possession in Europe's Conquest of the New World, 1492–1640*. Cambridge: Cambridge UP, 1998.

Shakespeare, William. *Antony and Cleopatra*. Shakespeare, *Norton* 2643–721.

Shakespeare, William. *As You Like It*. Shakespeare, *Norton* 1625–81.

Shakespeare, William. *Cymbeline*. Shakespeare, *Norton* 2974–3054.

Shakespeare, William. *Hamlet*. Shakespeare, *Norton* 1696–784.

Shakespeare, William. *Henry IV, Part One*. Shakespeare, *Norton* 1188–254.

Shakespeare, William. *Henry IV, Part Two*. Shakespeare, *Norton* 1333–405.

Shakespeare, William. *Henry V*. Shakespeare, *Norton* 1481–548.

Shakespeare, William. *King Lear*. (Conflated text.) Shakespeare, *Norton* 2493–567.

Shakespeare, William. *Macbeth*. Shakespeare, *Norton* 2579–632.

Shakespeare, William. *The Merry Wives of Windsor*. Shakespeare, *Norton* 1265–320.

Shakespeare, William. *A Midsummer Night's Dream*. Shakespeare, *Norton* 849–96.

Shakespeare, William. *The Norton Shakespeare*. 2nd ed. Ed. Stephen Greenblatt, et al. New York: Norton, 2008.

Shakespeare, William. *Othello*. Shakespeare, *Norton* 2119–91.

Shakespeare, William. *Pericles, Prince of Tyre: A Reconstructed Text*. Shakespeare, *Norton* 2734–91.

Shakespeare, William. *Richard II*. Shakespeare, *Norton* 983–1043.

Shakespeare, William. *Romeo and Juliet*. Shakespeare, *Norton* 905–72.

Shakespeare, William. *The Tempest*. Shakespeare, *Norton* 3064–115.

Shakespeare, William. *The Tempest*. Ed. Stephen Orgel. Oxford: Oxford World's Classics, 1998.

Shakespeare, William. *The Tempest*. Ed. Virginia Mason Vaughan and Alden T. Vaughan. 3rd Ser. London: Cengage Learning, 1999.

Shakespeare, William, The Tempest: *A Case Study in Critical Controversy*. Ed. Gerald Graff and James Phelan. Boston: Bedford / St. Martin's, 2000.

Shakespeare, William. *Timon of Athens*. Shakespeare, *Norton* 2270–323.

Shakespeare, William. *Titus Andronicus*. Shakespeare, *Norton* 408–63.

Shakespeare, William. *Twelfth Night*. Shakespeare, *Norton* 1793–846.

Shakespeare, William. *The Two Gentlemen of Verona*. Shakespeare, *Norton* 111–57.

Shakespeare, William. *The Winter's Tale*. Shakespeare, *Norton* 2892–961.

Shakespeare's Globe Theater. "Rebuilding Shakespeare's Globe." *Playbill: Doctor Faustus by Christopher Marlowe*. London, 2011.

Shapiro, James. "'Tragedies naturally performed': Kyd's Representation of Violence." In *Staging the Renaissance: Reinterpretations of Elizabethan and Jacobean Drama*. Ed. David Scott Kastan and Peter Stallybrass. New York: Routledge, 1991. 99–113.

Shapiro, James. *A Year in the Life of William Shakespeare: 1599*. New York: HarperCollins, 2005.

Sheerin, Brian. "Patronage and Perverse Bestowal in *The Spanish Tragedy* and *Antonio's Revenge*." *English Literary Renaissance* 41.2 (2011): 247–79. http://dx.doi.org/10.1111/j.1475-6757.2011.01085.x.

Siemon, James R. "Sporting Kyd." *English Literary Renaissance* 24.3 (1994): 553–82. http://dx.doi.org/10.1111/j.1475-6757.1994.tb01498.x.

Singer, Charles J., et al., eds. *A History of Technology*. Vol. 2. Oxford: Oxford UP, 1956.

Skura, Meredith Anne. "Discourse and the Individual: The Case of Colonialism in *The Tempest*." Rpt. in Shakespeare, The Tempest: *A Case Study* 286–322.

Slights, Camille Wells. *Shakespeare's Comic Commonwealths*. Toronto: U of Toronto P, 1993.

Smith, Bruce R. *The Acoustic World of Early Modern England: Attending to the O-Factor*. Chicago: U of Chicago P, 1999.

Smith, Bruce R. *The Key of Green: Passion and Perception in Renaissance Culture*. Chicago: U of Chicago P, 2009.

Smith, Bruce R. "Shakespeare @ the Limits." *Shakespeare Studies* 39 (2011): 104–13.

Smith, Irwin. "Theatre into Globe." *Shakespeare Quarterly* 3.2 (1952): 113–20. http://dx.doi.org/10.2307/2866501.

Smith, Molly. "The Theater and the Scaffold: Death as Spectacle in *The Spanish Tragedy*." *Studies in English Literature, 1500-1900* 32.2 (1992): 217–32.

Snider, Alvin. "Hard Frost, 1684." *Journal for Early Modern Cultural Studies* 8.2 (2008): 8–32. http://dx.doi.org/10.2979/JEM.2008.8.2.8.

Sofer, Andrew. *The Stage Life of Props*. Ann Arbor: U of Michigan P, 2003.

Spenser, Edmund. *The Faerie Queene*. Ed. Thomas P. Roche, Jr. London: Penguin, 1978.

Sponsler, Claire. "Medieval America: Drama and Community in the English Colonies, 1580–1610." *Journal of Medieval and Early Modern Studies* 28.2 (1998): 453–78.

Stallybrass, Peter. "Patriarchal Territories: The Body Enclosed." In *Rewriting the Renaissance: The Discourses of Sexual Difference in Early Modern Europe*. Ed. Margaret W. Ferguson, Maureen Quilligan, and Nancy J. Vickers. Chicago: U of Chicago P, 1986. 123–42.

Standish, Arthur. *The Commons Complaint*. London, 1611.

Standish, Arthur. *New Directions of Experience By the Avthovr for The Planting of Timber and Firewood*. London, 1613.

Steadman, John M. "Falstaff as Actaeon: A Dramatic Emblem." *Shakespeare Quarterly* 14.3 (1963): 231–44. http://dx.doi.org/10.2307/2867808.

Stern, Tiffany. *Making Shakespeare: From Stage to Page*. London: Routledge, 2005.

Stewart, Alan. "'Euery Soyle to Mee Is Naturall': Figuring Denization in William Haughton's *English-Men for My Money*." *Renaissance Drama* 25 (2006): 55–81.

Stockholder, Kay. "'Yet can he write': Reading the Silences in *The Spanish Tragedy*." *American Imago* 47.2 (1990): 93–124.

Stockton, Will. *Playing Dirty: Sexuality and Waste in Early Modern Comedy*. Minneapolis: U of Minnesota P, 2011.

Stodder, Joseph. "Magus and Maiden: Archetypal Roles in Greene's *Friar Bacon and Friar Bungay.*" *Journal of Evolutionary Psychology* 4.1–2 (1983): 28–37.

Stone, Christopher D. *Should Trees Have Standing? Law, Morality, and the Environment.* 3rd ed. Oxford: Oxford UP, 2010.

Strong, Roy. *The Cult of Elizabeth: Elizabethan Portraiture and Pageantry.* Wallop: Thames and Hudson, 1977.

Stubbes, Philip. *The Anatomie of Abuses. 1595.* Ed. Margaret Jane Kidnie. Tempe: Arizona Center for Medieval and Renaissance Studies, 2002.

Summit, Jennifer. *Memory's Library: Medieval Books in Early Modern England.* Chicago: U of Chicago P, 2008.

A Survey of London by John Stow, with an introduction and notes by Charles Lethbridge Kingsford. Vol. 1. Oxford: Clarendon, 1908.

Tassi, Marguerite A. "The Player's Passion and the Elizabethan Painting Trope: A Study of the Painter Addition to Kyd's *The Spanish Tragedy.*" *Explorations in Renaissance Culture* 26.1 (2000): 73–100.

Taylor, Gary. "*Hamlet* in Africa 1607." In *Travel Knowledge: European "Discoveries" in the Early Modern Period.* Ed. Ivo Kamps and Jyotsna G. Singh. New York: Palgrave, 2001. 223–48.

Tennenhouse, Leonard. *Power on Display: The Politics of Shakespeare's Genres.* New York: Methuen, 1986.

Test, Edward M. "*The Tempest* and the Newfoundland Cod Fishery." In *Global Traffic: Discourses and Practices of Trade in English Literature and Culture From 1550 To 1700.* Ed. Barbara Sebek and Stephen Deng. New York: Palgrave, 2008. 201–20.

Theis, Jeffrey S. "Primitive Architecture, Temporary Dwelling? Cells, Caves, and Environment in *The Tempest* and *Cymbeline.*" Shakespeare's Green Scenes. 2011 SAA. Bellevue, Washington. TS.

Theis, Jeffrey S. *Writing the Forest in Early Modern England: A Sylvan Pastoral Nation.* Pittsburgh: Duquesne UP, 2009.

Thirsk, Joan, ed. *The Agrarian History of England and Wales.* Vol. 4. Cambridge: Cambridge UP, 1967.

Thirsk, Joan. *Economic Policy and Projects: The Development of Consumer Society in Early Modern England.* Oxford: Clarendon, 1978.

Thomas, Brinley. "Was There an Energy Crisis in Great Britain in the 17th Century?" *Explorations in Economic History* 23.2 (1986): 124–52. http://dx.doi.org/10.1016/0014-4983(86)90010-0.

Thomas, Keith. *Man and the Natural World: Changing Attitudes in England, 1500–1800.* Oxford: Oxford UP, 1996.

Totman, Conrad. *The Green Archipelago: Forestry in Preindustrial Japan.* Berkeley: U of California P, 1989.

Traister, Barbara Howard. *Heavenly Necromancers: The Magician in English Renaissance Drama*. Columbia: U of Missouri P, 1984.

Traub, Valerie. "Prince Hal's Falstaff: Positioning Psychoanalysis and the Female Reproductive Body." *Shakespeare Quarterly* 40.4 (1989): 456–74. http://dx.doi .org/10.2307/2870611.

A Trve Declaration Of The estate of the Colonie in Virginia. Vol. 3. London: Rpt. in Force, 1610.

"Tudor, adj. and n." *Oxford*.

Turner, Henry S. "Life Science: Rude Mechanicals, Human Mortals, Posthuman Shakespeare." *South Central Review* 26.1–2 (2009): 197–217. http://dx.doi .org/10.1353/scr.0.0047.

Vergil. *The whole .XII. Bookes of the Aeneidos of Virgill*. Trans. Thomas Twyne. London, 1573.

Vergil. *The .xiii. Bookes of Aeneidos*. Trans. Thomas Twyne. London, 1584.

Virgil. *Eclogues, Georgics, Aeneid 1–6*. Trans. H. Rushton Fairclough. Revised by G.P. Goold. Cambridge: Harvard UP, 1916.

Vitkus, Daniel. "'Meaner Ministers': Mastery, Bondage, and Theatrical Labor in *The Tempest*." In *A Companion to Shakespeare's Works: Volume IV, The Poems, Problem Comedies, Late Plays*. Ed. Richard Dutton and Jean E. Howard. Malden: Blackwell, 2006. 408–26.

Wall, Wendy. *Staging Domesticity: Household Work and English Identity in Early Modern Drama*. Cambridge: Cambridge UP, 2002.

Walsh, Brian. "'Deep Prescience': Succession and the Politics of Prophecy in *Friar Bacon and Friar Bungay*." *Medieval and Renaissance Drama in England* 23 (2010): 63–85.

Warde, Paul. *Ecology, Economy and State Formation in Early Modern Germany*. Cambridge: Cambridge UP, 2006. http://dx.doi.org/10.1017/ CBO9780511497230.

Warde, Paul. *Energy Consumption in England and Wales, 1560–2004*. Naples: Consiglio Nazionale delle Ricerche, 2007.

Watson, Robert N. *Back to Nature: The Green and the Real in the Late Renaissance*. Philadelphia: U of Pennsylvania P, 2006.

Wayne, Don E. *Penshurst: The Semiotics of Place and the Poetics of History*. Madison: U of Wisconsin P, 1984.

Wells, Stanley, and Gary Taylor. *William Shakespeare: A Textual Companion*. Oxford: Clarendon, 1987.

West, William N. *Theatres and Encyclopedias in Early Modern Europe*. Cambridge: Cambridge UP, 2002.

Whigham, Frank. *Seizures of the Will in Early Modern English Drama*. Cambridge: Cambridge UP, 1996. http://dx.doi.org/10.1017/CBO9780511518973.

Williams, Deanne. "*Friar Bacon and Friar Bungay* and the Rhetoric of Temporality." In *Reading the Medieval in Early Modern England*. Ed. Gordon McMullan and David Matthews. Cambridge: Cambridge UP, 2007. 31–48.

Williams, Michael. *Deforesting the Earth: From Prehistory to Global Crisis*. Chicago: U of Chicago P, 2003.

Williams, Raymond. *The Country and the City*. New York: Oxford UP, 1975.

Williams, Raymond. *Culture and Materialism: Selected Essays*. London: Verso, 2005.

Willis, Deborah. "Shakespeare's *Tempest* and the Discourse of Colonialism." Shakespeare, The Tempest: *A Case Study* 256–68.

Wilson, Katharine. "Transplanting Lillies: Greene, Tyrants and Tragical Comedies." Melnikoff and Gieskes 189–203.

Wilson, Richard. "Voyage to Tunis: New History and the Old World of *The Tempest*." *ELH* 64.2 (1997): 333–57. http://dx.doi.org/10.1353/elh.1997.0020.

Wilson-Okamura, David Scott. "Virgilian Models of Colonization in Shakespeare's *Tempest*." *ELH* 70.3 (2003): 709–37. http://dx.doi.org/10.1353/elh.2003.0030.

Wineke, Donald R. "Hieronimo's Garden and 'the fall of Babylon': Culture and Anarchy in *The Spanish Tragedy*." In *Aeolian Harps: Essays in Literature in Honor of Maurice Browning Cramer*. Ed. Donna G. Fricke and Douglas C. Fricke. Bowling Green: Bowling Green UP, 1976. 65–79.

Wood, Gillen D'Arcy. "Introduction: Eco-historicism." *Journal for Early Modern Cultural Studies* 8.2 (2008): 1–7. http://dx.doi.org/10.2979/JEM.2008.8.2.1.

Woodbridge, Linda. *The Scythe of Saturn: Shakespeare and Magical Thinking*. Urbana: U of Illinois P, 1994.

Woolf, Virginia. "Notes on an Elizabethan Play." In *The Common Reader*. Ed. Andrew McNeillie. San Diego: First Harvest/ HBJ Edition, 1984. 48–57.

Yates, Julian. "Humanist Habitats, Or, 'Eating Well' with Thomas More's *Utopia*." In *Environment and Embodiment in Early Modern England*. Ed. Mary Floyd-Wilson and Garrett A. Sullivan, Jr. New York: Palgrave, 2007. 187–209.

Zamir, Tzachi. "Wooden Subjects." *New Literary History* 39.2 (2008): 277–300. http://dx.doi.org/10.1353/nlh.0.0027.

Zucker, Adam. *The Places of Wit in Early Modern English Comedy*. Cambridge: Cambridge UP, 2011.

Index

design of the Fortune in relation to the Globe, 107–8; documents governmental opposition to theatre construction, 45, 78, 109; documents support for the construction of the Fortune, 108, 109; on the proposed destruction of the Curtain, 111, 137; on the meaning behind the Fortune's name, 107

Sanchez, Melissa, 165n36
Sanders, Julie, 150n38
Sanders, William, 167n61
Sandys, George, 57
Saunders, Corinne, 145n61
Schalkwyk, David, 165n37
Schama, Simon: on the antagonistic relation between forests and civilization, 153n9; on the conservatism of forest law, 64; on "cultural reafforestation," 5, 140n10; on the practice of using sticks to negotiate a contract, 165n39; on the relation between trees and architectural columns, 161n41; on rumours about the Spanish Armada's landfall, 151n39; on the use of trees and wood in Christian iconography, 161n39
Scolnicov, Hanna, 152n7
Scott, Charlotte, 166n45
Scott, James, 4
Sebek, Barbara, 165n36
Seed, Patricia, 164n23
Shakespeare, William, 16, 28, 81, 84
Shakespeare, William, works of: *Antony and Cleopatra*, 21; *As You Like It*, 20, 21–2, 23, 71, 138, 154n24; *Cymbeline*, 24–5, 148n9; *Hamlet*,

18, 107, 154n25, 167n61; *Henry IV, Part One*, 9, 76, 82, 155n32; *Henry IV, Part Two*, 22, 82, 155n32, 155n36; *Henry V*, 4, 5, 22, 23, 28, 29; *Henry VIII (All Is True)*, 83; *Julius Caesar*, 107, 144n44; *King Lear*, 21, 167n64; *Macbeth*, 9, 22, 24; *The Merry Wives of Windsor*, 30, 59–61, 65, 67–83, 87, 90, 97, 106, 107, 109, 112, 132; *A Midsummer Night's Dream*, 21, 22, 23, 89, 130, 166n47; *Othello*, 9; *Pericles*, 126; *Richard II*, 9, 21; *Romeo and Juliet*, 21; *The Tempest*, 30, 68, 105, 112–13, 114–18, 121–33, 135, 163; *Timon of Athens*, 21, 22; *Titus Andronicus*, 21, 22, 89–90; *Twelfth Night*, 21; *The Two Gentlemen of Verona*, 22; *The Winter's Tale*, 24–5, 93
Shapiro, James, 15, 16, 160n29
Sheerin, Brian, 162n47
Shewring, Margaret, 168n6
Sidney, Henry, 95
Sidney, Philip, 95
Siemon, James, 161n35
Singer, Charles, 154n26
Skura, Meredith, 113, 121
Slights, Camille Wells, 156n41
Smith, Bruce, 21, 145n65, 146n69, 160n23
Smith, Irwin, 146n77
Smith, Molly, 160n29
Snider, Alvin, 142n19
Sofer, Andrew, 160n21
Spanish Tragedy, The (composite text with unattributed Additions), 30, 84–102, *91*, 103–4, 105–6, 107, 108, 109–10, 111, 112, 113, 132
Spanish Tragedy, The (Kyd), 30, 84–8,